THE ENDLESS
CRISIS

AMERICA IN THE SEVENTIES

A Confrontation of the World's Leading
Social Scientists on the Problems, Impact and Global
Role of the United States in the Next Decade

A Seminar under the Auspices of
The International Association for Cultural Freedom

Edited by FRANÇOIS DUCHÊNE

SIMON AND SCHUSTER · NEW YORK

PUBLISHED BY SIMON AND SCHUSTER
ROCKEFELLER CENTER, 630 FIFTH AVENUE
NEW YORK, NEW YORK 10020

FIRST PRINTING

The extract from the paper by Michel Crozier, here titled "The
Lonely Frontier of Reason," was previously published in the May
27, 1968, issue of *The Nation* under the title "America Revisited"
and is reprinted here by permission. Zbigniew Brzezinski's paper,
"America in the Technetronic Age," appeared in the January 1968
issue of *Encounter* magazine.

SBN 671–20517–X TRADE
SBN 671–20518–8 CLARION
LIBRARY OF CONGRESS CATALOG CARD NUMBER: 70–107252
DESIGNED BY EVE METZ
MANUFACTURED IN THE UNITED STATES OF AMERICA

CONTENTS

I

II–POST-INDUSTRIAL SOCIETY

III–GLOBAL POWER OR SELF-RESTRAINT

[*A picture section begins on page 151*]

3

ABOUT THE PARTICIPANTS

Identified below are only those participants at the International Committee for Cultural Freedom seminar held at Princeton, New Jersey, whose remarks and papers are included in this book. It is not meant to include all the participants in those proceedings.

ORLANDO ALBORNOZ is professor of sociology at the Central University of Venezuela. He is co-author, with David Riesman, of *Estudios Norteamericanos; perfiles políticos.*

GEORGE W. BALL, formerly Under-Secretary of State and United States Ambassador to the United Nations, works as an investment banker. During the 1968 Presidential campaign he served as foreign-policy adviser to Hubert Humphrey. His study of foreign policy, *The Discipline of Power,* was published in 1968.

DANIEL BELL is professor of sociology at Harvard University and author of *The End of Ideology.* He serves as chairman of the Year 2000 Committee and as co-editor of *The Public Interest.*

WALDEMAR BESSON is professor of political science at the University of Constance. He has written *Die politische Terminologie Franklin D. Roosevelt, Grundzuge der amerikanischen Aussenpolitik von Roosevelt bis Kennedy,* and *Die grossen Machte.*

DAVID BLUMENTHAL, a senior in the Government Department at Harvard University, is Editorial Chairman of the Harvard *Crimson.*

WILLIAM GORDON BOWEN is professor of economics at Princeton University and provost of the university.

5

SAM BROWN, formerly a student at Harvard Divinity School, was student coordinator for Eugene McCarthy's 1968 Presidential campaign and has represented the Peace Corps and the Agency for International Development in India and Southeast Asia. At present he is one of the coordinators of the Vietnam Moratorium Committee.

ZBIGNIEW BRZEZINSKI is professor of government and director of the Research Institute on Communist Affairs at Columbia University. His books include *Political Power USA/USSR*, and *Alternative to Partition: For a Broader Conception of America's Role in Europe*.

ALASTAIR BUCHAN, former director of the Institute of Strategic Studies in London, is the author of *NATO in the Sixties*.

MICHEL CROZIER is professor of sociology and study director of the Sociology of Organizations project at the Centre National de Recherches Scientifiques in Paris. He is the author of *The Bureaucratic Phenomenon*.

HAROLD CRUSE is visiting honors lecturer at the University of Michigan, Ann Arbor. He is the author of *The Crisis of the Negro Intellectual*.

RALF DAHRENDORF is professor of sociology at the University of Constance. His books include *Gesellschaft und Demokratie in Deutschland*.

MARION COUNTESS DOENHOFF is editor in chief of the German newspaper *Die Zeit*.

PIERRE EMMANUEL is director of the International Association for Cultural Freedom. He has published poetry and essays.

LOUIS FISCHER is professor at the Woodrow Wilson School of Public and International Affairs at Princeton University. He has written biographies of Gandhi and Lenin as well as *The Soviets in World Affairs* and *Men and Politics.*

JOHN KENNETH GALBRAITH, former United States Ambassador to India, is professor of economics at Harvard University. He is the author of *The Affluent Society, American Capitalism,* and *The New Industrial State.*

GINO GERMANI is presently Monroe Gutman Professor of Latin American Affairs and a Member of the Center for Population Studies at Harvard University. Formerly, he was professor of sociology at the University of Buenos Aires, Argentina, and President of the Asociación Sociológica Argentina (1962–1966).

GINO GIUGNI is professor of labor law at Bari University. He has written several books on labor and is a contributor to the Italian journal *Il mulino.*

OWEN HARRIES is senior lecturer in political science at the University of New South Wales, Australia. He has contributed articles to *Foreign Affairs, Survival,* and other periodicals.

ANTHONY HARTLEY is editor of *Interplay* magazine. Formerly with the foreign department of *The Economist,* he is the author of *A State of England.*

LILLIAN HELLMAN, playwright and essayist, author of *The Little Foxes, Toys in the Attic* and *An Unfinished Woman,* is currently teaching at M.I.T.

STANLEY HOFFMANN is professor of government at Harvard University. His books include *The State of War* and *Gulliver's Troubles, or The Setting of American Foreign Policy.*

ROY INNIS is national director of the Congress of Racial Equality, member of the board of the New York Urban Coalition, fellow of the Metropolitan Applied Research Center, and co-publisher of the *Manhattan Tribune*.

KARL KAISER is professor of political science at the University of Bonn. He has written *German Foreign Policy in Transition* and *Bonn between East and West*.

CARL KAYSEN is director of the Institute for Advanced Study in Princeton, New Jersey. He has taught at Harvard University and served as an economic adviser to President Kennedy. He is co-author of *The American Business Creed* and *Anti-Trust Policy*.

GEORGE F. KENNAN, former United States Ambassador to Russia and Yugoslavia, is professor at the Institute for Advanced Study, Princeton, New Jersey. His books include *Russia and the West under Lenin and Stalin, American Diplomacy, 1900–1950,* and *Memoirs: 1925–1950*.

HENRY KISSINGER is special assistant to President Nixon for foreign affairs. A Harvard professor, he is the author of *The Necessity for Choice: Prospects for American Foreign Policy* and *The Troubled Partnership: Prospects for the Atlantic Alliance*.

JAN KOTT, formerly of Warsaw University, is visiting professor at the State University of New York at Stony Brook. He is the author of *Shakespeare, Our Contemporary*.

LARS LANGSLET is research assistant at the Institute for the History of Ideas at Oslo University, member of the Norwegian Academy for Language and Literature, and editor of the quarterly *Minervas Kvartalsskrift*. He has written *Kirken i dialog*.

ROBERT J. LIFTON is professor of psychiatry at Yale University. He is the author of *Death in Life: Survivors of Hiroshima,* and *Revolutionary Immortality: Mao Tse-tung and the Chinese Cultural Revolution*.

EUGEN LOEBL, formerly Deputy Minister for Foreign Trade of Czechoslovakia, was director of the Czechoslovak State Bank. He is the author of *The Intellect and Wealth of Nations* and an *Analysis of Political Trials*. He is currently teaching at Vassar College.

ALLARD K. LOWENSTEIN is a lawyer and the United States Representative from the Fifth Congressional District of New York.

MOCHTAR LUBIS is publisher of the Indonesian daily *Indonesia Rays* and author of *Twilight in Djakarta*.

JOHN J. MCCLOY, lawyer and banker, was formerly Assistant Secretary of War, President of the World Bank, and United States High Commissioner for Germany.

JOHN MADDOX, former assistant director of the Nuffield Foundation Science Teaching Project, is editor of *Nature* magazine. He has written *Spread of Nuclear Weapons* (with Leonard Beacon) and *Revolution in Biology*.

ALEJANDRO MAGNET is Chilean Ambassador to the Organization of American States and author of *Orígenes y antecedentes del Panamericanismo*.

DAVID MARQUAND is Labour Member of the British Parliament for Ashfield. He has taught at the University of California and is a frequent contributor to British periodicals.

MINOO MASANI is a Member of the Indian Parliament, chairman of its Public Accounts Committee, and deputy leader of the Swatrantra Party. He was formerly chairman of the United Nations Subcommission on Discrimination and Minorities. He has written *A Plea for the Mixed Economy*.

LEO MATES, former Yugoslav Ambassador to the United States, is director of the Institute of International Politics and Economy at Belgrade.

MARTIN MEYERSON is Chancellor of the State University of New York.

ABDUL GAFOOR NOORANI is an Indian constitutional lawyer. He is the author of *Our Credulity and Negligence*.

SIMON NORA is an economic adviser to the French government. He has written *Pour une Politique étrangère de l'Europe* and *Rapport sur les Entreprises publiques*.

JOHN B. OAKES is editor of the editorial page of *The New York Times*. He is the author of *The Edge of Freedom*.

SABURO OKITA is president of the Japan Economic Research Center.

ANDREAS PAPANDREOU is an economist and the former chairman of the Panhellenic Liberation Movement. He has taught at the University of California, Berkeley, and has written *Introduction to Macroeconomic Models*.

AURELIO PECCEI is an Italian economist. He is president of Italconsult and vice-chairman of the Olivetti Corporation.

MARTIN PERETZ teaches social science at Harvard University. He was national co-chairman of the McCarthy for President Committee and has contributed articles to several periodicals.

NORMAN PODHORETZ is editor of *Commentary* magazine and author of *Doings and Undoings: The Fifties and After in American Writing* and *Making It*.

ROBERT POWELL was chairman of the National Student Association.

JAN G. REIFENBERG is Paris correspondent of the daily *Frankfurter allgemeine Zeitung*.

ARTHUR M. SCHLESINGER, JR., is Albert Schweitzer professor of the humanities at the City University of New York. An adviser to President Kennedy, he has written *The Age of Jackson, The Age of Roosevelt,* and *A Thousand Days.*

JEAN-JACQUES SERVAN-SCHREIBER is publisher and editor of the French weekly *L'Express* and author of *The American Challenge.*

EDWARD SHILS is professor of social thought and sociology at the University of Chicago and fellow of King's College, Cambridge, England. Among his books are *The Present State of American Society* and *Political Development of New States.*

ALESSANDRO SILJ is Deputy Director of Information Service for the European Economic Community.

SULAK SIVARAKSA is editor of the Thai periodical *Social Science Review.* He is the author of *Love Letters from America* and *Plato's Dialogue.*

R. M. SOEDJATMOKO, economist and writer, is Indonesian Ambassador to the United States.

IVAN SVITAK, writer and philosopher, is a member of the Institute of Philosophy of the Czechoslovak Academy of Science. He is currently at the Research Institute on Communist Affairs at Columbia University. He has written *Human Sense of Culture.*

ENRIQUE TIERNO GALVAN, recently retired as professor of law at the University of Salamanca, is one of the leaders of the Socialist opposition to Franco.

BRIAN WALDEN is Labour Member of the British Parliament for Birmingham. He is a former Parliamentary Private Secretary of the Treasury.

C. VANN WOODWARD has been Sterling Professor of History at Yale since 1961. He is the author of *Origins of the New South (1877–1913)*, *Reunion and Reaction,* and *The Strange Career of Jim Crow,* among others.

PREFACE

THE CONTENTIOUS MILLENNIUM

A PREFACE

This book is a record of a four-day international conference held at Princeton in December 1968 to discuss "The United States, Its Problems, Its Impact and Its Image in the World." "We're meeting here," said John Kenneth Galbraith, opening the conference, "at one of those periods, of which 1933 was one, 1948 another, when there has been a major change in the equilibrium of American politics." This seems in retrospect almost understated in the light of the uneasiness and self-questioning that came to dominate the proceedings. To sum up a meeting of ninety-odd people in one idea is always invidious; there cannot have been many participants, however, who did not acknowledge they were meeting at a point which André Malraux, contemplating the convulsions in France during May 1968, had called a "crisis of civilization."

This in itself was an object lesson in the speed at which political mood changes. The conference was arranged by the International Association for Cultural Freedom.[1] During the early 1950s, the Association's forerunner, the Congress for Cultural Freedom, had

[1] At the end of the Princeton Conference, Mr. Shepard Stone, the president of the International Association for Cultural Freedom, made the following statements, among others, in a press conference:

As you probably know, there was a Congress for Cultural Freedom, with many distinguished people in it, for many years. In 1966, it was revealed that CIA funds had been financing in large part the organization. At that time, many members of this organization, not only from the United States, but from Europe, Asia, Africa, distinguished scholars, came to the Ford Foundation and said, "This is a great institution and we want to carry on because we believe it's important,"

been militant in the battle for liberal values against the Marxist "poverty of historicism." By the late 1950s, with Stalinism exposed by Khrushchev himself and Russian tutelage and the one-party state becoming visibly unpopular throughout Eastern Europe, liberal values seemed to be carrying the day. An appeased sense of rationality triumphant spread through the intellectual establishment of the open societies, at least the more affluent and utilitarian of them. Yet at Princeton, less than a decade later, the prevailing themes were the poverty of utilitarianism, the new *trahison des clercs*, the pseudo-rationalism of technocrats, and the threat of violence. Hegel himself could hardly have expected a synthesis to breed so promptly its own contradictions. It was not surprising that Raymond Aron's *mot* "nothing fails like success" became part of the coinage of debate.

During the fifties, the vast majority in Western establishments were materialists in the foreshortened sense of assuming, for practical purposes, that quality would arise from quantity, the fulfillment of the individual from collective economic progress. "Let God take care of my physical ills, and I will take care of the rest," Chamfort said long ago, and the administrators of the Western world were tempted to feel they were filling this godlike role. In practice, material progress has opened the door to new opportunities, but also new frustrations and ambitions, expressed most spectacularly by the New Left. The principal virtue of the New Left

---

and asked the Ford Foundation to help. The Ford Foundation made an appropriation over a five-year period. The only funds in this organization since the beginning of 1967 have been Ford Foundation funds, and I'm now glad to say that in recent weeks I have received information that a number of European foundations are also going to support the International Association for Cultural Freedom. I can't emphasize too strongly what I'm saying, that since the beginning of 1967 there hasn't been another penny of money in this organization. I myself didn't join the organization until September 1967. I had previously been at the Ford Foundation.

Q.: How much did the conference cost?

Stone: I judge somewhere between seventy thousand and eighty thousand dollars.

Q.: How many people attended?

Stone: We think about ninety from twenty countries.

has been to hasten recognition of the insufficiency of material progress once it has done (or partly done) its work.

The New Left seems to have no coherent program, and to be demonstrably easily satisfied with the histrionics of self-righteousness. But at Princeton, as in a wider field, it forced more urgent consideration of social injustice and of the "quality of living." Two men, generations apart, George F. Kennan and Martin Peretz, who agreed on nothing else, both denounced the shortcomings of a civilization dominated by commercial standards and complacent, in its concentration on middle-class consumption, about social and political maladjustments and urban blight. Many moderates had been saying the same things for years, but their pleas, biased toward planning, consensus and reason, failed to capture the center of attention. Where they fell short, the New Left, by being often unreasonable, has succeeded in creating a "problem" on which technocrats and administrators, as vocational problem-solvers, are constrained to concentrate.

The very success of these methods has been a reminder that no new world is born painlessly, rationally or all of a piece. The idea of violence haunted most of the older generation at Princeton (anyone, that is, over the age of thirty). One after another they deplored the narrow "exclusiveness" of the young and the blacks, so unlike the universalist approach of the early socialists; also their "hedonism"; the "desacralization" of authority, leading to risks of authoritarianism; and, in general, the way left-wing violence might call to the far more potent violence of the right—prefascist anarchy summoning fascist order. The classic calm of Princeton's Whig Hall and the decencies of debate there were troubled by decidedly non-Whig visions of violence: black violence, student violence, police violence, bureaucratic violence done to the individual and the reciprocal intellectual violence of young and old.

Typically enough, the student spokesmen at Princeton did not offer analysis so much as affirm their revolt against liberal institutions which "though keeping legislative promises, have been unable to keep their larger promises to American society." As Sam

Brown said, they found it difficult and even immoral "to remain calm and analytical" as the older liberals did in the face of Vietnam, the arms race, and race *tout court*. Martin Peretz (like the veteran Spanish socialist Tierno Galvan) traced the troubles of American society to the fusion of money and government powers. Common to them all was a revolt against the managers, public and private: "the individual has increasingly seen that the great corporations take for granted" that they will "shape in some degree to their convenience the individual's view of his life, his boss, his needs. . . . Similarly, in the public sector, the individual has ceased to assume that the great bureaucracies, particularly those in the area of foreign policy—the Pentagon, the State Department— are subordinate to the Presidency, the Congress and the voters." There is something in this of the old Populist rejection of elite government, but also of the new fear of the ascendant technocrat, which goes beyond the radicals.

Much of the dread of the coming technological society is based on the belief that it will be thoroughly, even scandalously, elitist. Sometimes the elite is the machine itself: "the first ultra-intelligent machine is the last invention that man need ever make, providing that the machine is docile enough to tell him how to keep it under control."[2] Usually the elite is the small caste of computer-controlling technocrats, as in Zbigniew Brzezinski's familiar picture of managers working themselves to death and of "spectacles (mass sports, TV) providing an opiate for increasingly purposeless masses." The very nature of the industrial system nurtures such feelings: there is "the newspaper that *must* be filled; the plant that *must* be used, the institutions that *must* grow."[3] Why not, then, the battle cry of the New Left against the military-industrial complex, that there *must* be Vietnams? Doctrines of manipulation build on paranoid patterns of thought latent in wide sections of

[2] Irving John Good, fellow of Trinity College, Oxford, in *Advances in Computers,* quoted by Arthur Clarke in *Man and the Future,* ed. James E. Gunn (Lawrence, Kans.: University Press of Kansas, 1968), p. 262.

[3] Sir Geoffrey Vickers, "The End of Free Fall," *The Listener,* London, Nov. 4, 1965, p. 691.

society. Administrations proliferate. Legislatures decline. Heads of government steal the limelight more and more from their most senior colleagues. The memory of Caesar and of bread and circuses in the breeding grounds of Western culture stirs again. The progress of technology promises to centralize power still further. Lasers, test-tube life, artificial intelligence, data banks, mind control and so on become futuristic nightmares previously only the province of fiction. Yet nightmares are ambiguous: do they represent the power of the danger or the power of the human reaction against it?

The paradox is that the late sixties have demonstrated not only the strength but also the growing weakness of governments. In America, a determined and initially isolated minority, opposed to the stagnating Vietnam War, compelled the incumbent President to give up his otherwise automatic second term in office. In France, in May 1968, student riots and labor strikes nearly toppled that apogee of charisma, General de Gaulle, as if the year had been 1848 and the leader a mere Louis-Philippe. General de Gaulle's career, superficially an epitome of the trend toward authoritarianism, in fact provides a textbook instance of its limitations. For all his quasi-absolute power, de Gaulle had been effective only while public opinion was behind him. With its support, he could quell the colonels and settle the Algerian War by what seemed no more than a flux of television speeches. Without it, as in the long-forgotten miners' strike of 1963, the farmers' agitation in the middle sixties, the early phases of the *événements* of May 1968, and again in the shopkeepers' demonstrations of spring 1969, he was helpless. It may be argued that he was no real dictator and the totalitarian regimes are made of sterner stuff. But these too have been so shaken in Eastern Europe that without Russian bayonets they would have been swept away. Society may be slow-moving, and the need for violence to shake the complacency of government disquieting. The fact remains that authority seems entrenched only in countries like the Soviet Union that combine a powerful state tradition with political backwardness in the public.

Daniel Bell has commented that what matters is not "who"

governs, but "how," and that so long as the structure of power remains, changes of personnel are secondary. But if the powers-that-be are vulnerable to anything that stands for resistance to the abuse, or even exercise, of authority, this alone changes the "how" of government. The American bureaucracy was as roundly defeated as Johnson in the 1968 Presidential campaign. Something of the same principle even applies, *mutatis mutandis,* to industry. Big business cannot long afford to ignore the signs of the times if the apparent disaffection of the young for science, engineering and management persists.[4] In the U. S., it is already trying to adjust to the moral fervor of the young and the new climate of independence. "It's much easier to work with a beard or at night for IBM than for General Motors, because they need mathematicians more." In short, the changing ways in which people feel, though hard to quantify, are a major factor in the "structure" of society. Though the apparatus of administration grows ever more monstrous, the establishments in open societies seem less and less able to perpetuate the old elitist traditions of government. The mass-educated society is not the old largely passive one: an innovation which is already turning into anachronism many inherited assumptions about it.

Recognizing this does not necessarily lead to heartening conclusions. The vulnerability of the "system"—both public and private

[4] *The Times* of London on March 28, 1969, reported statistics used by Dr. H. G. Judge, principal of Banbury School, Oxfordshire, in a lecture at the Royal Society of Arts, to the effect that, in Britain, "the number of sixth form students reading science dropped from 32,700 to 31,700 between 1962 and 1967, while the number in the non-science group doubled from 38,300 to 76,100." Sixth forms are the top forms in British secondary schools. More recent figures (*The Times,* July 31, 1969) suggest that the proportion of science students is now rising again in Britain. But Dr. Nevitt Sanford, director of the Institute for the Study of Human Problems at Stanford University, in *Campus 1980—The Shape of the Future in American Higher Education,* ed. Alvin C. Eurich (New York: Delacorte Press, 1968), notes the increase among students at Stanford stating a preference for teaching and government as against business. Less than 3 percent of the freshmen at Stanford in 1966 stated a preference for business.

—to social processes it very partially controls can be used as evidence of the growth of an ungovernable society, a kind of New York City magnified to continental proportions. Daniel Bell has suggested, at Princeton and elsewhere, that basic changes are becoming perceptible in advanced society, and American society in particular. The "post-industrial" development is the best-known part of his thesis. In its simplest form, it means that services are coming to dominate the economy; and, more significant, that theoretical knowledge is becoming the engine of progress in society. It follows that the universities hold a key place in society and hence, increasingly, in politics too. But the "post-industrial" is only one of three "dimensions" in Bell's analysis. The second, and very important one, is that America is becoming a "communal" society. In the nineteenth century, wealth and benefits were distributed impersonally by the automatic operations of the market. If a man succeeded or failed, he alone seemed responsible. But as the realization began to spread that this justice was too rough, government took over more and more of the responsibility for full employment, welfare, education, research and, through them, for whole industries, regions and classes of people. At the same time, deprived minorities like the blacks have become more and more insistent that "equality of opportunity" is not enough, and demanded "equality of result." More and more pressure groups, ethnic minorities, farmers, labor unions, localities, educational and scientific establishments, the military and others have come to expect the federal government to arbitrate their competing claims, and to blame it for their frustrations. This plurality of thrustful minorities and factions generates a clamorous and contentious form of corporate politics. It is possible even to conceive of a point where conflicts cease to be local to their sector and polarize all society around the issue of violence itself.

This danger is increased by the third dimension of change in Bell's thesis. He has tellingly illustrated this by the example of "Coxey's Army" of unemployed who, in the winter of 1893–94, set out for Washington from various parts of the United States.

Only four hundred arrived. Seventy years later, the civil-rights movement delivered 250,000 demonstrators to the gates of the White House. America has always had a record of local violence, for instance in labor struggles, but since the Civil War these have rarely affected the over-all political stability of the country. Bell's argument is that America has been protected from its own vitality, as European countries have not, by the sheer size of the continent relative to the means of communication. This cushion of "insulated space" no longer exists.[5]

In some ways, this may mean only that American political structures and problems are growing more like those of other countries. The relatively small and centralized states of the Old World have long been "communal" from lack of "insulating space." Central governments there have for some time been umpires between rival groups because the political systems have long been unified and focused on the capital, and state responsibility for welfare in particular has been growing for over half a century.[6] In fact, America's unique problem, underlined by Kennan, is that its chaos of local authorities is almost eighteenth-century in European terms. The "communal" or corporatist system works well in Europe only in highly disciplined states like Sweden or Switzerland, but it is inefficient, rather than violent, in France, Britain or, until recently, Italy. Bell's analysis in itself may simply point to the need for new institutional arrangements in the United States—a greater federal involvement in social affairs and, as he suggests, a devolution in details to regional and local bodies. What gives it an alarming air is partly that, as Harold Cruse pointed out at Princeton, the American melting pot has not finished cooking yet—the blacks, the browns and the reds, Negroes, Mexicans and Indians,

[5] See Bell's "Notes on the Post-Industrial State," which appeared in the issue of Winter and Spring 1967 of *The Public Interest*. The phrase about "equality of result" is Nathan Glazer's, quoted by Bell.

[6] Social-security expenditures represent about 15 percent of GNP in all the European Economic Community countries and Britain, as against only 8 percent in the United States. See the EEC Commission's *Selected Figures: The Common Market Ten Years On*.

THE CONTENTIOUS MILLENNIUM

are still not truly in the mixture—and partly the streak of irrationalism in the New Left.

Some of the behavior of the New Left is "rational" enough by traditional standards—the revolt against paternalism, the fervor for social and racial equality. But these do not explain the life style of the movement—its passion for passion's sake, its cult of the immediate moment, its contempt for analysis and piecemeal reform. Students today remind George Kennan of their revolutionary predecessors in Russia before 1917 and do seem at times to have walked out of the pages of Dostoevsky. If the accounts of people teaching and studying in Paris and Bologna are to be believed, large parts of these universities have been reduced to chaos. In many places, anarchy is seeping through to the secondary schools. The strident hunt for tyranny even in the "repressive liberal tolerance" of the Anglo-American universities overflows into histrionics and psychodrama. If all these were disciplined by a program, they might still not be regarded as central. But the only point made by an elder and taken up by one of the most articulate spokesmen of the young at Princeton, Sam Brown, was Anthony Hartley's objection that the New Left seemed more concerned to mount guerrilla raids on society than to elaborate a program of government by which it might itself be judged.[7] In fact, there is a religious rather than political ring about the ideal of "participation" described by Edward Shils:

Participation is a situation in which the individual's desires are fully realized in the complete self-determination of the individual and which is simultaneously the complete self-determination of each institution and of society as a whole. In the good community, the common will harmonizes individual wills . . . Participation is the transformation of expanding sentiments and desires in which all members realize their sentiments simultaneously. Anything less is repressive.

[7] See pp. 180–81; also p. 284, where Sam Brown denies he or his fellow radicals at Princeton are adequate spokesmen for the New Left.

In this light, student disturbances are a passion play for "the dream of a regime of plenitude" present, but only distantly present, in the old laissez-faire and socialistic visions of economic fulfillment and fraternal love.[8] True, student movements since the romantic upheavals of pre-industrial Germany in the 1830s have all tended to have this millennial quality. The difference now is that the students, once a small minority, are becoming numerous enough to be the affluent society's equivalent of the old factory proletariat.[9]

Thus, together, corporatist politics and millennial emotions for instant utopia can be composed into a disturbing picture of the future, particularly if one assumes any close relation between students' behavior at college and their later attitudes as paid-up members of society. Early industrialism produced anarchism and fascism, and recoiled from both after paying a heavy price for the latter. The post-industrial society might have to accept them as endemic, and face recurring outbreaks, much as traditional society suffered the plague. Urban society is infinitely more self-aware and alive to social injustice than the traditional society, but it could be inherently less stable. The steady abuse of privilege in a world of scarcity could be replaced in a world of plenty by the periodic aberrations of the many.

[8] Edward Shils, "Of Plenitude and Scarcity," *Encounter,* May 1969, pp. 42 and 57.

[9] An exaggeration; there are 7 million students in the United States and 24 million industrial workers. Nevertheless, the upheavals of 1968 reflect the social and demographic rise of youth. The young mature earlier, have more freedom, enough money to be a powerful consumer market, and are absolutely and relatively more numerous than in the recent past. Forty-six percent of Americans were under 25 years old in 1965; 39.5 percent were under 20, as against only 31.5 percent in the EEC in 1966. About half of the young each year now go to some kind of college in America. Even in most of Europe, where the percentages are lower, there has been, and is, a hectic growth in the number of students. Indeed, the most glaring contrasts between the changing student body and the unchanging university framework are probably in Europe, particularly in France and Italy, where they have played a major role in recent troubles. The trend will continue unless there is a reaction of improbable proportions.

However, any social movement worth its salt is only the tip of an iceberg. This means that authority is paralyzed in dealing with the minorities when these manage to identify with mass attitudes or frustrations. Yet it also means that once the moderates are satisfied, the fanatics are thrown back where they came from, on the fringe. Bomb-throwing anarchists frightened established society out of its wits in the 1890s, but accomplished nothing permanent because they shocked the working class itself. The anarcho-syndicalists of the next decade also made the bourgeois tremble at the thought of a revolutionary general strike, but were unable to unleash one. In the 1930s, Communism throve because the unemployed were desperate, and in the forties because of the disgrace and ruin of the *anciens régimes* in war; but once the workers prospered, its politics became the kiss of death. Anarchists, anarcho-syndicalists and Communists did not change that much: what changed a great deal was their unacknowledged basis of support. On all the evidence and precedents, the same holds true of the world's latest excitements. It was calculated in 1968 that the militants represent about two percent of the student body in the United States, their immediate circle of support some eight to ten percent more.[10] The proportions become larger only occasionally, on well-selected issues. Student violence hits the headlines; the many examples of student restraints upon violence, even at Berkeley, in Paris or at the London School of Economics, do not. Again and again, in the university politics of the past two years, the focus of the struggle between the administrations and the militants has been the uncertain center of student, and to some extent faculty, opinion. It may seem a strange center, as the workers seemed half a century ago; but its motives and standards are not those of the extremists. It will not accept leadership from elders simply because they are senior; it may take a freer attitude than previous generations toward sex (perhaps) and drugs (cer-

[10] *The New York Times,* reporting a survey of 860 campuses by the Educational Testing Service of Princeton, N.J., Nov. 10, 1968. Quoted in Arnold Beichman's "Letter from Columbia," *Encounter,* May 1969, p. 15.

tainly). But this center can be mobilized to carry out tasks which fulfill its ideals of social justice, the quality of living, and even efficiency. People who have worked closely with radical, but not extremist, youth often agree that they are far more competent and mature than anyone assuming traditional standards had reason to expect. If the motives and aspirations of the invisible majority of the young are even partially met, the spectacular militants are likely to be left high and dry, as other apparently triumphant irrationalists have been in the past.

It is not, then, simply the power of technocrats, nor the millennialism of youth bored by affluence, which can explain the upsurge of conflict in societies many assumed to be pacified by wealth. A number of alternative interpretations sketched in broad psychological or cultural terms were put forward at Princeton. Michel Crozier stressed the students' fear of the cold light of reason they themselves accepted as controlling an increasingly man-made world. Norman Podhoretz saw the old minority opposition to the "American dream" of middle-class success growing into a potential majority. Edward Shils talked in terms of the growth of individuality undisciplined by the juvenile prevailing values. Robert Lifton pointed to the failure of technology to replace the moribund traditional cosmology with equally rich symbols, leaving people with "a sense of emptiness, of a counterfeit quality to existence." All these views more or less struck an equation of conflict between rising curves of collective pressures and individualism, a formula enunciated most explicitly, at the political level, by Galbraith: "We face today a basic contradiction between, on the one hand, the disciplines—including the disciplined belief —required by the necessarily massive organization, public and private, of the modern industrial state, and, on the other, the enormous reliance on educated, qualified scientific personnel and the apparatus for providing them, which trains people in the critical modes of the intellectual and causes them to question the subordination of personal to public goals."

The mass society is a new phenomenon. In practice, industrial

civilization clung to old oligarchic features long after these disappeared from the political vocabulary. It is only now that in the
richest countries the acutely poor have become minorities and the
numbers of students are creeping up to large fractions of their age
groups. The distance between the image of democracy and the
reality of social stratifications has only now begun to shrink
enough for the tribulations of the mass society to emerge in their
own right. One of those tribulations is simply due to the *mass* of
society as such.

There were masses in traditional society, of course, but until the
eighteenth century the vast majority were peasants scratching the
soil for food, on the margin of subsistence. There were *disettes*
and near-famines right through the eighteenth century in a country
as rich as France. Such people were far too bowed down by the
struggle with nature to be active members of society at all. They
were the substratum on which the small active society of the time,
the ruling classes, rose. To judge by Gregory King and Vauban,
whose estimates around 1700 were accepted as plausible by
contemporaries, the oligarchy in England and France then num-
bered less than 100,000 families each.[11] Scattered across ill-
communicating provinces, this governing class was largely local
despite the incipient centralization on Paris and London. In the
Germany of nearly three hundred "states," and in Italy, it was
even more so. Its frames of reference were essentially small.
Gentry exercised real but limited power. Rivals at court knew each
other's strengths and foibles with often bitter intimacy. The exercise of privilege and the competition for power were as earthy and
constraining in their way as poverty and personal subordination
for the subject masses. Neither lord nor peasant had need to prove
himself by *actes gratuits,* except possibly the military, and even

[11] Gregory King's table can be found most conveniently on p. 25 of G. N.
Clark's *The Later Stuarts* in the Oxford History of England series (1st edi-
tion, 1947 reprint). Extracts from the preface of Sébastien de Vauban's
Projet d'une dixme royale (1707), Ristampe Anastatiche di Opere Antiche e
Rare, Edizioni Bizzarri, Rome, 1968.

these had periodically to justify their heroic sense of honor on naked steel.[12] There was no room for the Victorian vagueness of

> Infinite passion and the pain
> Of finite hearts that yearn.[13]

If there is room for it now (though in angrier ways), this is largely because of the emergence of a vast middle-class mass equally far from the extreme constraints of both poverty and power.

The triumphs of the highly productive industrial society have turned the submerged nine tenths of the traditional society, the old "subjects," into the majority of self-conscious citizens of today. The immense diffusion of education and the emancipation from personal subordination to social superiors, made possible and even required by the wealth-producing system, have also given individuals an autonomy of outlook on themselves and the world, a novel inner sense of mastery and rights. *"L'appétit vient en mangeant":* the revolution of rising expectations that is more effective in rich than poor societies has made people more demanding than ever before. It is not surprising that the "belief felt" of the times is a kind of individualistic expansionism impatient of trammels and restraints. Yet the very division of labor that has freed the individual from personal bonds is increasingly coming to limit his freedom of action in impersonal ways. The fact that the old subject nine tenths of society have emerged into the light of citizenship means that even if the population had not hugely increased (which it has), the community would, in a sense, be up to nine times larger than two centuries ago. This whole order of magnitude of change makes the old automatic "participation" of the few as anachronistic as the isolation of the rural masses. Both are replaced by a vast number of people crowding into the middle stations of society where the natural pride of personal self-deter-

[12] The first writer to make propaganda for the *acte gratuit* was that cosseted and hypochondriac bourgeois, André Gide, in his *Caves du Vatican* (1914).

[13] Robert Browning, "Two in the Campagna."

mination is frustrated and insulted by the mediocrity of one's responsibility and power. This goes further than politics, as much of the discussion at Princeton implied. The frustration of individual ambitions when crowds of people pursue them simultaneously is typified just as much by urban sprawl as by the "manipulation" stressed by the New Left. The division of labor and the centralization that goes with it work in what might be called the "achievement gap" quite as clearly as in the bureaucracy derived, as Ralf Dahrendorf and Daniel Bell showed, from the protection of social and political rights.

One of the troubles of the mass society is that a crowd of people all seeking the same objectives may, and indeed often do, produce results that more or less frustrate the objectives of each individual in the crowd. The extraordinarily rapid increase in the number of cars, roads, garages, used-car dumps, secondary residences, seashore and inland resorts, airports and so on reflects an ever-growing demand for greater physical and psychic space. The millions of people who buy motorcars to express their yearning for mobility and freedom do not do so in order to queue in traffic jams. Nor do the settlers in the suburbs consciously intend to increase the wastelands and rubbish dumps, which the Civic Trust in Britain estimated in 1964 were growing at a rate there of 3,500 acres a year.[14] Urban sprawl is, in fact, an embodiment of the complications and distortions of individual purpose in a mass society. People pour into the great centers to make the most of their personal chances of wealth, power, romance, "the golden life in the culture" and even "togetherness." But because they want either a larger private kingdom or relief from the stresses of the cities, great numbers of those with means move as far out of town as easy transport will allow. Inexorably urban and semiurban areas fan out till in the end most suburbanites have the worst of both worlds: the clutter of the urban life and the relative isolation and cultural poverty of the rural one. They even have disadvantages that belong to neither: the one-class suburb with, especially in the

14 There were 150,000 acres of heaps, holes and miscellaneous wasteland in Britain that year, and the rate of growth is increasing.

United States, a very high turnover of inhabitants, commuting raised to the level of a major activity and, above all, the loss of the sense of "community." This is often treated as a nostalgic leftover from rural utopias that never were, a Jeffersonian dream ignoring the nasty realities of the past. But evidence is beginning to accrue that "extreme lack of contact with other human beings causes extreme and well-defined pathologies like schizophrenia and delinquency. . . . The way of life we lead today makes it impossible for us to be as close to our friends as we would really want to be. The feeling of alienation and the modern sense of the 'meaninglessness' of life are direct expressions of the loss of intimate contact."[15]

The question of mass in society has been examined mostly in material terms. It has been asked how fast food production can be raised to meet demands and what are the maximum numbers of people the earth can feed. It has been pointed out that only seven percent of the world's land surface is used for living by men and even that the whole population of the world could still be stood on the Isle of Wight. The emphasis in town planning has been to run after growth that has already occurred and provide overdue facilities of transport, welfare and housing. But if the problem is psychological and results from the contradictions of the growing demands of individuals on the one hand for the services great centers provide, and on the other for the "psychosocial space" great centers tend in part to constrict, purely material factors take second place.[16] It may be socially dangerous as well as uncom-

[15] Christopher Alexander of the Center for Planning and Development of the University of California at Berkeley, in *Environment for Man*, ed. William R. Ewald, Jr. (Bloomington, Ind.: Indiana University Press, 1967), pp. 67 to 102, and comments by others following. Professor Alexander's essay is interesting not only for its own thesis but for the evidence collected from other sociologists' essays.

[16] Food and Agricultural Organization, *Yearbook of Food and Agricultural Studies: 1956*, Part One (Rome, 1957), for the 7 percent figure. It is quoted in *After Imperialism*, by Michael Barratt Brown (London: Heinemann, 1963), pp. 1–2.

fortable to let things ride until many luxuries of space and freedom now taken for granted have been lastingly impaired. Yet to act may ultimately mean policies going as far as disincentives on the growth of population and certain forms of economic expansion. The issue of cities is more complex, difficult and explosive than society—no doubt defensively—has been content to assume.

Another effect of mass society—insidious because it makes it hard for the individual to come to terms with himself—is the achievement gap. This is the contrast between his sense of potency, standing high up on the giant shoulders of the culture, and a half-conscious vertigo about his impotence to operate in person at such heights. Television, radio, universities, travel, books, records and the other paraphernalia of modern mass culture give more people than ever before an apparent view of the commanding heights of the present, past and future, of politics, art and science, of the inner mind and outer space. In fancy, it has never been easier to imagine oneself into any experience or to embrace reality from a great height, "as the hawk sees it or the helmeted airman."[17] Lifton said of the "Protean style" at Princeton that "one can, in a sense, be anyone and no one" and shift from experience to experience "with relatively diminished psychological cost," but this is only true locally; for the personality as a whole, there is a considerable cost. The visions are borrowed vision: "the one thing" Proteus "had great difficulty in doing . . . was to carry out his own authentic function." When the individual has to face his personal challenge and opportunity, the odds are that these may seem both trivial and daunting. This has always to some extent been so, but now, as in so many other areas, the ancient scales of comparison have been fantastically overloaded. The modern logic of the division of labor, combined with extreme centralization, changes supply and demand and may well reduce even the individual's statistical chances of success. A century ago, before Wagner and others professionalized the orchestra, the middling pianist

[17] W. H. Auden, *Poems* (London: Faber and Faber), 2nd edition (1933), Poem XXIX.

devoted to his art might win modest local fame and, in those days, be fairly content with it. Now he is mentally competing with the Barenboims (or Beatles, as it may be) from the first time he buys a record. There are far more aspirant competitors these days, but world communications reduce the relative numbers needed to reach into every corner of the market to the superlative, or happy few. They have not been automatically, as in Stendhal's day, selected by the injustices of the social order. As Crozier pointed out at Princeton, this deprives the individual of the psychological protection of ignorance or alibis. In this way, the culture of self-awareness democratizes both self-dramatization and the secret fear of failure. It is particularly alarming for the young: their histrionic radicalism, thinly overlaying anxiety, is almost to be expected.

Moreover, when man is regarded as a bundle of molecules and genes, and his psychic life is seen as a war of the energies of self and environment, the logic of his own outlook drives the individual to see himself as a temporary fusion of larger forces indifferent to himself. The erstwhile "subject" has been released; and now feels himself merely an object. He may at the political level be taught to believe he is a sovereign citizen, but his own imagination reinforces his insignificance in society by an isolation in the mind. Human beings become, on such assumptions, aggressive lonely animals seeking out their own purposes. Though greedy for "love," they seem so many predatory egos even to themselves. Their loves are an accidental coming together, their constant departures a proof of their self-absorption. It is striking how much of modern art is consumed by themes of self-devouring consciousness. The theater of noncommunication—Beckett, Pinter, *et al.*—is almost purely an essay in the logic of such a culture. Man's acquisition, through molecular biology, spare-part surgery and test-tube genesis, of the knowledge to control himself as a machine will possibly aggravate, but has not created, this loss of certainty about himself. As Pierre Emmanuel put it at Princeton: "We tend to accept more and more the idea that man is not a person looking for his unity, his oneness, but is a succession or even a simultaneity of fragmentary perceptions in a fragmented surrounding. And at the same time we accept the idea of 'scientific' control of this fragmented individual!"

Man in middle-class mass society has doubts about his significance in the community; and, no less painful, doubts about his significance in his own eyes, within his mental universe. This loss of stature is potentially dangerous: fascism is a disease of people who feel insignificant. Yet "crisis" is not a proper word for the situation. It suggests a limited problem, and specific solutions applied over a finite period. This is not the challenge. If there is a crisis, it is one which (in the twentieth century, at least) is likely to be without end. It will be more like adjusting to a new way of life than solving a problem. The metamorphosis of the past two centuries has given men the ability to mold their environment almost at will, and transformed the *condition humaine* without their knowing quite what such power implies. The vacuum is less in the frequently quoted loss of traditional values, which are inapplicable today, than in the need to generate new ones, matching the changed character of society and the greater self-awareness of mankind. In the nature of things, changing all the time, "solutions," complete and definitive, do not exist. There are only ways, more or less creative and constructive, of learning to adapt to and even anticipate the ever more complex consequences of man's own choices.

Daniel Bell suggested at Princeton that the problem was "how you humanize a technocracy and how you tame the apocalypse." If one is to tame the apocalypse, it will certainly be necessary to humanize the technocrats. It is no accident that, as Lifton remarked in the debate, the quality of living is "a terribly hard subject to talk about, because most of our social science and psychological systems exclude it." Today's establishment is humanitarian enough in one sense; but by today's standards it is a very narrow sense. The elite has been raised to the pinnacle of a pyramid based on everyone's hope of salvation through wealth, and it necessarily reflects these values. "We can guess, though we cannot prove," one well-known town planner has said, trying to define criteria for open spaces in urban areas, "that filling in San Francisco Bay would raise the temperature of the metropolitan area by five or ten degrees and blanket it with a layer of smog which could cost tens of millions annually. But these arguments will command little support until they can be scientifically demonstrated and measured."[18] When it seems necessary to discuss the ruin of one of the natural wonders of America in terms of the dollars lost which might balance the dollars gained by wealthy real-estate men or municipalities, one is nearing the threshold of historic *gaffes* like Marie Antoinette's about cake. One day, no doubt, this kind of accounting will seem as brutal as the early factory owners who herded their workers in slums. They too were serving a kind of progress. The world has long since moved beyond dogmatic economic laissez-faire when it results in slumps and unemployment. The time is approaching when its impact on cultural priorities must be controlled as well.

There are, of course, huge economic interests to be overcome (such as the automobile and oil industries and real-estate interests which favor highways rather than rapid transit in cities); but they have been overcome before when political awareness has reached a sufficient pitch, as in the New Deal. However, the awareness is not only political. To have Keynesian policies, it was necessary first to have Keynes. Now that the need is in many ways to go beyond the Keynesian categories of the administrators, it is necessary to elaborate new ones. The sheer volume of society has driven the administrators down the path of least resistance to think in aggregates, whereas the voter thinks mainly of himself. That leaves a rich field for cross-purposes and tangled wires and may explain much of the diffuse dissatisfaction in society which sours the triumphs of Keynesian economics. There must be much more investigation of the paradoxes of the disparity between individual wishes and collective consequences in the mass society; more study of loneliness and community in different environments, and of

[18] William L. C. Wheaton in *Environment for Man* (see note 15 above), p. 176.

changing demands for psychosocial space and the consequences for work, leisure and town planning; more research into the population problems of megalopolis and the effects of different approaches to social welfare, as the floor of rights steadily rises, on social behavior: in general, an improvement in social accounting comparable to the improvement in economic accounting in the last generation.[19] There is a limit to what benevolent doctors of social science can achieve. Allard Lowenstein at Princeton referred to the Dutch Provos: their emergence showed that the human hunger for spontaneity and testing limits revolts against the most benevolent organization. Eliminating elite rule cannot eliminate this: majority rule in a highly ordered society could seem equally "paternalist." Nevertheless, it will be difficult or impossible to go beyond generalized measures, inherently insensitive to individual aspirations, if new concepts and basic data are not developed. There is a vast field for pioneering social studies here, and for a supporting role in particular by the foundations.

Ultimately, the aim should be to serve the diversity that the coming of a service-society and of the age of leisure should in any case encourage. The age of leisure has had a surprisingly bad press. Dennis Gabor's verdict, in *Inventing the Future,* is that "of all the dangers confronting civilization . . . only the Age of Leisure will find man psychologically unprepared." Like him, Kahn and Wiener in *The Year 2000* quote Keynes's *Essay in Persuasion,* which dwells "with dread" on the "readjustments of the habits and instincts of the ordinary man, bred into him for countless generations, which he may be asked to discard within a

[19] The growth of social indicators will probably be as important to the post-industrial society in auscultating its tensions as economic indicators are to the Keynesian economist trying to manage growth today. The use of computer consoles will greatly help the spread of questionnaires, so that it will be possible to obtain information now out of reach or too expensive to gather. A recent study in a New York ward, seeing crime as the victims saw it, produced results startlingly different from the police records. Such developments could lead to referendum politics and further eat into the role of the representative political system and legislatures inherited from the past. See *Toward the Year 2018,* ed. Foreign Policy Association (New York: Cowles Education Corporation, 1968), pp. 89–90.

few decades. . . . Must we not expect a general 'nervous break-down'?"[20] Visions of a passive majority rotting on the hoof in front of television and of a dynamic minority wreaking vengeance on the herd by periodically running amok no doubt account for much of the current alarm. If, in the real-life utopia, people want not the old work-weary dream of idleness, but to feel fully alive, almost anything is possible, including the burning down of society. Such fears of the future may well be rooted in too narrow a notion of what "work" is, and a consequent underrating of its tendency to survive in all conditions.[21] In the Middle Ages, chess was re-

[20] Dennis Gabor, *Inventing the Future* (Middlesex: Harmondsworth, 1963), p. 10; Kahn and Wiener, *The Year 2000* (New York: Macmillan, 1967) p. 198.

[21] Hours of work have fallen relatively little in the advanced industrial countries since the Second World War. Kahn and Wiener have calculated (*Year 2000,* p. 125) that if the trend continues, Americans would still be working an average of 1,700–1,900 hours a year by the turn of the century, against about 2,000 hours annually for the average full-time worker today. (According to the EEC Commission, hours in Western Europe are roughly the same, varying between 1,900 hours in Britain, Germany and Italy and a maximum of nearly 2,100 hours in France.) This change would be only half the rate of change in the last century if Fourastié's estimate is correct that, in France, hours of work fell from 3,900 hours a year in the nineteenth century to about 2,250–2,350 hours a year in the 1960s (Jean Fourastié, *Les Quarante Mille Heures* [Paris: Laffont, 1965], p. 12). It is possible, even probable, that when enough people have begun to sate their first-generation hunger for goods, they will turn to leisure more than they have, so that the drop in working hours, when it comes, may be quite sudden. But leisure is expensive, except for dropouts, and this may continue to slow the trend. In any case, the working year could be greatly cut and still remain one important focus of people's use of time. A person working seven hours a day four days a week, taking public holidays and eight weeks' vacation a year and a sabbatical every seventh year would still be working the equivalent of 1,000 hours a year. Yet that is not unlike what many American academics could do today if they wished. Moreover, if one takes hours worked not in a year but in a lifetime, years spent in education and retirement are important. An individual working 1,000 hours a year from age 25 to 55 will furnish a lifetime of 30,000 hours' work; another doing 2,000 hours from 15 to 65 will have furnished 100,000 hours—more than three times as much. The Age of Leisure may come more slowly than some have speculated.

garded as a licentious form of leisure, leading knights to brawl and gamble; today, Soviet grandmasters reputedly train for grueling matches by cross-country running. The example may seem slightly rococo, but it demonstrates an important principle: anything which seems important enough for some people to concentrate their energies on it, and for society to encourage them, of itself constitutes "work." Work, in fact, is any substantial activity supported by society.

This allows for an extraordinary range of work—a diversification already reflected in the rapid growth of "services"—and for a complete transformation in its way of life. There are vast ranges of occupation in which many people could—and do—find fruitful purposes: education, all the kinds of welfare, artisan production, international relations, culture, tourism, entertainment in all forms, highbrow and low—even, no doubt, politics and sitting on committees. The common characteristic in all these is that they tend either to fulfill the individual or to seek to improve relations between people. In the past, men have concentrated on accumulating the goods they lacked. The result is, today, that even in a humanitarian achievement like the British Health Service there is a serious lack of personalized care, and, more domestically, that it grows harder and harder to buy good bread or find a good plumber. There is no reason why a great many men should not find satisfaction in being good bakers or good plumbers, if their dignity therein were acknowledged. Any society in which nurses and teachers are among the worst-paid professions has plenty of scope for evolution along these lines. An immense effort of education and new kinds of incentives, particularly in terms of status, will be needed. At the same time, a society focused on the relations between its members does not suggest a hell of boredom. For a civilization obsessed by the soullessness of the conveyor belt, it should even have substantial attractions.

Growing leisure, in short, is likely to be only one aspect of a "post-industrial society" becoming more centralized in some ways and more diverse in others. The trend toward centralization is evident in the development in all industrial countries of a whole series of government-industrial-scientific complexes, of which the military-industrial is only a prototype. The American conglomerates, which throve on defense and space contracts, are now following federal funds wherever they lead, notably into urban and social fields, where they claim the market may swell to over $250 billion a year by 1980.[22] This trend, tending to reinforce the fusion of economic and political powers in society, will reanimate fears of being ruled by roundheads; but the diversification of work and the greater education of the many can provide a counterbalance.

This would profoundly shift society's scale of values. Orlando Albornoz remarked at Princeton, for instance, that the United States Negro always appears in Latin America as an entertainer or a sportsman, never a leader of society. But in a world where leisure values rank higher, leisure may serve him "doubly as a source of symbolic achievement and as a literal resource in his middle-class status."[23] As society climbs out of the worst economic constraints and as activities diversify, so should the avenues multiply to prestige, private fulfillment and even power.

Political institutions will need to reflect these complex changes. "Participation" expresses the new sensibility of a society more and more suspicious of external authority and elite rule and may even, within limits, satisfy it. Trade-union forms of participation will no doubt develop in the coming years in plant, university and elsewhere. Voluntary associations will play a larger role. "Noise

[22] "With the federal investment in urban renewal for 1968–78 amounting to $250 billion, predictions that the market for urban civil systems will reach somewhere between $210 and $298 billion by 1980 may prove accurate."— Ida R. Hoos of the Space Science Laboratory of the University of California at Berkeley, "Systems Analysis as a Technique for Solving Social Problems —A Realistic Overview" (Berkeley: University of California Press, 1968), p. 1. The "predictions" Dr. Hoos mentions are to be found in an article in the January 1968 *Finance Magazine,* "The Economic Spectrum as Related to National Goals—Identification of New Business Opportunities, 1967," by the staff of the vice-president for marketing, North American Aviation.

[23] Max Kaplan, "Leisure as an Issue for the Future," in *Futures* (Guilford, Surrey, England), Vol. I, No. 2, pp. 94–95.

Begins to Count" was the title of a recent article in *The Economist,* for instance, describing the growing influence of the noise-abatement lobby in Britain.[24] Voluntary associations will also be needed to maintain a far closer watch, and in part control, over local authorities. In the man-made and unmade society, politics should come nearer the heart of the man-at-the-driving-wheel than, say, a balance-of-payments crisis or Keynesian macroeconomics, which remain obdurately the preserve of specialists.

There are, nevertheless, limits to participation through decentralization in a society where communications and the scale of operations inevitably centralize issues. Even "quality-of-living" conflicts frequently defy decentralization. London's third airport, *"le Bang"* of Concorde or the effects of large numbers of nuclear-power stations on the ecology of the Mississippi basin are not local, but national, issues. Oil slicks fouling hundreds of miles of coastline are not national, but international, issues. Moreover, most citizens, quite rightly, want to "participate" only selectively at certain times and on certain subjects. Compulsive participators are born politicians, the anti-elite of today preparing to take over the establishment of tomorrow. Some system of occasional and differentiated participation at the national level is needed for citizens who are not primarily politicians but do feel strongly about specific issues.

Theoretically, legislatures should provide this. But, for a variety of reasons, they have in most nations become less and less representative of their electors, more and more part of the elite system of government at the center. They are also patently the weaker party in that system, as the executive widens the scope of its activities; and they are increasingly bypassed by new technologies of direct contact between the head of government and the voters. Television gives the President or Prime Minister unrivaled means of showing himself to the viewers. But, while the means of communication from the top to the base of the pyramid are so good as

[24] *The Economist,* March 22, 1969, pp. 66–67.

to produce symptoms of Caesarism, the channels upward are almost nonexistent. The result is that a static electricity of irritation builds up out of which, in critical periods, opposition groups, or demagogues, can make lightning, often by violence, or by provoking the police to violence, on television. In this way, opposition groups establish excellent communications between themselves, but almost invariably outside the institutional system. There is no normal channel of communication within it. Minorities must be able to make their demands for reform more effectively within the system. As Eugen Loebl pointed out at Princeton, "Times have changed since the old days when the minority oppressed the majority. . . ." The majority can (as about the poverty of the old) be passively or (as about race) actively oppressive. The fact is that most establishments, when forced to face an issue, are more flexible and less conservative than the voters. To that extent, they do lead and educate, and should not be bypassed by, say, a Swiss form of referendum.[25] On the contrary, they need to be stimulated to exercise their function more often. One way to provide this stimulus might be to introduce an institutionalized system of petitions. Assuming a minimum number of signatures, formal petitions could compel public hearings of given issues in congressional or parliamentary and even external, but officially recognized, commissions. They would not, like the referendum in Switzerland, seek to enforce decisions; they would only make governments face the fact that they alone cannot decide what issues should be given an airing, and when. That, particularly in the European context, would already go some way to filling what is increasingly felt as a gap. In the open society, debate is the great solvent of politics and a tremendous form of pressure on government. In America, where congressional hearings are already a political institution, a public television network to broad-

[25] Thirty thousand signatures can force a referendum on an issue in Switzerland. The Swiss electorate has nearly always voted against innovation (some of the innovations are admittedly rather eccentric). This works in a highly cohesive society like Switzerland; it might merely make matters worse in countries where there is more open conflict.

cast hearings may be more urgent than any form of referendum. Neither is a panacea, but they would help to give a fresh sense of communication, within the system, between electors and elected and to adapt politics to the new technologies. They might even give a new force to legislatures as effective critics of government.

Social and political prescriptions are important, but they should not obscure, as they sometimes do, the equally formative cultural factors. It always looks more practical and positive to seek concrete explanations of events and suggest precise action on the structure of society and the state. Yet the flavor of a civilization is again and again determined by large, irrational and unexpected movements that capture the imagination. Socialism, Communism and Fascism were all surprises in their time, and the shock waves of the New Left rumbled through Princeton. It is in terms of values that much of history is made, and this is as evident in today's "revival of ideology" as in less technological eras. The life style of today's young is often taken as a sign of the unexpended energies of youth in an affluent society, but in fact the revolt against all allegiance to father, teacher, king or God has roots in two centuries of romanticism, most of them spent in a far from affluent environment. The systematic straining against the known limits of life has been part and parcel of the explosion of the agricultural, nature-dominated civilization into the technological man-made one. This is even true of the romantic image of materialism: "the materialist's idea of progress is an idea of *progress without limits.*"[26] Potential limitlessness is the hallmark of romantic culture, as instant limitlessness is that of today's student radicals. But if there are no clear limits to technology, there are limits to the relevance, for instance, of communications more instantaneous than satellite TV. There are also, more important, limits to the human personality. While a small but spectacular minority try desperately to breach the limits of the ego, it is striking that many of the literary

[26] E. F. Schumacher, scientific adviser to the National Coal Board, article on "Economics in a Buddhist Country," in *Roots of Economic Growth* (Gandhian Institute of Studies, India, 1962).

masterpieces of our century—Shaw's *Heartbreak House,* Eliot's *Four Quartets,* Auden's *The Sea and the Mirror,* Sartre's *La Nausée,* even in a negative way Beckett's *Waiting for Godot*—all tend to demonstrate the frontiers of the ego, or at least uncover a world in which the cultivation of the ego appears infantile. Indeed, it is precisely through a refusal to contemplate their own limits that several of these artists were forced into acknowledging frontiers they had thought to ignore. Auden's and Sartre's works, for instance, turn on a kind of nervous breakdown. At one point in the curve of romantic self-cultivation, the ego fails to live up to expectations and collapses under the strain. There follows a period of "alienation," at the end of which the artist comes back to life through a minimal but intense and concentrated awareness of the fact of "existence" as such. Sartre's anti-hero, Rocquentin, for instance, apprehends existence by suddenly perceiving the mammoth immobility and immanence of a great tree root in a municipal park, and forms from this a kind of rededication to living, almost without enthusiasm, but acceptant, even "committed," and with a hard core of unsentimental respect, virtually lost by the greedy romantic, for being alive. *"Une petite mélodie s'est mise à danser, à chanter"* at the back of the jazz record played in the café which has been his nearest place to home: *"derrière ces sons qui, de jour en jour, se décomposent, s'écaillent et glissent vers la mort, la mélodie reste la même, jeune et ferme, comme un témoin sans pitié."*[27]

The work of all such writers replaces the romantic worship of the ego by a sense of contract, of the restraints of life and relationships. It goes beyond both the utilitarianism of the "scientific observer" and the Dionysiac romanticism that has been its compensation in art. This is true even of Eliot or Auden, whose Christianity might be thought to hark back to an older age of family, church and state. The strength of their best poetry is that it stands up, as an argument about experience, and specifically modern experience,

[27] Jean-Paul Sartre, *La Nausée,* Livre de Poche edition (Paris, 1968), pp. 245–46.

without their faith having to be accepted. The key notion, in all such works, is that of dialogue, of relationship. This is, interestingly enough, the same concept that philosophers of the computer, such as C. West Churchman at Berkeley, have been reaching, and have been forced to reach for, to distinguish humanity, or man working with the computer, from the manlike computer able to react *objectively* like a human being.

The obvious objection is that such writers are too singularly eminent, all highbrow and some dead, and that, whatever they are or are not, their values are middle-aged; but this is precisely the point. Industrial, mass civilization is indeed new; and, as Shils suggested at Princeton, in psychic terms newness strangely resembles infantilism. The religion of life without limits does not merely complicate living in society; it also, and more importantly, destroys any standards by which the individual can live with himself. It is viable as a temporary expression of youthful vitality; inherently unstable as a permanent value. Youth is likely to go on being Dionysiac in a man-made, mass society freed from the constraints of nature, but this cannot continue into later life without being personally as well as socially disintegrating. Mature industrial civilization may well evolve a culture that explicitly recognizes the ages of man, like the Greeks and Hindus, or Shaw, in his own peculiar way, in the last part of *Back to Methuselah*. If so, the Dionysiac side of youth can be recognized, but its transience stressed, which would limit its pretensions. The condition is that there should be some visible progression from the values of youth to those of maturity. Given the values of the utilitarian establishment, this is at present lacking. To influence the young of the future, it will be necessary to have an elder generation more alive to spiritual factors, both in thought and in action. This is perhaps the most important challenge to intellectual leadership in the new civilization of man face to face with himself.

The Achilles heel of the post-industrial society may in the end prove to be not the domestic scene at all but the international one

—if, by the end of the century, it is still easy to distinguish them. It is a truism by now that every year the world becomes more tightly knit in a mesh of material and psychological interrelationships, and each country becomes increasingly dependent upon the good working of the system as a whole. But the large number of societies involved, the great variety of their stages of economic and political evolution, and the lack of generally accepted mechanisms and rules, all tend to make the flexible evolution that is hard enough to attain in a single nation more elusive still in the world at large. Most highly evolved civilian communities, provided their public opinion is independent enough, are unlikely to lose their balance if they are open to a healthy outside world. But if the international context is itself unhealthy, and all countries are thrown off balance together, it becomes infinitely more difficult for any one of them to reestablish its equilibrium, and a vicious circle of instability and hatreds can be set off, leading to catastrophe. The fragility of this situation has been demonstrated twice this century. The 1914 war broke out because the oligarchies of the European powers had no notion of what their inherited military codes, rigged out in modern dress as Social Darwinism, would mean in an industrial setting. Fifteen years later, the slump, wholesale unemployment, and even perhaps the Second World War, were rendered inevitable because the economic establishments did not have the faintest idea of the consequences of interdependence for mass societies once things began to go wrong. It is as well that technology, in part, and in part the bitter experience of such "cultural lags," have led what Karl Kaiser calls "transnational politics" to be somewhat more solidly ordered today.

The young are not the only ones haunted by technology in the shape of the Bomb. It has turned war from the accepted arbiter of shifts in the power balance to a kind of modern Black Death terrorizing rulers and ruled alike. It so inhibits the superpowers themselves that, Carl Kaysen said at Princeton, the United States had "an awesome and incredibly expensive and increasingly useless military power." A well-known dictum has it that the nuclear balance of terror "decelerates history." Yet it actually accelerates another kind of history: it has created something like the king's peace when the European monarchies curbed the feudal aristocracy and "New Men" rose to exploit—ruthlessly—the powers not of war but of civil life. Thus, its effect is not to deny the "balance of power" but in the most literal sense to civilize it and make international politics often more like internal ones than in the past. The king's peace is most imperfect. In fact, its operation depends on the constant hazard of its own breakdown. But while it lasts, the industrial world, at least, is in an almost confederal condition of nonbelligerent norms.

This civilian logic of politics has been reinforced by the postwar generation of leaders who have built up the most powerful international mechanisms yet devised. The "capitalist" industrial powers in particular have set up joint money and trading arrangements to prevent the financial and commercial protectionism of the disastrous period between the First and Second World Wars, and these have become retaining walls of peace and the open society. Regional integration, in the European Common Market, and even world social policies, in the United Nations agencies, have at least been begun. Such organizations work better in economics than in defense, and between "capitalist" powers than between "socialist" ones, or than between rich and poor. But collectively they have internationalized the management of the "capitalist" world (at least) in a way that would have been inconceivable at any previous time in history.

Another important, though less immediately constraining, development has been the decline in the sense of the usefulness or prestige to be gained by grabbing someone else's territory. This is far from universal, as the occupation of Czechoslovakia has shown—though even that was hesitant and shamefaced. Elsewhere the signs of another outlook have been multiplying. This is partly due to the discovery, with Keynes, that wealth is better harvested on the home farm than far afield. It is also rooted in deep cultural changes. Algeria and Vietnam have shown that some small

45

countries at least have become sufficiently aware of their own personality to worst major powers. The reactions of the French and American publics have shown that civilian societies have little stomach for long wars when they do not seem vital to the homeland and, not least, when the spectacularly unsurburban activities of war are televised through all the suburbs. What one is witnessing, at both ends of the scale, different though the outlooks are, is the growth of human self-awareness and resistance to pure power politics. The world has changed a great deal in this respect even since the heyday of imperialism from 1880 to 1900. It is no accident that despite the record in Latin America or, more so, Eastern Europe, it is, as Brzezinski said, difficult to describe American or even Russian politics in classic imperialist terms. The same may be said of Alastair Buchan's remark that the United States could not impose itself on the world without changing its social system in ways it would not be willing to consider. Cultural factors like these may, in the end, be the most important of all.

For all these reasons, the international system seems more solidly structured than it was. Yet the roots of this lie in the fifties rather than the sixties, and in some ways it seems less secure now than then. This is largely because ten years ago most of the world was only half on-stage. During the fifties the superpowers bestrode the Cold War like colossi, but even Russia, despite its ideological challenge and the Korean War, was still largely isolated in its "socialist sixth of the earth." China had barely begun its revolution, Japan was in ruins, picking up the pieces. The Third World either was ridding itself of Europeans or, like Latin America, was a backwater. Europe, though dwarfed, remained the cockpit of the world. As a result, America's complementary policies, one of containing the Soviet Union, the other of building up politicoeconomic cooperation with allies behind the *Lebensraum* offered by the nuclear frontier, worked within a simplified context. The erosion of the cold war, the rise of Japan and China, nationalism and the failure of containment to work in Vietnam as in Europe, have subtly changed all that. International politics itself, so dominant in

46

the fifties, has given way somewhat to the revival of internal social pressures and "ideology," above all perhaps in the United States. The world, and the interrelations between domestic and foreign policies, have again become complex and untidy after a whole generation when grand designs seemed possible and in order.

These cross-currents were in evidence in the discussion on America's impact on the world at Princeton. The majority of speakers, in reaction against Vietnam, argued for American "self-restraint": "we cannot play the role of cosmic Metternichs" and "the policeman of the world cannot and will not be the innovator of the great society." This feeling that the defense of Cold-War frontiers, à la Dulles, had become partly too much for American power and partly irrelevant was summed up in Brzezinski's prescription of "selective disengagement." It was, however, balanced by skepticism about far-reaching agreement with Russia. Stanley Hoffman did not believe

> we will get a return to the pure bipolarity of conflict or to a condominium of the superpowers—it's hard to see how it could be established or maintained. Our range of alternatives is narrower. Either the present international system will be perpetuated, in which case, unfortunately, since there is very little to choose between partly impotent superpowers and largely impotent smaller states, there will be recurrent crises and overstraining of the superpowers, or there will be an attempt to establish a more structured international milieu with more middle powers, more hierarchies responding to different kinds of power—military, economic, technological, monetary—more regional decentralization, a world in which competition will continue, but within limits and restraints.

This sense that the world system needs to be better structured in a way which corresponds to its complexities, and pessimism about the developing countries and the attitude of the industrial ones to them, led to the stress being placed on the "creation of a community of developed nations." There was remarkable unanimity on this—or, at any rate, lack of opposition to it—which is in itself a

47

sign of the times. It is rare for intellectuals to see so much eye to eye (though the young said significantly little on foreign affairs), and it was important that they did so. Yet behind this agreement on aims lie a large number of questions about means.

Owen Harries posed a number of questions about "selective disengagement." How selective would it be? What criteria of selection would be applied? Where would the line of selection fall on the map? While the United States is talking of pulling in horns, for instance in Africa, the Soviet Union is seeking to build up influence from India to Algeria, Nigeria and even Peru, and the Red Navy is becoming ubiquitous. Concentrating on Vietnam and the cities, and aware of the pitfalls of "influence," American opinion can bear with this now. But cumulatively it could undermine the relatively young sense of security born of the Cuban missile crisis of 1962 and produce reactions, even overreactions, in a few years' time. If not, and selective disengagement is carried through, where will it end? Alastair Buchan feared, from a European point of view, that the United States might discover it had no vital interests outside North America. Kaysen replied in effect that this was too strategic a view and that in cultural and economic—that is, civilian—terms the United States is more than ever present in Europe. No doubt the United States will not become wholly isolationist. But the preoccupation with the not-so-great society means more than acute competition for federal funds between the cities and the Pentagon. There is a sense in which all fundamentalist movements, like the New Left, are isolationist. It is true that student movements bear remarkable resemblances throughout the world. But this assumes an international order rather than promotes it, much as the Workers' International stopped short at speeches. There has been a regular pendular swing in the twentieth century between movements for international organization, which tended to underrate social pressures (after both wars), and internationals of good will (the workers before both wars, and now the students), which in their emphasis on "man" and "values" tend to underrate the need for international mechanisms. There is a pres-

48

sure, explicable but unfortunate, to regard the two as competitive rather than complementary.

Questions also arise about a "community of developed nations." The difficulties of international cooperation have grown, even among present partners, partly as a result of the very progress made. The further joint management advances, the more it uncovers the sensitive roots of social differences between peoples and of national conceptions of sovereignty. A prime example is provided by the European Economic Community, where the prospect of changes in exchange rates, themselves based in the last resort on social and political differences between member countries, have heavily strained the common price system for agriculture. Other examples can be found both inside and outside the European Community, in money, trade and technology. Such differences are not insuperable, if the will to overcome them is present. But how much more difficult it is to extend such systems to countries between whom politics are based on mistrust. The occupation of Czechoslovakia has shown that it will be very hard for the West to pursue economic cooperation with the smaller Eastern European countries to any point where the Russians fear it can affect their political and military domination of the area. The limitations of cooperation between the rival superpowers themselves may be relaxed, but so far there is not much to prove it in any of the fields —space, arms or oceanology—where they are in a class by themselves. There are even problems between the United States, as the world's dominant economy, and Japan as its most dynamic one. Their economic and financial interrelations are intense, but anti-Japanese protectionism is growing in the United States and the Japanese have been keeping up a stubborn resistance to attempts by American industrial giants to invest and produce in Japan. If the two countries fell foul of each other's economic nationalism, this could profoundly affect Japan's foreign and defense policies a decade hence.

In some ways, the major problem today is the slow but potentially chaotic diffusion of power in a world where nuclear engineering is spreading and growing cheaper. This applies even to the Big Two themselves. Russia, having learned the lessons of America's strategic mobility as an "offshore island," is beginning to emerge from its Eastern European glacis, into Asia and onto the high seas. It is for the first time becoming a world power in the same sense as the United States, and this can potentially change politics everywhere. Whether the aim is to extend Russia's reach as a great power or as an ideological competitor with China, or more likely both, America's former freedom of maneuver will be increasingly challenged.

So, however, is Russia's, by the emergence of the Far East as a major center of world politics. China is expected to be able to produce intercontinental missiles from 1972–73 onward. If it attains significant nuclear status by the 1980s—and it seems set to do so from the middle seventies on—the relationships between the superpowers will be infinitely more complex. Even a move as necessary as an improvement in Sino-American relations—called for by all the Asian members of the Princeton conference—will arouse Soviet suspicions.* Damping reciprocal mistrust between two nuclear powers is tricky enough; the permutations of three may call for talents of a still higher order.

Then there is Japan. Saburo Okita described at Princeton its fantastic economic record in recent years. It looks as if between 1966 and 1969 Japan will have increased its annual GNP by $60 billion a year! In 1966 her product was about equal to France's. In 1969, three years later, it is about equal to that of France and Italy together. Such achievements make it plausible that by 1975 Japan will have a GNP two and a half times that of China, and by 1980 one comparable to the six Common Market countries put together and two-thirds that of the Soviet Union. Its small physical size may disqualify it—like Europe—from being more than a heavily armed neutral, even if it abandons its present policies and acquires nuclear weapons. But a Far Eastern polity built around four states

* See "Asia: Dialogue with China," pp. 260 following.

with vast resources (the United States, the Soviet Union, China and Japan) could fall back all too easily into the classic complexities of the balance of power.

To this picture of an industrial world subject to the king's peace but laboring under increasing diversities and strains would have to be added the effect of the growing intercommunication of cultures and opinions across frontiers. The New Left, which spans such a diversity of societies, seems a portent in this regard. It only radicalizes, after all, attitudes long familiar in the U.N. General Assembly—aspirations to freedom of the human personality, anti-colonialism and a visceral hatred of the powerful, the wealthy and even, by extension, the white. It is true but irrelevant to point out that Saudis cut off thieves' hands, that Indians oppress their untouchables, Nigerians Biafrans, and so on. The bias in world opinion is a fact, and hypocrisy the tribute of governments to it. Carl Kaysen was surely right when he said that

> we are, for better or worse, becoming members of a single moral community. There's no doubt that the rational course of action in a selfish and material sense for all rich countries is to ignore the poor majority of the world and let them stew in their own juices. In every rich country, the United States, France, the United Kingdom, Germany, the Soviet Union, Czechoslovakia, the strongest internal political forces currently push in this isolationist direction. But I also think there is a deeper force, which I can describe only as a sense of moral community, that makes this in the short run difficult, and in the long run impossible.

This community is also practical: whatever the limits of foreign aid, stressed by Leo Mates, all rapidly growing poor countries, from Taiwan to the Ivory Coast and Venezuela, have for one reason or another had abundant foreign exchange. The process can work also in reverse: the community of revolt between the poor and radicals in the rich countries potentially knows no frontiers. Perhaps the most revealing aspect of the Arabs' campaign against Israel has been its international setting, in Athens and Zurich airports, in Robert Kennedy's assassination, and now in reported contacts between El Fatah and anti-Semitic Black Power groups in the United States. In a world wracked by instabilities but technologically one, radicalisms will increasingly interact. They may not lead to race war. They are, however, likely to rivet the attention of governments on their domestic scene, and make them even less sensitive to each other's needs than they are now.

The nuclear dangers of such a world may restrain all its major powers, as they do the superpowers today, and lead to the permanent encysting of local conflicts. But the complexities, and dangers of accidents, such as slumps, which make bad situations worse, call for more organically political safeguards than the Bomb. "As between peace or uncontrollable violence among themselves, the choice of the developed societies will continue to be peace for some years, perhaps until the end of this century, and the decision thereafter, peace or war, will follow inexorably from the dispositions that they have adopted meanwhile."[28] They need, in Marion Doenhoff's words at Princeton, "to turn the technical nuclear peace into a political peace." That means, if this is possible, the creation of mechanisms and rules which can enjoy a widely accepted political legitimacy.

Currently, the emphasis is on agreements between the two superpowers. Two-power agreements, if they can be reached, are obviously invaluable as an extension of the nuclear balance that has been one foundation of the postwar peace. It is certainly worth trying to limit both the arms race, which is subject to increasing risks and falling returns, and the commitments in the Middle East of the superpowers, which have already largely lost control. If Russia takes China seriously as a threat, it may be more willing to cooperate than some experts assume. Yet its present policies are highly ambiguous, expansionary in some respects, conciliatory in others, and provoke considerable uncertainty and suspicion. This

[28] F. H. Hinsley, "On the Present State and the Future Development of the International System" (a review of Osgood and Tucker's *Force, Order and Justice*), in *World Politics,* Vol. XX, No. 4 (July 1968), pp. 705 ff.

is a question not only of will but of power. The present Soviet regime, conservative and rigid, may in the medium term be more vulnerable to the seismic tremors of politics—on the long Chinese frontier, in Eastern Europe, even at home—than other more flexible societies. Its continuity of policy cannot be taken for granted. Even if it could be, neither superpower is keen to accept controls on its own actions, whereas these actions, for instance in the nonproliferation treaty, are apt to impose restraints on others. It is hard to see a "dual hegemony" acquiring political legitimacy in the eyes of others who, like Andreas Papandreou or the Latin Americans at Princeton, regard the superpowers from a wide variety of points of view and on very different issues as conservative guardians of a more or less repressive status quo. Two-power agreements can be one element in a complex of "hierarchies" of arrangements, but do not constitute a framework on their own.

Hence the need to continue promoting the politico-economic system developed by America and its allies as another building block of a future world system. This is the only structure embodying the civilian logic of politics which is strong enough to cut across the prospective muddle of power of the seventies and eighties. Despite achievements like the Kennedy Round, this structure has been in the doldrums lately, in part because of the divisions of European purpose during General de Gaulle's reign. The "community" approach has developed mainly in the North Atlantic area because of the uniquely close cultural, political and economic ties between America and Western Europe. The European paralysis since 1963 has correspondingly helped to create a sense that international solutions are on the wane. Americans have become irritated by the Europeans' incapacity to act. Europeans have become both fearful of America's preponderant power and jealous of its non-European priorities. The exchange between Waldemar Besson and Carl Kaysen at Princeton was typical of this rather neurotic relationship, and unthinkable both in tone and in substance a decade earlier, though the disparities in power were then at least as great. If the Europeans can, in the post-de Gaulle

53

era, free themselves of their present sense of paralysis, the relationship might improve quite markedly again.

If Britain does become a member of the European Community, Americans will assume, as George Ball pointed out, that a more effective and united Europe will emerge. Such a uniting Europe should be better able to help strengthen the world's monetary system as financial movements become more and more intense. It should be able to encourage the appearance of at least a few European "transnational" corporations using their European base to establish themselves in the United States and elsewhere. It should be able to make a significant effort in some, at least, of the new technologies, such as data systems, breeder reactors, oceanology, satellite communications and even aerospace. The system of international management established in postwar conditions can then be brought up to date to meet the problems of the seventies. The core of international cooperation, in the North Atlantic, can be expanded, and other nations, in different ways and for different purposes, gradually attach themselves to it.

This could be of particular importance vis-à-vis Japan. Japan's foreign trade has been growing, in most years of the past decade, at twenty percent a year. A Europe of relatively shrunken states facing competition from a giant Japanese economy would no doubt retreat into protection, leaving the Americans and the Japanese not too happily face to face. A North Atlantic system based on two reasonably balanced pillars, North America and Western Europe, could more easily hope to continue to integrate Japan as an equal third in money, trade and the new technologies. Japan and Western Europe, included as economic giants which cannot be serious nuclear powers in a broad and varied politico-economic system, might be able to play a major role in the emergence of a civilian dialectic of contractual relationships cutting cross the diplomatic dialectic of virtually impermeable great powers.

The emergence of such a system would depend on nationalism's not gaining the upper hand. It need not; Western Europe is too diverse and Japan too dependent on the good working of the world economy for contentiousness to be very attractive to either if the system works. Its magnetism would depend in part on its willingness to help the poorer nations, in part on developments in the Communist states. At least, it would open up opportunities in both directions. Without it, the prospects for a "community of the developed nations" look fairly dim, and the eighties and after might be uncomfortable decades in which to live.

In many ways, the responsibility lies currently with the Western Europeans. As the main reservoir of politically unmobilized or poorly mobilized resources, their capacity, or incapacity, to mobilize them more effectively could make a real difference. If they do improve their performance, they could be a catalyst of broader "Western" cooperation. For this reason, the next few years, when Europeans see how far they can unite now that de Gaulle is no longer there, either to stop them or to provide excuses for inaction, may well be one of the testing times of man's capacity to control the current transition from a nature-dominated to a man-made world.

Despite—or because of—the Bomb, the Cold War and the fear of slumps, a great deal has been accomplished since 1945. The great blot on the record is the almost Victorian indifference of the rich countries to the poor. Still, the industrial nations, pursuing their own purposes, have laid the foundations of abundance at home and perhaps of a workable international system in the world. Today's revival of ideology is a direct result of these very great achievements. The younger generation, brought up in standards of affluence and equality, is all the more outraged by exceptions from them and, knowing only the successful industrial society, more alive to its frustrations. It is customary to stress the gap between the generations and present it as almost unbridgeable. Yet, in some respects, the aspirations of the one stand on the achievements of the other and extend them. If, for instance, there is one theme common to the domestic and international scenes, it seems to be the changing role of force in human affairs. There has been a partial but very significant shift away from the old forms of force and authority toward new standards of self-determination. That could be crucial at the dawn of the society of collective free choice where, if old habits of behavior survive, they could turn individuals' real power of choice to ashes, perhaps even radioactive ones.

The past twenty-five years have produced new constraints on naked, military power. Nuclear deterrence, at one end of the scale, and the will to independence of societies large and small, at the other, have greatly narrowed the scope of traditional forms of power. The civilian and rationalist ethos of industrial societies makes even people with no special moral objections to war regard it as increasingly irrelevant as well as frightening. Many of the young have intensified this into a burning hatred of power politics as such. The shift is not universally present in the same degree. If all advanced countries have to some extent been affected by the spirit of the times, they have patently not been equally affected, as events in Czechoslovakia have shown. The Middle East too was rightly cited by Minoo Masani at Princeton as an example of the continued relevance of armed force in many situations. Indeed, the pace of change in human behavior may still prove too slow for the magic-making world of the new technologies. Nevertheless, might violating widespread notions of right is becoming an increasingly double-edged weapon. The civilian dialectic of politics has gained somewhat at the expense of the military one.

Something of the same psychology is now affecting the quite different context and dialectic of domestic affairs. The tactics of the New Left illustrate this very clearly. If the New Left are "twice the men" on television and, even away from it, bear witness as if the cameras were still trained upon them, this is not merely to compensate for lack of constructive thought about government. It reflects a sound instinct that the authorities in open societies are helpless once rebels can easily appeal to the public's dislike of what it considers abuse of power. This is not new, of course; what *is* new is the impact of television on citizens with a growing sense of their own dignity and rights as individuals. This does not serve only rebels. The Parisian public backed the students in the early days of May 1968 when they seemed underdogs beneath the flailing batons of the gendarmes, and turned against them once they seemed about to impose their own will as Lords of Misrule. Still, either way, the politics of 1970 imply a public not necessarily uncooperative with, but more and more critical of, authority. It is going to be harder and harder to treat people, even unconsciously, as machines less effective than real ones, or as statistical units in vast social aggregates. This seems so widespread in the wealthiest Western societies that it justifies to some extent their appropriating the complacent epithet "advanced."

All life is balance, and there are dangers even in progress: broadly speaking, the current ones seem to be those of undirected anarchy capable of leading, if unchecked, to the disastrous habits of self-assertion of the early twentieth century. The dangers are most feared at present on the domestic scene, where they are probably most easily assimilated. In highly evolved civilian communities, the very factor that makes shock tactics pay, the wide-spread fear of civil violence, also makes them potentially counter-productive. There are built-in checks and balances in such societies. The greater danger is probably the uncreative international chaos, feared by Stanley Hoffmann, "of partly impotent superpowers and largely impotent smaller states." The international checks and balances are much more primitive than the domestic ones. In any given nation, institutions exist and the vast majority of people look to them to hold the ring. In the international society, they do not exist, and the whole art of politics is to devise substitutes for them. Inside a country, making a fuss, bearing witness, protesting and debating, all the politics of radical inspiration, make sense, may gain support, force reforms and even win power. Between societies, the difficulty is to agree on contracts, rules and mechanisms that have long ago made possible the kind of politics taken for granted at home. "The skill of making, and

57

maintaining Common-wealths, consisteth in certain Rules, as doth Arithmetique and Geometry: not (as Tennis-play) on Practise onely."[29] Men will need not only inspiration but rules.

FRANÇOIS DUCHÊNE

[29] Hobbes, *Leviathan,* conclusion of Chapter 20.

THE ENDLESS CRISIS

AMERICA IN THE SEVENTIES
A Confrontation of the World's
Leading Social Scientists on the Problems,
Impact and Global Role of the United States
in the Next Decade

THE TERMS OF REFERENCE

Introductory Remarks by the Co-Chairmen,
Jean-Jacques Servan-Schreiber
and
Carl Kaysen

JEAN-JACQUES SERVAN-SCHREIBER: It is proposed that we discuss the present domestic problems of the United States, together with the international problems of the world. This, it seems to me, is a very necessary conjunction. There are great similarities between the internal crisis of this country and crisis in other parts of the world. Both mark the rebirth of fear: fear of the other man, which is the basis of racism; fear of powerlessness, which explains in part the disarray of youth in many countries; fear of the increasing tempo of change in science, in industry, in the environment of our lives, which probably explains the fear of the future in all of us. It is essential to examine how we can strengthen the chances of reason in its duel against fear. From that point of view, America is now the crucial battlefield. Because your country is further on the path of industrial progress than many of ours, many of the crises you are living through today we shall increasingly have to face in the future.

We have witnessed in the United States since 1960 a remarkable progress of rationality. We have seen the science of decision-making take great leaps forward. We have seen an impressive refining of developmental methods for industrial growth; spectacular growth in the scope of education; the role and influence of the

61

intellectual elite become greater and greater, in government, business and the nation as a whole. But now, within the last three or four years, this remarkable progress of reason has been clouded by a resurgence of irrationality. The Vietnam adventure, violence in the cities, the passions on the race issue, the assassination of great moderate leaders, have altered the life and image of America. The biggest danger for all of us would be a retreat of reason in America before the instincts, the emotions and tensions of irrationality. In this complex world, and most of all in this country, with its power for good and evil, it is essential that reason, on the contrary, should constantly increase its zone of influence. It is because you are in the avant-garde that you are now in such a profound turmoil and debate publicly fundamental and elementary questions that were buried for centuries under tradition and dogma. The relationship between parent and child, between rich and poor, between black and white, between the organization man and life, between structure and spontaneity—all these basic questions that were solved by tradition you are now submitting to a formal debate.

What is the finite dimension and human consequence of industrial growth? What are the objectives of a modern society? What cultural ambitions should be ours after all those efforts of production? Upon the answers that you will find to this new set of questions will come a new definition of the relationship between man and society after the second industrial revolution. It seems to many of us that the debates and dissents going on in this country are proof that you are earnestly in search of that new social contract. And there lies, perhaps, the final reason of our common concern.

It seems to me impossible for America to focus its intelligence and resources on the rational solution of its internal crisis without a radical change in the present distribution of America's physical involvement toward the world. America cannot hope to discover the ways of its post-industrial society or invent its new social contract, if it feels responsible for restoring order in every single crisis that erupts anywhere in the world. If America is anxious and overmilitarized, reacting to all symptoms of revolution or changes in the rest of the world, the chances of reason in this country to win its running battle with fear will be small. The policeman of the world cannot and will not be the innovator of the great society.

CARL KAYSEN: There are three different kinds of reasons why the United States is in some sense the center of world concern today. The most obvious one is that it is at the peak of military, economic and perhaps even technical power. Whatever nation occupies that position occupies also everybody's thoughts, feelings, concerns and anxieties. Then, too, we have made the furthest movement, if not progress, in the direction of industrialization, of urbanism, and we tend to think that the urban industrial society is the universal solvent, the form of social organization to which every society tends, and therefore the United States is the picture, good or bad, which everybody can hold up before him.

Another reason we often forget is that our society, ideally and to a substantial if dangerously insufficient extent, embodies widely shared values: democracy, egalitarianism, material progress. That too makes us a model. It is fair to say that our social problem-solving mechanisms have worked fairly well for the past hundred years. They have certainly not worked perfectly, nor without high costs to some groups and people, but they have worked fairly well.

Three features, I think, have made this mechanism rather successful. The first is nonideological and rather open politics in which principle since the Civil War has played a relatively small role and interest in bargaining a rather large role. The second is a relatively free scope for the market system and the absence, on the whole, in this period, of social groups strong enough and well organized enough, to prevent on a broad scale the workings of the market when these were harmful to those groups. The third, and perhaps the most important was, until World War Two, a relative isolation from the rest of the world.

At the moment, trust in this mechanism, belief in its efficacy in solving the problems that we face, both domestically and internationally, is low. There is some kind of crisis of confidence in our form of social organization. It is, however, accompanied by a lack of plausible alternatives. I think it is this double difficulty—loss of confidence on the one hand, the unavailability of what seems to be a superior alternative on the other—that gives us a sense of unusual anxiety.

Domestically, it is no longer easy to believe that a system of market economy with only a moderate amount of government intervention directed at managing the aggregate level of demand will solve social problems. It is perfectly clear that that system does not solve the intertwined problems of race and poverty. We face a thorough change in the system and a set of relations between market and political guides new in our history. We also face a harder-to-define problem, a loss of faith in some sense, in the positive achievements of the system. Further wealth itself seems an insufficiently powerful stimulus to motivate the kind of social allegiance society needs.

At the same time, we are facing the consequences of radical changes in the international system. These reflect, I think, two basic facts, one economic, one cultural or moral. The economic fact is that the technology of military power has changed in such a way that there are only two serious military powers in the world, and there will be for as far ahead as anybody can usefully see, which I would say is ten years if he wants to be very bold, twenty if he wants to be insane. Yet as the cost and complexity of maintaining real military power increases, the political usability of military power decreases even more rapidly. So we have an awesome and incredibly expensive and increasingly useless military power. The relation between military power and the conventional goals of international politics has changed far more rapidly than our ability to think about that change.

The cultural fact is that we are, for better and worse, becoming members of a single moral community. There is no doubt that the rational course of action in a selfish and material sense for all the rich countries is to ignore the poor majority of the world and let them stew in their own juices. In every rich country, the United

States, France, the United Kingdom, Germany, the Soviet Union, Czechoslovakia, the strongest internal political forces currently push in this isolationist direction. But I also think there is a deeper force, which I can describe only as a sense of moral community, that makes this in the short run difficult, and in the long run impossible.

I
THE CRISIS

OF LIBERALISM

1

THE REVOLT AGAINST
THE ORGANIZATION MAN

JOHN KENNETH GALBRAITH: I suspect that we're meeting here in 1968 at one of those periods, of which 1933 was one, 1948 another, when there has been a major change in the equilibrium of American politics. In the year or so just passed, issues which have preoccupied American political discussions since at least 1948 have suddenly dropped out of sight. The consensus—if I may use that obsolete word—on the whole question of Communist containment disintegrated into a bitter dispute over one of its aspects, Vietnam. In the election there was almost no discussion of the old familiar economic and welfare issues which have done so much for my profession these past twenty years. I was for several months last year the chairman of Senator McCarthy's Economic Advisory Committee, which, in the past, would have been a position of some esteem. I never knew who the other members of my committee were; we were never asked a question. We took for granted from the beginning that our role was ceremonial.

What replaced the old, familiar, well-loved issues? First, there has been, of course, the discussion on civil equality. It has changed from a grace to be granted to a right to be asserted—and not necessarily peacefully, if peace, as so often in the past, means inaction. The second issue which burst on our politics with really remarkable suddenness was a sense of the individual in a highly organized world.

We face today a basic contradiction between, on the one hand, the disciplines—including the disciplined belief—required by the necessarily massive organization, public and private, of the modern industrial state, and, on the other, the enormous reliance on educated, qualified scientific personnel and the apparatus for providing them, which trains people in the critical modes of the intellectual and causes them to question the subordination of personal to public goals. There is a clash here, common to all the advanced industrial societies of the world, and I would suggest that we saw, during the last years and in this election, the first great manifestation of it. It is perhaps more visible in the United States because we are the most developed of the industrial communities and more than most wear our conflicts on our sleeve. But it is the same revolt that in France broke the impressive façade of Gaullist stability. And it is not selective in its association with political systems. In Prague the struggle is also between those who see life in terms of individual self-expression and those who defend the disciplines that, in one powerful view, successful socialist industrialization requires. Such, one senses, is the conflict between the writers, artists and poets and the needs of industrial discipline, real or assumed, within the Soviet Union itself. The day is not distant when organization men on either side of the Iron Curtain will exchange sympathetic confidences on how to keep their respective poets and students in line.

In the past, we've handled these matters in America by a system of myths which have served rather well as a substitute for truth. One myth, in the private sector, is that the individual is sovereign on the market, which instructs General Motors, General Dynamics, General Mills, etc. According to this, the supplying firm is wholly the public servant, never the public master. In our public life there is the equally hallowed notion of the citizen electing the legislator, the legislator instructing the Executive, who instructs the bureaucracy which, in turn, instructs the suppliers. With a rush of revelation that many might think overdue, we've had in the last year or so growing doubts about these imagined manifestations of sovereignty. They have come to be seen for what they are, as systems of belief designed to distract attention from the more disenchanting reality. The individual has increasingly seen that the great corporations take for granted that what the public wants in the way of automobiles, soap and cigarette filters is what the public will be persuaded it should have. They will also shape in some degree to their convenience the individual's view of his life, his boss, his needs, and will expect him to conform his existence to the goals of the organization he serves. Similarly, in the public sector, the individual has ceased to assume that the great bureaucracies, particularly those in the area of foreign policy—the Pentagon and the State Department—are subordinate to the Presidency, Congress and the voters. What is proclaimed as foreign policy is what the military and civilian bureaucracy believes it should be. Not even the power of the President here is plenary. As we all know, on military appropriations, for example, he fights at least a rear-guard action. Concern over the seeming autonomy of the military-industrial complex long ago roused even such an otherwise placid figure as Dwight D. Eisenhower. The frequently iterated and reiterated willingness of the military members of this complex to accept the prompt and permanent extinction of mankind in defense of ideological distinctions that they do not understand has added steadily to public alarm.

It has been customary to speak of the Vietnam War as the issue of the past year. It was really the symbol of the greater issue—how to set limits to the power of bureaucracy in the service of its own myths. The individual has seen, through Vietnam, a continuing succession of matters serving the purposes of the machine. Perhaps the most remarkable manifestation of this process has been the substitution of official truth for truth. What seems plausible within organizations, where disciplined belief is a requirement, looks fantastic without. It could be believed within the organization that we were in Vietnam to keep some solemn if highly ambiguous commitments. Outside, everyone knew it was the result of a succession of hideous miscalculations. It was possible for someone accepting the disciplines of the machine to see the Tet offensive a year ago as a victory. Outside, everybody knew it was a catastrophic defeat. It was possible within the machine to see the government in Saigon as a manifestation of Jeffersonianism, with moral overtones of Lincoln and Norman Vincent Peale. Outside, there has been a strong tendency to agree with Mr. Buchwald that its only real contribution to democratic and parliamentary practice has been the device of jailing unsuccessful presidential candidates for five years. Inside the bureaucracy, Greece can be the southern flank of the bastion of freedom. Outside, it is obviously a regressive and messy collection of military despots.

There has been an extraordinary lack, within the machine, of any sense of the danger of being divorced from the public. In the pristine days of the Cold War, the public did go along, and it was assumed that the organization would be similarly exempt today from the pressures of public opinion. Very little effort was made to see whether there was public support, not only for the military budget and the Vietnam War, but for the whole structure of our foreign policy. The national interest was involved, hence people had a patriotic obligation to go along. In any case, the needs of secrecy precluded explanations.

This exclusiveness has tended to build on itself. It has been ill-received in the intellectual and academic community. Students who are assiduously lectured on the virtue of thinking for themselves and assuming responsibility in the society, and who, to everyone's surprise, occasionally do, have been especially adverse. This has produced the assumption that the academic community is intransigently hostile and hence no effort need or can be made to defend foreign policy before it. For a major foreign-policy figure to appear before a major university audience in recent years would at minimum seem heroic and more likely wildly reckless. The Secretary of State [Dean Rusk] has taken further refuge in the notion that the young, having no recollection of Hitler, Munich and Stalin, cannot be expected to understand. But this exclusiveness operates not only against the universities and the young. The Senate Foreign Relations Committee has received only marginally more deference as the result of considerably more pleading. The excuse again is that the foreign policy is too delicate for public discussion. In effect, the machine has said of all outsiders, and above all of the academic community, "Well, they're beyond the pale; we'll just have to go ahead without them." This was, in one form or another, the fundamental point of the tension in this past year, the sharp edge of the by no means novel issue of the individual versus organization.

This issue the older liberals of my generation and the Democratic Party were peculiarly unable to understand. They've come very much to terms with big private and public organization. Once, American liberals were deeply suspicious of large organizations. In the form of big business it raised the specter of the social inefficiency of monopoly and of economic, social and political aggression against labor, the public and the democratic state. As large public bureaucracy, it might not be fully subject to public control. But the tradition that nurtured these fears has become, for all practical purposes, extinct. As a newer generation of liberals concentrated on fiscal policy and the new economics, improved welfare, education and civil rights, a new era of good feeling was imagined to have come to characterize relations between the liberal reformer and the industrial system. Far more than conservatives, American liberals in the last thirty years have worked to perfect the relationship between the bureaucratic state and highly organized industry. Liberals, not conservatives, have taken the lead in state regulation of the industrial environment to promote steady growth. Liberals saw the need for regulating aggregate demand—what is now called the new economics—before it was fully perceived by industry itself. The liberals served the industrial system in two further respects. First, public purchases are the foundation of stabilized aggregate demand: a large public sector of the economy developed. Second, the risks associated with advanced technology require government to pay for development or provide a market. The private corporation cannot underwrite it. Both of these ends are served by an arms race sustained by the vision of a relentless Communist menace. Liberals of the last generations have been wholly susceptible to these visions. As compared with conservatives, they have argued only for greater sophistication in meeting the Communist challenge, greater awareness of the social origins of Communist agitation and greater liberality in financing technological competition. The possibility strongly appeals to me that Soviet industrialization nurtures similar needs and that the resulting competition renders service—of an extremely dangerous sort—to both industrial systems.

It was the revolt against this identification of the older liberals with the impersonal power of organization which was the basis of a great deal of the tension at the Chicago convention and of the great difficulty of healing the divisions within the Democratic Party after the convention. It was also, I would say, the dominant factor in the election of Mr. Nixon. Though the new mood lost in the political arena, the remarkable thing is how close it came to winning. Although there was very little evidence of it as recently as four years ago, the reaction against a bureaucratically determined foreign and defense policy and unease about the extent to which one's life has been taken over by the large corporations were sufficiently strong to have won a substantial victory for either of its exponents, Senator McCarthy or Senator Kennedy, had either been a candidate. I'm not quite equating them in this regard, but there is very little doubt that either would have won. This suggests two things to me. One is that the lesson will not be lost. Future Presidents, recalling that one was forced from office, future Secretaries of State recalling that one was reduced to getting in and out of hotels like a burglar, future military men watching the revolt against the draft sweeping the campuses, future industrial firms reflecting on the fate of both their recruiters and recruitment, will have a more thoughtful view of the limits of organization. The other is that the struggle will certainly continue to be part of American politics in the years to come. I think the great point of vulnerability of the new Administration is its commitment to the Pentagon, to things like anti–ballistic-missile development, and the reaction this will provoke. Were I organizing opposition to the Nixon Administration, which, as a detached and impartial citizen, I would never dream of doing, I would concentrate heavily on that issue.

But we cannot fool ourselves. So far the revolt has been a revolt against. It has been a common and fair observation during this past year: "I can see what those fellows are opposed to. I only wish I knew what they were for." Coming to terms with organization will not be so easy as opposing it. On the affirmative question of how we come to terms with organization, thought has not yet begun. We cannot avoid organization. Derisory, dull and pompous as the goals of the great corporations may be, their world has nevertheless, in the United States, gone far toward eliminating the poverty which may be the one thing in life worse than dullness. Even today, the problems of the ghetto and cities are by-products not of the shortcomings of General Motors, but of the fact that in these areas we've lacked the competent organization we have in other parts of the economy. The question is not how we dispense with organization, as I fear some of my colleagues who have been associating with the movements I have been describing would say. The problem is how we come to terms with organization, how the individual can have some sense once more that organization is subject to goals more humane than those manifested in such a ghastly misadventure as the Vietnam War.

This is not a counsel of despair. Men once knew they were against capitalist exploitation and that they were against depressions. They were less sure what to do about them. So, with the vast public and private military and civilian organizations which have taken so much of our lives and no small part of our fate in hand, a good many million people have shown an instinct for resistance— a determination somehow to hold organization to account. This is impressive, and one day it will impress even those who cannot imagine the American people becoming roused over an issue that affects their self-expression or survival as distinct from their income.

MOCHTAR LUBIS: Has the recent Presidential election been a victory for individual choice or for the organization? Cannot the political machine still impose its will on the nation?

GALBRAITH: Certainly if the Republicans had had a free opportunity to select a candidate, he would not have been Mr. Nixon. He would have been Mr. Rockefeller or somebody else. If the Democrats had had a similar choice, he would have been Senator Kennedy, had he lived, or Senator McCarthy. On the other hand, I wouldn't want to draw too severe a conclusion from that. Few things in this world are perfect, and the discontent over this process, at least among the Democrats and potentially among the Republicans, was considerable. The Democrats will try to take steps in the next few months and years toward correcting it. I think they will be inadequate. One of the tragedies of the moment is that we are preoccupied with problems of the Electoral College, which are tolerable, whereas we need drastically to reform the nominating procedures within the party, which are being neglected. But in saying this is not perfect I don't want to imply that it is not likely to be improved.

ANDREAS PAPANDREOU: This is not critical of what has been said, but I would like to stress the problem of the structure of power, to which one seldom hears any reference. Do the citizens control the political authority in the United States? If so, to what extent? Does the political authority—the Administration and Congress—control the bureaucracy, the Pentagon being one instance only? This is possibly the source in the United States of the sense of powerlessness of citizens, either together or individually, to affect the course of events. This also has its counterpart abroad. Today there is a reverse colonization of the former colonizers in Europe, not to speak of the Third World. The allies and associates of the United States are powerless to affect its policies which decisively affect their own future. The heart of the problem is that somehow the process is beyond our control.

The Leviathan which has engulfed us all, this fantastic technological change commanding nature and us as well, is guided in ways we do not understand and by forces we have not yet had the courage to identify. In the openly totalitarian states, an elite takes responsibility, and is formally there to do that, using its wisdom and its values without concerning itself necessarily with the values

76

of the people it guides to a future it has predetermined. In the West, in a country such as the United States, no such formalized elites exist. But elites do exist, and guide life in fashions we have failed to define. There is indeed in our age the rise of the technocrat and bureaucrat, and he makes his alliances with forces in different countries in differing ways that determine our future. We have to understand and learn how to control these forces, how to make the citizen sovereign in his country and nations sovereign within regional groupings.

For this we need courage to identify the sources of power and speak about them. It used to be said that the working class was a carrier of change. It probably was, but is so no longer in advanced society. Are intellectuals possible carriers of change? The intellectual is in rather a bad position because, as in the Middle Ages, he is not free. He gets his research money from governments and support from institutions. He has to find a halfway house between living appropriately and taking his stand and making his mark. What characterizes the intellectuals of this period on the whole is lack of courage (I do not exclude myself). Hopefully, the forces which seem today disruptive—the minorities, the blacks, the students, the restless little countries that challenge the superpowers—may be the sources of change.

AMBASSADOR R. M. SOEDJATMOKO: Isn't the vital question whether new constellations of political support can be mobilized for new and more desirable policies? Does the political system have sufficient flexibility to deal with the crucial problems? Is there a chance of its breaking down?

GALBRAITH: This requires a statement of faith rather than a detailed analytical response. My instinct is that one can deal with all problems. If one abandons that notion, one deals with no problems. And if one has that instinct, then one excludes the notion of a breakdown.

SAM BROWN: Professor Galbraith has made a statement of faith. I think my generation, those in college today, do not respond with faith on this matter. We do not say, "Yes, the liberal institutions we've inherited will be able to cope with the problems we face." Also, we do not start on the other assumption, that they must fail. We look at the institutions we have, and at the problems we have, and we say that liberal institutions, though keeping legislative promises, have been unable to keep their larger promises to American society, and that a continuation of that trend can only result in a breakdown of those institutions. It is not adequate to have faith and rule out a breakdown, because it seems to me that liberal institutions in America are headed for a breakdown. To avert that you must find new ways to deal with the failure of the liberal establishment.

I would only add that when I walked into this room and observed the stereotypes college students attribute to liberal intellectuals being acted out around this table, I responded sharply. I hope I didn't respond so sharply to the stereotypes that I've been overly harsh in judging the content.

GALBRAITH: There's no question but that it is convenient for anyone with my political and intellectual associations to imagine problems can be solved within the liberal establishment. I withdraw the word "faith" and substitute the more pejorative and honest phrase "suspected convenience." That being said, like Mr. Dean Rusk I enthusiastically adhere to the proposition that there are enormous advantages in age and that this enables us to lecture people like Mr. Brown who remember neither Munich nor the Great Depression. Those of us who are, incredible as it may seem, relics of the 1930s, remember that there were then at gatherings of this sort overwhelming doubts that the system could survive. Such meetings were heavily preoccupied with economic questions. Now most of us have difficulty imagining those questions could once have been so difficult. It could be the same again. I am not suggesting it is. I merely state the possibility. One of the possible mistakes we make is in assuming the powerlessness of intellectuals. Eighteen months ago, some people—I can pick out three or four in this room, Arthur Schlesinger, Martin Peretz, Carl Kaysen, John Oakes—came together to view the possibility of defeating the State

Department and the Pentagon—I use those words deliberately—on Vietnam, by argument, by political action and I must say also by the enthusiastic cooperation on all matters of the government in Saigon. And what has happened? Popular opinion has been turned around, it has been brought to bear on the bureaucracy, and the bureaucracy has surrendered. If this can be accomplished in wartime, with all the passion of war aroused and the natural compulsion to salute when the flag goes up, then it surely can be brought to bear on other issues in peace. Look not at the strength of the military bureaucracy, but at its weakness as exemplified by General LeMay. Two years ago, General LeMay was a bona-fide American hero. Most of us would agree that in the reaction against the Pentagon and the bureaucratic state, he became the kiss of death to George Wallace. It's not out of the question to imagine this process being continued, to imagine heavy pressure being brought to bear on Congress, and a very large increase in the number of Congressmen and Senators who become energetically critical of the appropriations for the military and industrial complex. Recapturing power from the bureaucracy could become the foundation of a party program and reformist drive as full employment was in the past. The patterns are somewhat less clear for the private sector. So long as economists propagate the myth that General Motors is subordinate to the market, and the young believe it, we'll make little progress. But the moment we are persuaded that General Motors is the source of initiative in the economy and that St. Peter doesn't inquire of every entrant what he has done to increase the Gross National Product, economics will become a lesser part of our life, and social control of large organizations will be accepted as a possibility. We won't be the slaves of the assumption that all technology is good no matter how hideous it makes our lives. We won't be slaves to the assumption that the economic goals are automatically superior to aesthetic and environmental objectives. We will have in that area a progressive assertion of the individual versus the organization. I see enormous difficulties ahead, but we have had enough experience in the past

79

to show that the intellectual community, so far from being power-less in these matters, is the only source of power and one of the reasons for not opting out, for not saying difficulties cannot be solved within the framework.

EUGEN LOEBL: Before I came to this meeting, I had the opportunity to lecture in twelve universities all over this country and had contacts with many students and professors. What I found absolutely missing was the famous American pragmatism. I was pleased to see that the younger students in particular are looking for new approaches and new views. If youth is the future of your country, here is an element of optimism for these rather sad days. I may say that politically, in their readiness to engage seriously and wholeheartedly in problems, your students are on a higher level than ours in Czechoslovakia last year. Last year, our students, like yours now, were against the establishment; they pursued a negative critique, but had no positive answers to offer. However, this year in our country, students found a positive answer and so became the most dynamic political force, and still are—even under the occupation. That is one lesson: youth must have a positive program. But, as we have seen in Czechoslovakia, you cannot give the young a positive program like pocket money. Youth can have one only when the nation as a whole has a view of its future. Then the young people find their place themselves.

The other lesson is that while the intellectuals have no power as such, intellectual influence in the more highly developed societies is of tremendous importance. In our country, a few thousand intellectuals were able to unite the whole nation and were, unfortunately, even able to lead others in wrong directions. Why were they able to do this? Because they attacked the problems of our time—the problem of man himself—and did it not just as an abstraction or a slogan. They tried to project a social model in which the human personality, and especially creative intellectual work, has optimum space. I feel that this country still lacks such a motive. One should not tackle the problems of man through a single issue, even such an intractable one as race. Society has to be taken as a whole.

This or other organizations—under no condition government-sponsored ones!—should start to work out a perspective for the nation. One or more teams of experts of different disciplines should work out a project which would at least be a basis for a nationwide discussion. If one takes the Czechoslovak experiment as a kind of social laboratory, one finds it possible for intellectuals to unite a whole nation around ideals and realistic policies of humanism.

2

MORE CONTROLS AHEAD

GEORGE F. KENNAN: You don't need me to tell you with what concern and apprehension a great many people of my age view the situation in this country today. It would be hard for me to overstate this. There have been times, in this last year or two, when a great deal of what many of us used to associate with this country seemed to be in process of dissolution. We are faced with a whole series of national problems, each of which if not soon met in some reasonably adequate manner could bring grievous damage to our whole American civilization. Yet to none of them has our response been in any way adequate.

First, of course, there is the extreme disaffection and alienation from the body politic of the great mass of our Negro population: our greatest, most tragic, national problem. In close connection with it, there is the rapid disintegration and deterioration of our great cities as centers for cultural and political and in some respects even economic activity. As a sort of by-product of that, there is the recurrent disruption in these great cities, not just of individual processes of work, but of the very rhythm of urban life—the disruption of public life on the part of public servants and others whose regularity of effort is, after all, essential to the safety and comfort of the population. There is the steady and continuing process of destruction and pollution of our natural resources and the attendant deterioration of the physical environment for human life across this continent. There is the wasteful and chaotic nature of our transportation system. There is the domination of most of our great media of communication by the advertisers and the exploitation of these media for commercial purposes, purposes which have, if anything, only a negative educational value. Finally, in close connection with this but having aspects separate from it, there is the extremely disturbed and excited state of mind of a good portion of our student youth, floundering around in its own terrifying wilderness of drugs and pornography and political hysteria.

In every case, we are faced, as I see it, by a serious gap between traditional outlooks ingrained in the minds of leaders of opinion, legislators, political parties and the public at large, on the one hand, and the outlooks, insights and appreciations necessary to make a hopeful attack on the problem in question.

Everyone close to the problem of the urban Negro now realizes that the liberal dream of integration and an era of good feeling with which the American intelligentsia has comforted itself in recent years is simply not going to materialize. I am satisfied that there will have to be for the majority of black people a stage of voluntary separate development and local self-government to be lived through before we can hope to achieve any satisfactory relationship between them and the remainder of American society. Until the Negro finds his identity collectively in a community of his own, he is not going to find it individually, and until he does find it, it is going to continue to be difficult for him to relate himself to any of the rest of us on what would appear to him to be even and fair terms. But thoughts of this nature are strange as yet in many of the more influential and articulate sectors of American opinion, and the conceptual framework out of which such changes could take place in a constructive and orderly way is almost entirely lacking.

Again, in the case of our cities, we've seen a great deal of thought directed to how we can adjust to the blighting and disintegration of the central areas, but not so much to how we could avoid it. We have, it seems to me, come nowhere near the heart of the problem. This is how to preserve and restore the great cities for the performance of those cultural and social functions which they and they alone, unhappily, can perform in a modern society. Much attention has been given to alleviating poverty in the great urban ghettos, but I cannot conceive of any successful attack on this without an attack of at least equal vigor on poverty in the rural areas to the south from which this misery has been and is continuing to be imported into our great cities. It will be imported in even greater dimensions if all we do is raise living standards there.

Take the question of work stoppages, labor discipline in the great cities, the sort of thing that we've seen going on in New York this fall. I cannot see how anyone with these impressions in mind could fail to recognize that strikes where the comfort and safety of millions of people become a pawn to be used for interests that have nothing to do with the public interest are a destructive device of labor settlement. Such strikes ought obviously to be outlawed and replaced with better means of solving labor difficulties. We need here a very basic revision of our concepts of labor relations. But are these views sponsored by responsible public authorities or political parties? I think in general the answer is no.

Take again the question of pollution and destruction of natural environment and the related problems of transportation. It seems quite probable that restrictions far more drastic than anything we have seen to date will have to be placed on the operation of many industrial establishments. Thousands of communities will have to adopt radically different and much more expensive methods of sewage disposal, limitations will have to be placed on the packaging of commodities for general consumption in order to reduce the vast and absurd quantities of rubbish that our civilization is now producing. There will have to be a major shift, governmentally contrived and enforced, I fear, from the private automobile and the airplane to forms of public transportation that are cleaner and take less land out of use. People will have to turn, for example, from the search for some new and unspoiled natural area which they can devastate for a fourth airport around New York City to the search for changes in the transportation pattern which would make it unnecessary to build any such airport at all. But here too the concepts that would be necessary to envisage and to implement such changes are still largely lacking from our consciousness.

We can take finally the problems of the advertiser and the mass media and the related questions of student unrest and bewilderment. Does anyone seriously believe that the advertiser is really a person fitted by purpose, by function, by dedication, to be the custodian of what amounts to over half, I suppose, of the educational responsibility in this country? I'm told by educational authorities that the TV set is rated as at least as important as the school system in its effect on the minds of children. Now, either that TV set is going to have to be bodily removed from the American home or we are going to have to find something quite different to replace the stream of frivolities and inanities that flickers incessantly across it, holding endless numbers of children for endless hours in its hypnotic power and subjecting them almost without limit to its philosophic superficialities and its intellectual anti-discipline. I wonder whether we're not going to have a major restructuring of the experience of the American child and American youth if we are to retain the vitality of our society; and whether this will not have to be conceived and sparked, wherever nobody else is prepared to do it, by public authority of one sort or another.

But are we ready for this intellectually? It flies in the face, of course, of some of the most dearly held of our concepts about human freedom.

The purpose of these observations is simply to drive home the point that there is a great conceptual gap between the established outlooks of our society and a hopeful approach to some of our greatest problems. This is a gap which is not likely to be filled, either by the traditional postulates of American liberalism or by the angry and flamboyant demands of student radicals and black militants.

There is the further question of whether our present political institutions would be adequate as instruments for implementing such changes. Changes of such magnitude are going to require the imposition of some sort of public discipline in areas of life to which such discipline has never before been applied in our national experience, and where the very idea of applying it would be abhorrent to great numbers of people.

They are also going to demand—though this sounds contradictory—a radical decentralization of public authority such as we see in the New York City school situation today. There will have to be more power exercised by governmental bodies, but at lower levels and in a more decentralized way. The federal government cannot expect to regulate the initimate details of people's lives across the whole vast span of this nation without doing violence at a thousand points to the particularism of social groups and of geographic regions, without, in fact, impairing the very reality of democracy. But are state and local governments across the country prepared in any way to assume such tasks? Just look at New York City's problems. They involve two great governmental structures, one municipal and one at the state level in Albany, just within the confines of New York State itself; two other state governments; the host of smaller municipalities that are scattered across the whole Greater New York area in three states; and, finally, the great quantity of sub-municipalities within New York City itself. Can the challenges of this or any such area be successfully met without some rationalization of this wretchedly overcomplicated, anarchic system? Is the very institution of state government as we know it in any way adequate as the sole legislative and administrative entity standing between the federal level and the level of local government? Can we avoid for long some sort of redrawing of state boundaries, and even the creation of new regional authorities in certain fields?

The gap we have to fill is institutional as well as conceptual, and it's going to require revolutionary changes, I hope peacefully revolutionary, before it can be closed. So great are its dimensions, and so weak as yet the evidences of our capability of budging it, that there are moments when people my age are close to despair. But one knows also at this age that despair is not a feasible way of life, nor is it in the circumstances a justifiable reaction.

This country still has within it great resources of strength and vitality, resources of good nature, common sense, neighborly generosity, cheerfulness and humor, practical ingenuity—qualities that have endowed our people with their identity and given to our life the power and charm that it has had throughout most of our history. These qualities are visible today primarily in older people and not in younger ones; mainly in rural areas, not in urban ones; primarily among people who work with their hands, not among intellectuals. They would seem to be, on the face of it, the attributes of the declining element. But they do exist elsewhere, in a latent way, among many people in whose faces and behavior they are today regrettably undetectable. They are capable of being released. The liquidation of the Vietnam involvement and the termination of the agony of the Vietnam draft would alone release great quantities of them among the student youth. We must, therefore, tailor our external involvements to our domestic requirements. There can be no question, in my opinion, of the necessity of a very considerable retraction of external involvements in the interest of domestic progress.

This alone is not all that's needed. There is still the vital question of leadership here at home. The development of this leadership will not be easy, for the best of new administrations. There will be political debts to be paid, deeply rooted vested interests to be placated and overcome. A revolution in outlooks and in the framework of government can never be brought about suddenly in any useful way in such a country as this. But beginnings can be made, and beginnings can have their own momentum. New faces are about to appear on the governmental scene, on the national scene, and it implies no disrespect for the old ones to believe that the appearance of new ones is a good thing and comes at a good time. The great trick, of course, is going to be to improve the atmosphere and the reality of communication, on the one hand between governmental leaders and hundreds of thousands of worthy and troubled and devoted people who work in government, and on the other the millions of concerned citizens and above all educated citizens and ones in process of education. Many of the prerequisites for this improvement, it seems to me, are already here. Surely there are evidences that a great many people are tired of violence and anger and intimidation and demonstration and denunciation as preferred instruments of social change. These devices are wearing themselves out, even with the students. Millions of people, as I see it, are now in a mood to welcome a general movement of national unity, to see the decorum of our life restored, protesters mingle their efforts with those of other people instead of jeering and screaming as a means of achieving social ends. They would, in short, like to feel the pulse of returning confidence in themselves, in our value as a nation and in our possibilities for the future.

Even the right word might possibly begin it, as in 1933. The new Administration should and must be given a fair opportunity to show what it can do. If it should fail because others of us were not prepared to give it the requisite patience and tolerance, its failure would be one from which all of us would lose. If it should succeed, there could be in this country a release of constructive energies no smaller than that which poured out in England at the time of the Battle of Britain. Even the vast problems I have talked about would begin to lose some of their forbidding aspect. For other peoples, outside our own continent, it would be something far greater than anything we could ever achieve by force of arms.

MARTIN PERETZ: There are few writers from whom I've learned as much as from you. Nonetheless, there are times when a cool reasonableness, even of despair, is not much preferable to political hysteria. What troubles me is that what Ambassador Kennan says about young people, most specifically in the article in the *New York Times,** has an almost obsessive quality. If we look at what

* See *The New York Times*, Dec. 4, 1968.

has happened lately, it was the hysterics of the young which brought Vietnam to the center of the stage. I remember eight thousand of us around the White House in 1961, before the Vietnam adventure reached its climax. We asked for an end to testing, and everybody laughed. We were thought of as very marginal. When we started talking about Vietnam, we were also thought of as a very cranky group. The other day I came across a news clipping of a speech given by a man who first got me and some of my generation involved in politics, a very marginal, quixotic, cranky figure. His name was Stuart Hughes. He ran for the United States Senate and got two percent of the vote. But he made a speech in East Boston High School and warned, "There are now fifteen thousand troops in Vietnam and unless we do something very quickly, before long there will be a quarter of a million bogged down in an endless war." That was in 1962, seven years ago, when most of the present opposition of notables was entranced by dreams of counterinsurgency. I found in my own hand on the headline of that article (it was in slightly bolder words): "Tell Stuart to stop talking about Vietnam. Nobody knows where it is." But we young people knew a long time before you did. And we smoked you out by our hysterics, induced by watching enlightened liberals meticulously constructing the Vietnam disaster. In terms of each of the basic issues to which you have so eloquently spoken today—the cities, the waste of natural resources, the debilitating effect of television and public relations—as I look around this country, whatever the failures of the young, it is only they who, however confusedly, try to talk about these issues. They talk differently from Ambassador Kennan. They think there's a kind of easy answer in a glibly pronounced socialism. I think they're wrong. But they're right in saying that it's corporate power and the profit motive that have kept us so attached to debilitating and destructive means of organizing our society. So we should be pleased with the kind of hysterics that keeps invoking that archaic, old-fashioned word "capitalist."

Let me say one other thing. As I look at this coming Administration, I find it very difficult to be very patient with them even before they've started. The Nixon Administration, if I read my *Wall Street Journal* correctly, is planning one percent, one and a half percent increase in unemployment to stabilize the fiscal situation. That happens only to be 1,300,000 more unemployed, mostly black. It seems to me that this cool reasonableness, at minimum, is not infinitely preferable to hysterics.

KENNAN: You mentioned the demonstration in front of the White House against Vietnam. When I see pictures of student demonstrations, and hear the slogans shouted, I always wonder why the demonstrators think that people who *could* do the things they want *should* do them. Obviously not because they've been reasoned into it. Your opponent is hardly likely to be slayed by the wit and profundity of "Ho, Ho, Ho Chi Minh." The only argument here is implicitly that there are a great many of us and we are very stirred up and therefore you had better quickly get off the dime and do what we want you to do or else you're going to be faced with ugly reactions here in American opinion.

Now, this is all very well, but remember—since we're speaking frankly, you won't mind my doing so, too—you, the students and you, the black militants, are a minority. I wouldn't want to get in a screaming contest with the right wing in the United States. Someday they'll outscream you, and if you bring ten thousand people in front of the White House to show how angry you are, they'll bring a hundred thousand.

This is a very dangerous game. I cannot go along with a concept of public affairs the highest dream of which is apparently that the present political system remains unchanged, and we continue to have just such intolerable governments as we have had in recent years, but they are to be periodically kicked into doing something useful because they are afraid of the emotions which opposite policies would arouse in public opinion. If I were President and had to submit to the mob at the gate, rather than because I had been convinced intellectually, I would want to leave my job and go right out. If you think that this is the sort of President you've got, it's his departure you should be demanding—or a change in the political system. But why keep this system which satisfies you so little and cause it to function simply by a series of abuses and intimidations? This is not the way the affairs of a great nation can be conducted.

LILLIAN HELLMAN: George Kennan will remember that we met twenty-four years ago in the Soviet Union. Even then I respected his honesty and his talent, but I find myself bewildered by what he has said here tonight. George and I must have been born within a few years of each other, and so it is very hard for me to understand how two people of the same generation have come in the end to have such different conclusions about a younger generation. (Perhaps we have different views of our own generation.)

Mr. Kennan says that he thinks the new Administration in Washington should be given a chance. But is it a question of chance? Chance is rather too sporting a word. Perhaps it would be best to wait and applaud the Administration, if and when it deserves the applause.

When one speaks of a younger generation—and I have taught a great many students in the last ten years—of whom is one speaking? Some of them are fools, and many of them, I think, will be sellouts. But most of them are a better generation in knowledge and in spirit than we were. Moreover, we owe them a great debt. (As we owe the Negroes of this country a great debt in the last few years.) The most forceful protest made in this country about the crime we are committing in Vietnam has been done by the young. What has been done—little enough—about the crime of inequality has been done by the Negroes, most of them young, too. The rest of us, the liberal middle-aged, protested certainly on both issues, but we did not protest in time or in strength. Many young people and many Negroes don't talk what I think is sense. (Incidentally, I disagree with almost every word of what Mr. Innis said this afternoon.)* But youth is saying and doing many of the things that

* See pages 98 ff.

should have been said and done fifty years ago. I think, from what I've read and listened to, that George thinks the new young are mistaken and foolish. Maybe. But certainly it is their traditional right. Indeed I think there will be no future for any of us if we live in fear of the young and forgive the old. I wish I had been as bright as young people are today and I think many of you in this room must share that wish, and must have enough self-knowledge to recognize that sometimes our anger against youth comes because we envy them. In any case, whatever the arguments, there seems to me nothing that warrants despair—except possibly when one looks at the past of American liberalism.

KENNAN: If I find it more difficult to admire the behavior of the students, it's because at every turn I have a sense of *déjà-vu*. They are dreadfully like the Russian revolutionary students before the revolution. They tore down an existing governmental structure, which had its faults, but what they put in its place was something, in my opinion, worse. They themselves were the first victims of what they let loose on society. I'm not afraid of the demonstrating student. I'm afraid of the right-wing reaction which he's going to bring down over all our heads, his and mine.

HELLMAN: Joe McCarthy came without any student reaction.

KENNAN: But others can come with it, I think. The iron is entering into the soul of a lot of good people out in the sticks in this country. And this is what bothers me. It's perhaps a matter of temperament. But I look at these young people and I find their views silly and hysterical, without historical depth. I find them putting propositions forward which the most elementary knowledge of what's gone on in the world in the last forty or fifty years should knock out of their heads. I'm even disinclined today to talk with them, because I feel as though I am being constantly pushed down from being a university professor into a kindergarten teacher. There are certain limits to the elementariness of what you should have to say to people who are already in college. If they go on this way, they're going to destroy the very educational institutions on which they are presumably dependent for an education. I say "presumably" because I don't detect on the part of the student militants any particular desire for an education, and for the life of me I cannot understand why they are on the university campuses. If they want to cure the ills of society and the ghetto, the campus is not the place to start. Why don't they leave it and devote themselves full time to revolutionary activities? There's no reason why they should ruin perfectly good educational institutions in which other students might wish to study.

SAM BROWN: I need, as one who classifies myself as a militant student and am proud of it, to note very briefly some of the elementary lessons which we may have learned from your generation, Mr. Kennan.

We learned in 1960 that political hysteria is not limited to the student generation when we saw the missile gap created out of whole cloth, which Secretary McNamara later admitted. You must admit that this was political hysteria in the world beyond anything which we students are capable of and has had greater consequences on missile production at home and abroad and therefore in the world. In 1964, we then learned a lesson in political hysteria from Mr. Johnson, and that regardless of the hysteria created by the Democratic Party they are as ready to kill people as ever Barry Goldwater was. We learned in Vietnam a third kind of hysteria lesson, and that's the hysteria of wartime in the United States. We learned hysteria from the liberal establishment which in the first years of the Vietnam War supported it so strongly. (You stood to some degree as an exception to that liberal consensus in the country.) You must admit hysteria in Vietnam resulted in much more death than we students are capable of. Then we learned in Newark and Detroit and Chicago and San Francisco and Los Angeles a very elementary lesson about police hysteria and about the establishment who sanction hysteria. If we study the example laid down for us by the rational liberals who preceded us, we will see there a form of violence, of hysteria, which we are incapable of producing regardless of our fulminations against the establishment.

I'd only like to conclude by saying that I've never known what it was like to be in love with an older woman until Miss Hellman spoke a little while ago.

STANLEY HOFFMANN: Ambassador Kennan, you remarked that the student movement was a minority movement, as indeed it is, but as I see the American scene now, where would the support come from for the admirable aesthetic, rural, unpolluted vision that you defend? The central government in a country which is run by universal suffrage, and in which the media of advertisement and of profit have the power which they have, will more likely follow what it considers to be the wishes of the majority. In this respect community control is a very confusing notion, because, as Americans found out in the past, the community can be easily manipulated, highly conservative, highly conflicted, so that the solution of those conflicts would again have to be left to a central government that would be more responsive to the pressures for conformity than to the dream which you support.

If this is indeed the predicament, can one really blame those among the young who believe that there is no other way of being heard than a fairly loud one? Certainly there is something grievously wrong about destroying the universities, but can one really assume that there is absolutely nothing in them that ought to be changed? Even if the relationship in education has to be in part an authoritarian one, does this mean that all aspects of academic life are bound up with this, and that some democratic organization there isn't necessary or a good thing?

KENNAN: Of course student opinion should be heard. But when there is no respect for academic authority, this thing simply won't work. Just before coming here I saw on TV a brawl between a college president and a group of students who had surrounded him and who were hurling obscenities and missiles at him. He tried to defend himself physically. This is a disgraceful sight in the face of which there won't be any educational process. I certainly think there should be student councils, whose views should be listened to and taken into account. But you said, "How are they going to be heard otherwise?" I've been told hundreds of times by students,

"They won't listen to us." Well, it sounds like a petulant child. Of course people listen. And of course they hear. Suppose they disagree? Suppose they say students are a minority and find their views immature and, despite what has been said here, a bit on the hysterical side and lacking in background?

If these students are wise enough to solve the problems that they profess to want to solve, they oughtn't to be in a university at all. They should be mature enough to be in the middle ranks of life, as indeed they think they are. But if they are, then the whole educational process is unnecessary. You can't have it both ways.

ALLARD K. LOWENSTEIN: I know you've heard other views, but I think we are fortunate in the Western world that some of the evils in our culture inconsistent with our pretensions and ideals are being challenged at root by people with energy, vigor and determination to produce something better, even though they're not often equipped to know how to bring it about. It is healthy to see Americans denouncing what their government is doing abroad. One would hope to see a similar response by Indians about Kashmir, Nigerians about Biafra, and so on. Out of awareness that the world needs something more than a constant defense of each country by its leading intellectuals and political figures, we might begin to struggle to some really international solutions to world problems.

The closest thing that has arisen yet to genuine internationalism is what is coming out of young people. We are extremely fortunate that the next generation is in revolt against hypocrisies encrusted in the affluent world and is committed to basic social change. If this revolution had been directed in favor of racism, war or privilege, we would be in dark straits. Instead of regarding it as a threat, we should welcome the energy unleashed through people who have almost everything materially and, precisely because of that, find it inadequate for human beings.

Of course, this revolution runs up against the unbending resistance to changes in the assumptions of a Western world which has long been conservative. As a result, you have sometimes drift and sometimes a lurch into anarchy, a revolt against any institution, anything that doesn't automatically change when asked to. You get into difficulties of communication and of assessing what is a valid demand and what is a demand simply to make demands. But if we would roll with this challenge, accept the validity of much of it and really examine our own presuppositions, we would, I think, quickly make significant contributions to the educations of younger people. Too many of us don't do that; they simply reiterate their own previous assertions, and if the young don't accept them, the confrontation escalates.

There are two very different areas where liberalism and Western progress have been least effective. Thanks to technology and the development of capital in sufficient quantities to make money available for many things, we have now removed, for perhaps eighty percent of our people in this country and, in varying percentages, something like that in most of the developed world, the worst of the scourges of exterior injustice and misery. The worst of the failures of liberalism is that we've never been able to figure out how to extend that process of enlightenment and assistance to the remaining pockets of deprived people.

The other problem is that we've discovered that even after we've removed the exterior causes of unhappiness we don't produce a happy society at all. Unless we begin to figure out how we can make lives seem fuller, communication between people more easy, and give them a sense of participating in their own destiny, the revolution is going to say, "Even if you remove poverty and war, all you've done is leave us with a vacuous society." In places like Holland, where there's no war and very little racism, and young people still burst out in anarchic ways, that problem is even more important than war, poverty and racism.

If, here in the United States, we are really to face the deep scars we have, we must face the implications for our world policies. You can't spend seventy-two percent of your budget on military and foreign policy without money that needs to be spent elsewhere. The United States certainly can't enter into a period of total withdrawal from the world. But we must reeducate our people to what really safeguards this country from the dangers they fear. That is going to mean more funds spent on education, housing and so forth, which we've been neglecting in the past in deference to other concepts of the world.

When the United States sneezes, places far away get pneumonia. So we have an enormous obligation to reassess some of the hypocrisies our own young people are challenging. Dictatorship in Spain or dictatorship in Greece cannot be virtuous because it says it's anti-Communist if in fact what we're opposed to is oppression by dictators. The assertion that we must do something in the Dominican Republic or Vietnam or Greece or Spain in the name of outmoded notions of what the world is about will produce great chasms between the generations. The people coming along free of that kind of stereotype reject it, particularly when it leads to their being sent off to die in wars which they can see are not connected to the idealism and democracy they've been raised to believe the country should stand for. If we want seriously to cope with the revolution of the next generation, we have to understand this interlocking of foreign and domestic questions, economically and in terms of the perception of what is hypocritical and what is honest. America must again become the symbol of justice and decency in the world that we were becoming under Presidents Kennedy and Roosevelt.

If there's a lesson America has given the world this past year, it is, I hope, that the energies of youth, properly channeled, can become dominant in changing countries with an opportunity for freedom into actually free countries. By welcoming young people in their efforts, we could create some form of international community that would be not only the generational one of the affluent young revolting in Paris, or Italy, or here, but of all people concerned about a world in which the processes of change could be encompassed without extermination and death. If we don't do that, I think, the world will fall apart. What could be a greater calamity and misreading of the necessities of life than to assume this is inevitable?

3

BLACK POWER: *SEPARATISM*

ROY INNIS: Many of us black nationalists think we have the solution to the black problem. This is to draw up a social contract between the two main factions, black people and white people, sharing the same approximate piece of geography in America. We recognize only two factions in America—black and white. The first U.S. Constitution was a contract between competing white subfactions. The reason the U.S. contract has broken down is the lack of recognition of black-white relationships. We oppose totally the various Mickey Mouse solutions, like integration, which are a way of keeping us powerless and frustrating our legitimate aspirations. Even if possible, integration could in no way satisfy our need of self-determination. Integration, in fact, is not possible in the United States with the legacy of racism that exists. When I refer to "racism" I do not mean that conscious overt phenomenon we see exhibited in the South. We call the Eastmans, Faubuses and Talmadges honest racists. The kind of racism we find debilitating, and which stands in the way of any organization between separate black and white groups, exists in most of America among those who least suspect that they are afflicted by the disease. It's the institutionalized kind that operates almost automatically, like a perpetual-motion machine, relegating blacks in any relationship with whites. We define black power as a method for implementing the golden philosophy of black nationalism; and black nationalism, like all nationalism throughout history, is the control of one's destiny—social, political and economic. The example we love to use is that of the Jews in the old days of the pharaohs. The kind of oppression which led to that kind of nationalism is very similar to ours—oppression in the land of the oppressor. That kind of oppression leads naturally to a demand for separation. Moses talked about removing Jews from Egypt. We talk about removing blacks from the United States. I grant you it is not particularly pragmatic to load all twenty-five million of us back to our faraway ancestral lands; and we are dispersed in small pockets throughout America. So this leads to a new solution, an innovation enabling people to exist in society as two groups. We exist mostly in certain parts of the urban centers, the so-called ghettos. We prefer to call them little communities, the Harlems in New York City, the Roxburys in Boston, the Wattses in Los Angeles, all large homogeneous groupings of my people. We will become liberated when we control the instruments of society in these areas—the schools, police, welfare, sanitation, the economic and political institutions. We will then link up the identities of our Roxburys, Harlems and Wattses into a nationlike structure which is unique in that we will be islands not in the sea, like Indonesia, but islands in land.

We will have infinitely greater ability to succeed than the Americans at the start of their country. In 1781 it would have taken Benjamin Franklin in Philadelphia a longer and harder time to communicate with Alexander Hamilton in New York only one hundred to one hundred fifty miles away than for us, with modern technology, to communicate between our separate islands. We will be a nation of over twenty-five million people, with a Gross National Product approaching forty billion dollars, larger than most nations of the world. All in all, we will be able to maximize our interests in this way better than we ever could with the Americans. As for America, it will not exist in the way it exists now unless the contract between white and black comes about.

EDWARD SHILS: What would be the difference between the type of order which you establish and Botswana or Lesotho? How are you going to organize your sovereign state's relationships, constitutionally, legally, in international trade, money, defense and all the other paraphernalia of sovereignty?

99

INNIS: Our relationship with the Americans would be negotiable. We would prefer to be totally autonomous, like Mexico or Canada. But these things will grow in stages. The initial stage will be some local autonomy in the so-called ghettos. The next step would be to move toward a new constitution giving us a minimum of guarantees and a per-capita share of political power and such things. We will move successively to bigger and better things. We are aware of the cycle of history. Rome goes up and Rome comes down. The contract is renegotiated every step along the way in decline.

JAN KOTT: I am deeply moved by Mr. Innis' speech, especially by his comparison between the situation of the black people and the historical fate of the Jews. This does not stifle a fear that his comparison is also a subject for doubt. I remember very well the discussions before the war, during the quasi-fascist period in Poland, then during the Stalinist era and in the last few years. There was the same kind of claim about the necessity of separation because of the impossibility of integration. I have many friends who began to feel Jewish because they were denied the right to be Poles. I know very well how necessary it is to affirm the identity and dignity of being oneself. Half the Jews remaining in Poland have been forced to leave in the past year. The last hope for integration has been lost. That is historically true. But it was a solution of despair, not hope, and, after my European experience, I would like to ask Mr. Innis if his proposal of separation comes out of hope or despair?

INNIS: Let me suggest that the solution for the Jews in Poland did not work because it was not the kind of solution I am suggesting. It was not separation but mere segregation. We must make a clear distinction. If somebody else puts you apart and yet still controls your basic institutions and regulates the flow of goods and services in your area, you are segregated, not separated. You are separated only when you are France or Germany, in that each of these political subdivisions controls certain basic social, economic and political factors in its area. This was not true for Jews in

Poland, and we are not asking for the position of Jews in Poland.

WALDEMAR BESSON: We have a long and tragic history in Europe of minority islands of one nationality within the sea of another nationality. I am thinking of Germans within Slavic groups and of Slavs within Germanic groups. This kind of thing can exist for centuries, but it is precisely when the kind of nationalism Mr. Innis espouses comes to the fore that it proves impossible to live with it any more. One must take account of the likelihood that the very nationalism which prompts this kind of solution to the American racial problem would also make it impossible for the minority to exist peacefully among the majority.

ABDUL GAFOOR NOORANI: I'm a Moslem from India and it seems to me that in many ways the black-power movement is similar to Mr. Jinnah's demands for the partition of India. Before Mr. Jinnah came on the political scene as the unchallenged leader of the Moslems, they had merely demanded safeguards as a minority in a united India. But fear that, once the British departed, the Moslem minority would be swamped by the Hindu majority worked in favor of partition. Well, we have had partition and I regret to say it has proved no solution at all. How much worse the problem would be in America, where there is no compact territory with a Negro majority and the two nations would have to coexist side by side.

ORLANDO ALBORNOZ: Mr. Innis is no sociologist, because otherwise he would not entertain any illusions about his parallel societies. That idea is, to say the least, unrealistic. But if it were to succeed it would not help forward integration in other parts of the world, including the Caribbean, Brazil and Peru, where Negroes and Indians also live in parallel societies with the whites.

BRIAN WALDEN: I wonder if I might ask Mr. Innis some questions which I think are interrelated. He may not. First, what is going to happen if some black people, using their choice as individuals, want to live somewhere outside the black communities? Second, if these communities expand both in size and in expectation, is there a sort of treaty whereby you are ceded a few more city blocks, or is a separate city built somewhere for another one of these? Third, is the white community really going to like this situation, and do you care whether they do or not? Don't you see some disadvantages if our German friend [Mr. Besson] is right and people living within the same geographic area develop bitter resentments against each other? Finally, I understand you are a West Indian.* As you know, we have many West Indians in Britain. We also have a great deal of white racism and exploitation of colored people. They were not taken there by the oppressor; they went there. Can we relevantly preach the same kind of black nationalism there?

INNIS: Blacks who want to live outside the black communities would be similar to West Indians in England or Canadians in the United States: you really do it at your peril. My people living across the border, or their people living across the border in our area, will have to go by the local norms, as in all nations.

Territorial expansion is a serious problem, because the way history deals with it is by mounting an army and expanding. These guys have the biggest bombs and the biggest missiles—we can't quite do it that way. But there's an immense amount of American geography still uninhabited. I want to negotiate. The important thing is to get two peoples to be honest and see themselves as two factions and come to a table. Once you're at a table you pull the technicians in and do what is pragmatic for both your interests. Will the American whites like this and go along with it? Well, like and dislike are irrelevant. It's the pragmatic view which counts. Tactically, I have learned a trick from whites. They look at us in various categories, you know—jokingly we used to say the difference between field niggers and house niggers—and it's a very

* In a conference paper Señor Albornoz mentions "the significant part played in Negro political activity by a number of Negroes who came to the States from all the Caribbean area except Puerto Rico. They had been socialized under a different idea of what it means to be a Negro, so they reacted in a more independent manner once they were in the States." Stokely Carmichael, like Roy Innis, is a West Indian.

effective technique. If we look at whites in that way we will find that there are urban whites and nonurban whites. There are also whites who control something like eighty percent of the goods and services produced in this country. I will say to whites, "To which of your various interest groups does my solution make sense, either to maximize your interest or to cause the least threat to it?" I suspect we would find a tremendous segment, especially those with power, whose interests would best be served by defusing the chaotic confrontation that's coming on between blacks and whites.

CARL KAYSEN: What you say may be a feasible goal, provided you and your colleagues have the magic, the organizational power, the drive, the leadership to organize and successfully exploit the misery in which most black Americans live. But what I think you're not taking into account is that the white society you would make your new social contract with, should you succeed, would not be today's moderately, mildly watered-down liberal white society. It would be a much more mobilized and repressive white society, in which the power equation between, in your language, "you and us" would be more sharply drawn. Would you get a good bargain?

INNIS: Let me suggest that future blacks would also be more repressive. We'll be in a more defensible position under the kind of setup I suggest. Right now we have absolutely no defense, as these same repressive Americans run our institutions, schools, police, sanitation, welfare, health. I want at least to be in a better position to force a bargain.

JOHN B. OAKES: If I did not know that Mr. Innis was so sincere and so deeply involved in this, I would almost think he was attempting to bring the argument on black-white relationships to a *reductio ad absurdum*. The proposal he is making is impractical and unrealistic, immoral and a form of self-indulgence. He has approached the question as though the Negro problem were the only one facing the country. The entire scope of American internal turmoil is viewed in the light of a twenty- or twenty-five-million minority, a very large, important group, the Negroes, ten to twelve percent of the population of the United States, but not the only element in our country with problems. Mr. Innis specifically said that the blacks and whites were the only two important factions. I deny this. It puts a totally wrong light on the situation. There are far more whites below the poverty line than there are Negroes. In percentage terms, of course, the Negro is relatively much worse off. But the problem of schools, of economics, of oppression, if one wants to put it that way, is applicable to very large segments of the white community as well. The fundamental cure, and what black power is really aiming at, is the economic improvement of a large segment of the American population which has indeed been depressed for the past three hundred years. More attention should be focused on education and job opportunities, and the very important destruction of segregated housing. The New York school issue has exploded because the educational neglect of the Negro community is based on segregated housing. These matters are not simple and not easily solved. I recognize the powerlessness of the Negro community, and to the extent that black power creates political pressure to alleviate the situation it has a genuine validity. But my interpretation is socio-economic rather than political or racist. The point of view Mr. Innis is expounding is a racist point of view, the apartheid view. It is attempting to create a community philosophically separate and distinct from the white community in this country. To me this is the negation of everything that our country or, for that matter, the human race should stand for. Anyway, it is totally impractical. There are vast numbers of Negroes, probably an overwhelming majority, who would reject Mr. Innis' separate state, but even if they were not a majority, it certainly would be a very large minority. It is impossible to conceive of a country that could exist under the social contract, so called, that Mr. Innis proposes.

INNIS: The suggestion that my solutions are contrary to the American way I regard as a symptom of the serious fault in black-white relationships. The American way is the white way, and that's very good for whites. It has nothing to do with black people. The blacks are not the only segment in America, you said. I am not a sociologist, but it would be a serious error to apply an analysis coming out of a homogeneous setting, i.e., whites, to a heterogeneous setting, blacks and whites. Black people are not just another ethnic group like the Italians, Jews or Irish. We are a people with a different history, clearly identifiable, and different values, even now under this oppression. There are black and white subgroups, of course, but only two main groups, blacks and whites. Consequently, whites existing below the poverty level cannot in any way be related to us. I understand there may be other problems. But I refuse to mix my strokes. I refuse to mix black-white problems with the class problem or with the generation-gap problem, or with the individual-in-society problem. No. Our problem is unique.

Maybe black people will reject my solution. In 1770, the solutions offered by the Madisons and Jeffersons were not the solutions of the majority of White American colonists. The fact is, they had no solution. People have needs. Leaders structure solutions to satisfy those needs. People follow those leaders when those solutions start working, start satisfying their needs. We should not expect to have a consensus among black people. We cannot expect the average black to have a solution to his own problems. Nobody any time in the history of mankind ever had.

I consider myself a pragmatist. I hardly ever talk about final solutions—I cannot project my solutions to infinity. But if I can give black people in this country the capacity to choose for themselves, they will be in a better position to evaluate pragmatically in their own interests how they can best be organized with people sharing the same approximate piece of geography. The options given to us are three. We have been living under one, segregated, type of organization where white people control all the flow of goods and services and all the institutions in both black and white areas. The alternative was supposed to be integration; it didn't come about, and had it come about, I, the black, would have been outvoted in all situations. I would be a permanent minority of ten to fifteen percent in all the institutions. One of the most elementary political concepts is that you maneuver for higher ground so that in at least some situations you are the majority. Look at the states. Why do you need fifty states? Why not just one? Why do you need counties within states? Because in each of these, people end up as a political unit with some control of their own destiny. We must do the same thing. The third option we have—there might be others, I haven't heard them yet—is separation, which simply means controlling one's own destiny, one's institutions, schools, police and so forth, regulating the flow of goods and services in one's area—basic things people throughout history have tried to achieve. We have no obligation to define ourselves as Americans if that status doesn't produce the rewards that go with states.

ARTHUR M. SCHLESINGER, JR.: I suppose black nationalism in this country is one more expression of the peculiar worldwide revival of nationalism which has splintered the Communist empire, is dividing Belgium, leading to the possible secession of Quebec and causing Scottish and Welsh nationalist movements in Britain. But I must confess I agree with Mr. Oakes and Mr. Kaysen about the problems of parallel societies occupying approximately the same area. It seems to me a completely fanciful notion. I don't think it can provide a long-term solution to anything. One has only to consider what would happen to the Democratic Party, which has been on the whole, for the last generation, the instrumentality of social change in this country, if it were to be deprived of Negro votes which in so many states make it possible for Democrats to win. I was glad to see that Mr. Innis himself became, in his last time around, more agnostic about his Jim Crow solution and offered a formulation with which I am inclined to agree, that such proposals as his would create a capacity for self-determination in the black community enabling them to make their own judgment about their ultimate form of organization. Personally, I cannot foresee any solution in the long run except that of integration. I strongly disagree that black nationalism is a permanent strategy and that separate national states within the same geographical area are anything more than what Sorel used to call a social myth.

However, I do not share Mr. Oakes's feeling about the immorality of this myth. It is a mistake to suggest that the kind of views which Mr. Innis expresses do not play an indispensable role in the balance of forces necessary to produce social change. As a tactic there is a desperate need to build a sense of purpose in the black community. One means of doing so could be the transfer of authority, involving a revision in the structure of city government. I strongly endorse the decentralization in the New York school system. I agree on black police forces. But these are a matter for case-by-case judgment. Dual black and white unionism is a much more doubtful case. I regard all these as possible tactics. I welcome Mr. Innis' viewpoint in the expectation that, given the complexity of historical change, his argument for parallel societies may make possible the realization of a society in which integration can eventually take place on much solider and more equal grounds than in contemporary America.

INNIS: Mr. Schlesinger's remark on the loss of black votes to the white liberals may well be right. But what has this vote done for us as a people? Who has gained from these noble coalitions of blacks and liberal whites, blacks and trade unionists, blacks and Marxists? It is not black people. There'll be no great loss to us in this process.*

MICHEL CROZIER: This morning Mr. Loebl expressed his surprise at seeing American students turning away from pragmatism. I want to say how interested I am to see a black-power leader going the other way. I'd like to ask Mr. Innis a pragmatic question. There are situations where black people can elect the mayor of a city or where, with the help of business people, they can develop neighborhood corporations. Does he think such steps useful in the drive of the black people to develop a new kind of relationship and improve their bargaining position in tough conditions?

INNIS: I have reservations as to whether Carl Stokes becoming

---

* Stokely Carmichael was reported in *The New York Times* of May 22, 1967, as saying, "To ask a Negro to register with the Democratic Party is like asking a Jew to join the Nazi Party."

mayor of Cleveland is real progress. My organization was one of those that played a major part in his becoming mayor, but I was not deluded. I needed that image, of course, for myself, but I knew that in real power terms Carl Stokes as mayor was almost irrelevant. Power is really held by the institutional barons, the urban bureaucracy. In fact, my action in Cleveland is severely inhibited because Carl Stokes is mayor. It's not so easy to run out there and picket one of my guys!

I'm also deeply involved in the new wave of business in the ghetto. It is fraught with all kinds of dangers, because I suspect I am talking about one thing, and Nixon and the business guys about something else. Now, I believe my guys are so clear about what we want and so tough-minded that we will get our agenda through before they get theirs. But maybe I'm wrong, so let's not assume any great miracles will come about. Also, if we measure the rate of progress as one curve and the rate of increase in the problem as another, we will see that the progress curve is not catching up with the confrontation curve.

SAM BROWN: As a student observer, I'm struck with the difference between the discussion which has taken place here and the topics current among the university generation. The discussion here has centered largely on an attempt of white people to find out what black power means. But people now in school center discussion not around black power but around white racism.* We talk not about what the black community is asking and how to meet it, but about what the white community has done to the black and our responsibilities as white intellectuals, members of the establishment. We need to understand our own response to the black community, how that looks changed, what that means about

* Señor Albornoz, in his conference paper, writes of the Student Non-violent Coordinating Committee's (SNCC) Black Power Manifesto: "If whites want to help, they should do so by organizing themselves. They could go into white communities and work in them to reduce the misunderstandings between one group and another, not trying to 'rehabilitate' blacks. The Black Power leaders insist that there is no problem among Negroes; it exists only among whites."

police, schools, education in general, and cultural values. We need to understand our own background and the race hysteria which we all carry inside us. That is much more fundamental.

ROBERT POWELL: I would like to express my appreciation to Mr. Innis for sitting through the discussion that took place just now. I know that very few black students I've associated with would have sat through it. One of the problems whites have, particularly white liberals, is that the present situation they see is disappearing just about the time they're beginning to recognize it. We've been talking about building a cooperative society in which blacks and whites can live together. That's the situation black people faced ten or twenty years ago. The new situation is that Mr. Innis' new kind of society is not that far in the future. Black islands exist in this country already, in the city centers, in the South, wherever black people are collected, if you'll just look at the population figures and the map. They already exist and it seems to me what's being asked of white society is that black people be allowed to make those black islands a little more tolerable to live in. It means turning over to the black communities the police force, the schools and other political resources that ought to be theirs in what we call a democratic society but which now belong to the whites.

The choices posed here to Mr. Innis and people who speak with him are fraudulent. The choices are, build a separatist society or come build a society with us. The kind of America that I see and a lot of young people, students, see is an America in which we cannot build a cooperative society any more. I can't ask black parents to send their kids to white schools today. The teachers in those schools are just as racist, very often, as the bigots in North Carolina where I come from. It is not nearly so overt, but the destruction of black self-respect that goes on in white schools is abominable. The culture we want black people to join institutionalizes violence and racism and powerlessness. If I were a black man I would want no part of it. James Baldwin said, "Who wants to be integrated into a burning house?" Perhaps a lot of institutions will suffer as Mr. Schlesinger said, including, hopefully, the Democratic Party. That kind of suffering is long overdue, because the institutions we're fearful of changing are essentially racist. Not necessarily because people that run them are Nazis or hate black people but because they are totally insensitive to the fundamental problem of white racism in America. Until that changes it seems to me blind and unfair to give Mr. Innis and people like him the burden for creating the kind of white society in which they can live. It is our burden, not his. If we want to talk about integration—and my own long-term goal, too, would be integration—we will have to build a new kind of white society. That's the problem I'm interested in, not the black problem.

JEAN-JACQUES SERVAN-SCHREIBER: Senator Kennedy was very much oriented towards the blacks, among other groups. Did you lean to him or to Senator McCarthy in the Presidential campaign?

POWELL: I worked for Senator Kennedy, and not necessarily because of the pitch he made to black people. What I thought was heartening was his occasional, and unique, candor with white audiences about white racism. He told a group of medical students in Kansas how privileged they were and that if they wanted to do something they should get up off their rear end and organize a white community. He said the same thing to a group of businessmen. To that extent it was helpful. But you have to realize that the Democratic Party, in the state it's in now, will not allow a man to talk that kind of language in public, because the public won't buy it. One of the discouraging things about that campaign is that the second choice of many people who voted for Senator Kennedy in the primaries was Governor Wallace. They wanted to vote for somebody who was a fighter, not necessarily for his principles.

RALF DAHRENDORF: Would Mr. Innis care to say a few words about the causes and directions of student unrest and how these relate to his own concern?

INNIS: To be frank I never took student unrest particularly seriously until just now. This young man indicated to me that there might be some hope for whites in America through the young people. But I was involved with American students in the old civil-rights movement and I saw many of them going through a new fad, the peace movement and different kinds of unrest, and I got to feel something like disgust for that kind of behavior. I do not really believe the students are going through more than just another fad, another period in their lives. In about four or five years they will be in suburbia, they will be the institutional managers of my area.

ZBIGNIEW BRZEZINSKI: I can be brief, because I very much agree with Mr. Powell. The American white liberal, having won his victory over the conservative, is, on the racial issue, himself about to become conservative and attempting to impose on the Negro solutions the Negro has outlived. What I would like to see discussed is what precisely the white community is prepared to give up—not in order to go all the way with Mr. Innis toward two separate nations, but to make it more possible for the Negro to build his own community. If, in this process, the result becomes separation, I would not close my mind to it. But I would like to avoid debating the issue of Negro nationhood, because I think that freezes the Negro side into a posture of maximum demands and the liberals into a posture of negation. Let them build Negro communities, have their own police forces, hospitals, schools, labor unions, and see what happens in the process of doing that. I believe ultimately the result will be coming closer together, but I don't want to pose the issue in abstract terms now. There must be a necessary period of transition to see what can succeed.

MARTIN PERETZ: One of the problems that always comes up when one talks about minority groups and liberation struggles is who speaks authentically for the oppressed. Though my friend Bob Powell and Sam Brown feel they can talk about the black community as a monolithic unit, I don't think they can. I would even say there is some question as to whether Mr. Innis can talk about the black man as a unit, because there is a fundamental distinction between the position of the black man here and the position of colonial peoples living under a metropolitan power elsewhere. In the struggle of the Jews in Palestine or the struggle of the Indians against the Raj, the choices were severely limited. You had one option: you became an illegal resistance movement. What is happening among black people in America is nothing like this monolithic kind of movement. My own view from some long years of involvement with the civil-rights movement, especially in the South, is that these notions, while attractive to some, strike them, many of them, as utterly alien, futile. And some of my friends would say to you, Roy Innis, "You are kind of putting us on." The rural Negroes, in the South, seem to be taking the conventional road to political power. Faced with a very intransigent enemy, they try to organize simply on the basis of numbers and appear to be winning some share of legitimate power. In the urban communities where the enemy does not appear to be so obviously hostile, the situation is more difficult. There we get the kind of black movement that appears to be much more extreme and threatening to many white Americans.

What disturbed me about one of the things Mr. Innis was saying, and I found it interesting that Professor Brzezinski would find common ground of agreement with him, is that he was clear he wanted black control of the political institutions, but then there was a kind of hedge: who controls the economic institutions? He said something about the flow of goods and services, but was rather vague. And of course Professor Brzezinski did not say he was in favor of the black control of economic institutions. It seems to me there are two choices: either the central economic institutions of the United States stay something like what they are, which spells essentially corporate domination of the American economy, or you exempt or exclude the black community from the economic community dominated by American corporations. In the second case, the colonial precedent becomes terribly appropriate. It's a guarantee, for many, many years to come, of economic under-development for the black sector. However unhappy Africa's experience of independence has been, it was the only possible option there. Here, wretched as is the situation of the black people, they do see other, more conventional, integrated options. It is not clear to me that all blacks want out. I have found—it's a tentative observation, perhaps not a fair one—that blacks who appear to want to assert their blackness with peculiar intensity are those who might rather easily have molded into present American society. I remember Dr. King saying once that he didn't have to talk about blackness with that poignancy and passion, because he came of a long line of black Baptist ministers and there was no question that he was black. The pressure for separatism comes really from black intellectuals who might have made it in this very imperfect society of ours. Tensions between student black militants and Communistic black militants will, I think, reflect this reality.

NORMAN PODHORETZ: There has been a very lively debate going on within the black movement, at least since the early sixties. One school of thought has taken the position that "we do not wish to be integrated into a burning house," by which James Baldwin not only meant that the civilization was in some Spenglerian way doomed, but that it was a rotten civilization and that he did not wish his people to be acculturated to such a society. The other powerful thrust wants precisely to be integrated into this middle-class society which it does not regard as necessarily corrupting. I think that the play of these two forces has generated a good deal of confusion within the movement itself and has yet to be resolved.

HAROLD CRUSE: I see in the Black Power movement too much rhetoric and too many mechanical descriptions of what one might like to see in terms of group arrangements, but not enough analysis of the forces that one must contend with. I can't, for example, dispose as cavalierly of the students' movement as Mr. Innis does. What are we to do about black students who very much attack the role not only of white institutions but of black institutions? I'm very much in favor of the student movement, both black and white. I see in it the only possible source of future leadership on these questions. I see community organizations, identity organizations, economic, political organizations, et cetera, established in the black communities. I see blacks living outside these black enclaves as having important roles to play vis-à-vis them. I don't see Black Power movements in black communities having a dictatorial role over the lives of blacks who don't happen to exist in black enclaves. The Black Power movement as of this moment does not have the overwhelming support of the majority of black people in this society. That's a reality. It provides leadership in certain areas of social thought. But I don't see it exerting real influence over the majority of black people in this society until it develops a better analysis of the situation.

4

BLACK POWER: *PLURALISM*

HAROLD CRUSE: The Black Power thrust has many elements. It has what I call a bourgeois economic reform element, and a separatist land element, and an identity rhetoric, and group cultural values, and it also contains what we see in the streets, a revolutionary anarchist element. There is no one element that covers the whole range of Black Power ideas. However, fundamental to understanding it is seeing Negroes as a group seeking democratic parity within the American group and class structure. It is a group demand. We know, at least I know, that the Black Power separatists, the true-blue separatists, cannot win land in America. This is a utopian demand. But we still have to understand its origins. It is a historical demand. It goes back to the post–Civil War period, when the whole question of winning the civil war against the Southern slaveowners turned on whether these people would be expropriated or not. We know from history that they were not. The failure of the North to carry out complete land reform undercut all the efforts of the radical and revolutionary elements of the Civil War period to effect some kind of solution to the slavery, and subsequently race, problem. The land problem is a carry-over from that era. On the other hand, the identity rhetoric of the Black Power movement springs out of a deeply felt need on the part of most of the young generation of black people to establish a real cultural-group identity in America. Black-Powerites reject integration not on moral or ethical grounds, they reject it because it is manifestly impossible to achieve under our present group and class setup in America. If integration as a form of social arrangement were that easy to achieve, there would be no need for separatist sentiments or for disappointment about the American ideal. Therefore the Black Power concept is also a cultural concept and has to be viewed from that point of view. Then we have the revolutionary anarchist wing in the Black Power movement. All of these elements are in uneasy alliance with each other; but ultimately it is the reform element in Black Power that we should watch very carefully, because there has been a rapprochement between powerful corporations in America and Black Power spokesmen. Corporation spokesmen, being very realistic people, more so than intellectuals, see very clearly the value of the dangling dollar held before those who are begging for economic rights. The capitalist understands the wishes and aspirations of other would-be capitalists. It was for that reason that the first Black Power conference, held in Newark, New Jersey, last year was financed by the biggest corporations in the country.

ENRIQUE TIERNO GALVAN: Is Black Power an example of the traditional class struggle?

CRUSE: No, it's not. One of the fundamental errors is to superimpose such European concepts on American realities. The black problem is only peripherally a class problem. It is basically an American ethnic-group problem. It could not have developed in Europe or in any other society as it has developed here. Essentially, Black Power is a belated attempt on the part of the black movement to get an economic and political share in the American pot. The Negro movement has always been aware that immigrant groups coming to America manage to maintain enough solidarity to establish some level of economic and political power. The young don't get involved as some white radical students in arguments about socialism and capitalism, or property, exploitation, profits and so forth. They see it in clear honest terms of the power a group has in America. The problem of the Negro is that for many reasons this group development has been delayed by the division in the black leadership about whether to aim for separation or integration.

But the Black Power movement itself does not divide simply into two factions, one believing in separatism, the other in it as a tactic. There is a middle ground, an implied objective of cultural pluralism which at one time was strongly favored by American sociologists as the most democratic method of accommodating diverse ethnic and cultural groups. I am a cultural pluralist fundamentally, and I see the recent Black Power thrust as another means of achieving this end.

C. VANN WOODWARD: Mr. Cruse is right to point out that the numerous European ethnic groups have organized themselves to make their wishes and needs felt. But it is misleading to compare the problems of European immigrants with those of the old black minority, because the Europeans never had the same race prejudice to contend with. The Irish, the Italians, the Jews, wanted not separation but integration. I wonder if the Black Power movement is simply temporarily opting for separatism or if it does in fact mean what it says in opting for permanent separatism. I am afraid that I see tendencies toward its becoming identified with nationalism of this withdrawing and separatist sort and I am concerned that it should not finally opt for them.

ORLANDO ALBORNOZ: The real force behind the concept of Black Power and the eruption of racial tension is the continuous displacement of Negroes from the South towards the Northern cities since 1960. Between 1900 and 1960 the Negro proportion of the total population in the North and Northeast rose from 1.9 percent to 6.8 percent, while in the South it fell from 32.3 percent to 20.6 percent. Once in the Northern cities, most of the blacks end up in ghettos. There they suffer from a high unemployment rate and organizational instability, especially in the family, from low income and low educational standards and enormous psychological tensions due to discrimination in a society which, despite the undeniable progress of Negroes, exhibits a "white" image. No wonder Malcolm X wrote as early as 1964 that "the most dangerous North American Negro is the one who has been locked up in the black ghettoes by the Northern whites."

DANIEL BELL: There is an old Jewish proverb that says, "For example is no proof." We all operate by illustrations and some kind of anecdotal evidence. Yet this slurs over the large basic magnitudes of social change, which shows there has been considerable progress in the United States. You will find, for instance, that there has been a rather extraordinary change in the situation of the blacks since 1960. One million have moved out of unskilled occupations into semiskilled and skilled occupations at a time when even the number of unskilled whites is increasing. The number of middle-class blacks is increasing at a very rapid rate, and, as one would expect, the number of blacks in colleges is increasing even faster. In fact, it has grown by as much as ninety percent over a period of six years—starting from a low base figure, to be sure, but still moving upward. This picture is much more complex than some of the simplicisms put forward would suggest.

LOUIS FISCHER: I notice that in sports in the United States Negroes do not ask to be segregated, because in sports they are equals and possibly superiors of white men in track, baseball, basketball, football. There is a suspicion that elsewhere the Negro feels himself noncompetitive or inferior and, in order not to show this inferiority to the community, wants to withdraw into his own community to protect himself. Perhaps as he progresses in education, he may want to come out of that segregated community and compete as an equal or superior with the white man.

CRUSE: If you recall, back in 1947 when Jackie Robinson was first picked up by the Brooklyn Dodgers there was protest by certain black baseball fans that this undermined black baseball. It didn't last very long. Since, there has been no argument against black participation in the major leagues or in other areas of sports. But Black Power theorists are for the most part little concerned with the peripheral areas, sports or entertaining or any of the others where Negroes participate. Their ultimate aim is the black community's political and economic control of its welfare.

AMBASSADOR SOEDJATMOKO: For someone who has lived under colonial rule, Black Power seems a very normal phenomenon. The search for a sense of identity, for dignity and pride, is an essential precondition of the liberation of a person or a group. As in the nationalist movements in the colonial period, there are a great many manifestations of neurosis and unreality in the rhetoric of the Black Power movement. It is only after independence gained through power that it becomes possible for a group or nation to establish realistic relationships with the outside world or other groups. The difficulty in the United States, of course, is that the Negro community cannot find a territorial expression of its sense of identity. This leads to absurd notions like the idea that a separate black identity in the United States could, on the precedent of Israel, possibly be obtained through the United Nations. Yet, one should recognize the inherent legitimacy of the search for Black Power. This leads to two conclusions, I think. One, we should not be frightened by the rhetoric of Black Power, because though some goals of Black Power are unattainable, they are necessary, rhetorically, to mobilize the black group and make it effective. The other is that integration will become psychologically possible only after sufficient power has been generated to overcome the deep sense of inferiority that is one of the great problems of the black community. The only way to prevent the radicalization of the Black Power movement into absurd positions is a timely adjustment of the political system. My doubt is, has the American political system the flexibility to adjust in time?

CRUSE: The white American has always seen America only from a white-European point of view. He has blurred the white and black and Indian encounter characteristic of the whole Western Hemisphere. His high culture, at least, has ignored the other native strands, in American music or American drama or American dance or American folklore, which are basic ingredients of the country's special physiognomy. He has oppressed the black people culturally as well as politically. The European expansion into the United States was the beginning of a great social experiment that ultimately produced the colossus of the Western Hemisphere. But the flaw in the democratic ideals was slavery. The American has been forced to face this defect from time to time: he faced it in the Civil War, in the Revolutionary War, again during the Reconstruction, and intermittently in the twentieth century. Now he's facing it again in a much more profound and pressing way. My feeling is that the great American experiment is fast approaching a crossroads in the nineteen-seventies and eighties.

As a result, the Black Power issue is a touchstone for the whole emergence of America as a finished nation. Without wishing to appear racially provincial or chauvinistic about black concerns, I do feel many of the problems of America rest on this. Take the political powerlessness of which Negroes complain. What is the difference between black political powerlessness inside the black community and the general white powerlessness expressed by Mr. Papandreou? Everybody in America is powerless politically. The two-party vice in which Americans find themselves when they try to break out of traditional political patterns is common to both black and white.

This has its counterpart abroad. I don't deny America the right or responsibility to "dabble in everybody's affairs." It is called to play a leading role in the world, if only because it is favored by wealth, resources, social ideals and so forth. But America is like the keeper of a grand house with an itch to oversee all the problems of the world, pretending it is truly master in its house, when in fact it is only a very poor keeper. It is becoming the colonizer of its old parent Europe and trying to become the colonizer of the newly emerging nations of the Third World. It is playing a distorted role because the unsolved problems inherited from the past are falsifying its sense of purpose.

ROBERT LIFTON: I am very taken with the remark of Harold Cruse connecting aspirations for Black Power with aspirations for a sense of power among many whites. I think that is a fundamental insight that's been enormously neglected by American intellectuals. Both are part of one large historical crisis. It's useful to look back on American history like Mr. Cruse, but there are some more immediate turning points. I for one would look back toward the use of nuclear weapons in Hiroshima and Nagasaki, because of the image of historical extinction let loose upon the world and in response to which much of current behavior among young people has to be understood. Another factor is the feeling of moving toward the automated society. One cannot talk about America without this bit of general historical perspective. We are in the middle of a historical crisis of forms all of which—institutional, psychological, interpretative, aesthetic—affect the individual and groups. The Vietnam War may not be fundamental, but it cannot be overemphasized as a symbol of wrong and destructive policies which might lead to historical extinction and the loss of autonomy within an organization. You have a problem of powerlessness of which the black subculture is a very special group. This suggests that the situation is more revolutionary than some have suggested.

RALF DAHRENDORF: I am a little puzzled by talk of black rebels and student rebels as if they were defending the same kind of cause. It is true while you were having coffee I watched a student being taken to the dean's office because he had staged a one-man demonstration outside this building against racists. Nevertheless, I feel that black powerlessness and white powerlessness are not really the same. Black powerlessness, or rather Black Power, is part of a move towards greater equality of citizen rights in the traditional framework of American values. On the other hand, white powerlessness, the situation in which many citizens feel that while they have the right, and even the economic opportunities, to participate, somehow they are unable to achieve any ends or change anything in society, is a new problem. The two are very different. There may, though, be a relationship between them in that the very kind of organization necessary to bring about citizenship rights for everybody is what makes it so difficult to exercise those rights once you've got them. Take the market mechanism. The market mechanism has been unable to bring about equality in the countries where we live. So a certain amount of intervention took place. But this required the setting up of organizations which in effect make it very difficult for the individual citizen to control economic or political affairs. The same might be said to some extent about Parliament. Parliaments in many of our countries seem singularly unable to provide the initiative or control required to allow the individual citizen effectively to exercise his rights. The same might be said about individual participation in many organizations and on many levels—the legal system, for instance. In short, the problem of color and of equality is very much an historical problem with which we can probably cope in our traditional institutions, but in coping with this we create a new type of problem, which we are facing in student rebellion and the widespread feeling of powerlessness. I suggest that we distinguish between the two a little more.

GINO GIUGNI: There are different degrees of power and powerlessness. There is a difference, of course, in the distribution of power among social classes, but my impression is that there is also unevenness in the distribution of power among ethnic groups. Is the white community really a community, or a juxtaposition of many different ethnic communities? My impression is that integration has been real among the groups which emigrated here let's say until the first half of the last century. But the wave of integration beginning at the end of the last century gave birth to ethnic groups which are not so well integrated, though they borrowed some of the American values, mostly Protestant, which they found. Thus, in my country, Italy, nobody is racist, but when Italians come here as immigrants, they become immediately archracists. The dilemma for the Black Power movement is whether to aim for a strong ethnic group acting as a pressure lobby, like the Jews or Italians, or to have more general goals such as a broad social revolution which would give it a message to the whole population of this country and, indeed, to the world. If it chooses the first, it will emphasize some negative aspects of this society and help produce an America that is not a nation but a federation of ethnic communities. If it chooses the second, the Black Power movement could be meaningful for the history of mankind.

MINOO MASANI: I happen to be chairman of the U. N. Subcommittee on Discrimination and Minorities and studied your racial problem here in this country in 1950–52. Let me say that as a student of this subject I find a remarkable amount of advance and change during these years. It may be much less than we would desire, but to feel that integration is not advancing is a mistake. Integration is advancing, even though slowly. There are less and less members of the pure African race in this country, and I can look forward to a day, maybe not in my lifetime, when the United States will catch up with the Brazilian pattern. I had the chance to be ambassador in Brazil and I admired the way in which this process of integration had been carried very much further forward than you have been able to do in this country.

In which part of the world do people have more power to share in determining their destiny than in the United States? I'd be glad to know of such a country. Or is it because the American people by and large do not follow the wishes of some of us that we think they are powerless? According to a Louis Harris poll yesterday in *The New York Times,* seventy percent of the American people are conservatives, while only seventeen percent are liberals. Would we think they were more powerful if seventy percent had voted liberal and only seventeen percent had voted for a conservative candidate? There's very much more of the organization man in Western Europe and in our countries than in the United States. This very seminar is a testimony to the live debate, the dissent, we find better expressed in American periodicals of a high order than anywhere else in the world.

ALBORNOZ: We have a number of Negroes in Latin America, and minorities like the Indians, but they have not become conscious of their role in society, and this is why the Negro situation in the United States has become so important in Latin America. The United States is the frame of reference of our life. The United States, in Latin America, is a colonial power. It certainly intervenes in our local affairs and controls the flow of goods. We submit to American technology. We tend to be so overwhelmed that we ignore the many tensions of American society. It is as a revelation of these that the Negro problem interests Latin Americans.

When Stokely Carmichael comes to Havana and Castro gives him a long farewell speech; when we read about riots in the United States and how Negroes are treated in the South or the cities and about the policy of Mr. Wallace and General LeMay; we become aware that American society is powerless to solve this problem, and this affects its pretensions to leadership of the Western Hemisphere. We fail to understand the continuance of the Negro problem, and poverty, and violence in cities, and the killing of leaders, and Vietnam and the Dominican intervention, and why Che Guevara was killed with the help of the CIA. How can the United States help our problems when it cannot solve its own?

We are so close to the United States and so desperately trying to change our own relationship with it! So we are very sympathetic to the Negro. We differentiate very clearly between the white and black social structures in the United States. Whenever we see a Negro in Latin America he is a boxer or baseball player or cabaret singer, never a leader in society. Many people in Latin America think matters would be improved if the leadership of the United States were not only white. But the Negro problem has been overpublicized in Latin America. Many Latin Americans think American society is going to pieces. They are just waiting for the Negroes to break down the American structure and inaugurate a better relationship between Latin America and the United States.

II
POST-INDUSTRIAL
SOCIETY

5

BEYOND THE PROLETARIAT

DANIEL BELL: A number of years ago, I coined the phrase "the post-industrial society." This is not, let me emphasize, a statement as to what a complete society will be like in the future.* It is a statement about a change in one fundamental axis of a society. Every society in some way or another has a bone structure which defines it. Historically in the West we've had a society which has been organized around property and land, and this was the basis of stratification of society. In the Communist states, autonomous political power is the organizing principle in society and the source of power. In the post-industrial society, there are many different dimensions. In part this is because the majority of people don't work in industry any longer: already the majority in the United States work in service occupations; the professional and technical class is becoming the largest rising class in the labor force. More basic still, the future sources of innovation in society depend increasingly upon the codification of theoretical knowledge. One can see this perhaps most crucially in the nature of industry. There has been a radical change in the relationship between science and industry, roughly speaking, in the last decade and a half or so. If you look at the major industries—steel, automobiles, electricity, aviation, telephones—all are nineteenth-century industries in their pattern of organization and in the fact that those who created them were talented tinkerers, people like Siemens and the dynamo, or Edison and electricity, Darby and steel, Bell and the telephone, or

* See Mr. Bell's paper, pages 186–92.

the Wright Brothers and aviation. They were people who worked quite independently of the laws of science, independently of Faraday or Maxwell and those who worked with the property of metals, and so on. The first modern industry, in fact, was the chemical industry, because one has to have a theoretical knowledge of the properties of the macromolecules one is manipulating in order to know where one is going. The way that Carothers invented nylon, or Shockley the transistor, provides a big contrast with older industries in the relationships between science and technology. One finds, too, even in matters such as state policy, that theory now serves as a guide to practice. We have the extraordinary situation of a British Labour Government deliberately engineering a recession in order to redeploy resources on the basis of some theoretical considerations. You may blame the theorists or not, but you have there a situation in which theoretical knowledge has become a new paradigm of society. This obtains in all advanced industrial societies. It's more evident perhaps in the United States, somewhat evident in the Soviet Union; by the year 2000, perhaps, Japan will be a post-industrial society with all the dimensions involved; England, France, Germany are perhaps moving along in the same direction.

If this is the case, clearly the key institution—not in the sense of power, but in the sense of importance for innovation—will be the universities. I've made the possibly fanciful claim that in the next fifty years the universities will perhaps replace the business firms as the major institution in society. Not that the business firm will disappear; simply that research corporations, laboratories, scientific stations, universities will become the main source of innovation and direction in society.

In a basic sense—here, I suppose, I'd still be a Marxist—what is involved is a change in the character of a system. Now, if one deals with the character of a system, one doesn't ask who rules, because that's transient. The "who" is always a matter of a momentary struggle for power between different persons and different social groups; the important factor is "how" you rule, what is the basis of rule. I would argue that political changes in this country and in other countries are related to three different kinds of social systems, in which people are located differentially in the system according to the relationship formed by the different modes of moving into the society. The most traditional mode is that of property, transmitted through inheritance; and the family then becomes the key social unit. There is political office as a basis for wielding wealth, status and power. Lastly, there is skill, which comes largely through education. It's rather interesting that one can take, perhaps too mechanically, the same paradigm and show these in international relations. A society at the beginning of industrialization seeks markets for products. In advanced industrial society, the relation turns on the export of capital. In a post-industrial society, the relation is skill. What strikes me as most evident about Monsieur Servan-Schreiber's book *Le Défi Américain* is essentially this: American "imperialism," to the extent that it is imperialism, is no longer interested in the export of products. It has some interest in the export of capital; but the export of skill—managerial skill, technical skill—becomes the dominant aspect, if you will, of the post-industrial society, as against the export of capital, which would be an older form of imperialism, or the export of products. One of the sources of industry's lack of interest in large parts of the Third World comes from the fact that these have lost so much of their importance. The relationship to Europe comes from the fact that Europe has advanced skills in the key areas of science-space industries, which are computers, electronics, lasers, cryogenics and various other elements of the new technology.

If one thinks of social conflicts in a post-industrial society, it is clear what the equivalent of working-class conflicts will be (in fact these are already present). They will be the conflicts of a meritocracy, in which achievement or skill or education alone determines the place in society. There is the conflict between the scientist and the military, which we have had in this country for about fifteen years, quite often hidden in the labyrinth of Washington; there is a conflict between technocrats and politicians; a conflict between elites and masses who want their own form of participation; and sometimes even a conflict between teachers and students. One of the reasons why the university is at the center of social upheaval today is that it has become burdened with a function it had never envisaged, that of the prime gatekeeper of society. Where a university used to reflect the status system of society, it now becomes the determinant of the status system. It has life-and-death powers over individuals and can determine their lives on the basis of grades and other such matters, and becomes so to speak a superheated cockpit of these kinds of conflicts. If there is a problem for the future, particularly for intellectuals, it would seem to me a double one which is part of the emergence of the role of the university in a post-industrial society. It's how you humanize a technocracy and how you tame the apocalypse. Having seen some of my students attain the apocalypse, I would submit that it is much easier to humanize a technocracy. There is always the saving grace of age.

MARTIN PERETZ: I was to have written, like Mr. Bell and Mr. Brzezinski, a paper about the future, and I was to stand here like Moses looking toward the Promised Land or Condorcet pointing to the "Tenth Stage." If you will read my paper, you will find I haven't done that.* I think the present bad enough, and to envision the future in such conditions is to envision something infinitely worse. Some of the non-Americans will have discovered a degree of rancor and acrimony, though not personal rancor and acrimony, between generations of social scientists. Not everybody in the younger generation is unhappy with the work of the older generation, but if I gauge from contemporaries who are historians or economists, or from my own own experience in political science, we think our elders have been working with the administration of the system without really posing the basic normative questions. The younger generation have a sense that their elders have participated in what one writer has called a great American celebration. If this group had met ten years ago, the kind of discussion we

* See Mr. Peretz' paper, pages 199–203.

engaged in yesterday on race could not have taken place. Ten years ago we were certain that no strident ideological demands would be made against the system. Today that looks like an intellectual fad—like Art Nouveau or the novels of Vladimir Nabokov. The essential reason for it was, I think, hostility to Communism. As a result, established social science neglected the importance of economic possessions, of economic inequality, in the structure of the present; therefore, these are slighted in its visions of the future.

I find it curious that both Bell's and Brzezinski's writings elevate the pragmatic and application-minded intellectuals to the crucial group in the functioning of the future society. Without trying to teach Daniel Bell his Marxism—he apparently went through greater rigors of Marxist training than I—it would seem to me that when intellectuals make intellectuals the linchpin of the future, we might at least contemplate the notion that this is an ideology. It is not an ideology of a ruling group—because, assuredly, this group of intellectuals flailing around for some sense of purpose could not possibly be a ruling group—but, rather, an ideology of the ruling group's servants.

The universities of the future would, I hope, try to elevate to the center of their discussions normative considerations of social choices. The question should be, *Where should* the future take us? It is, after all, not all that clear where it *will* take us. To state the question in a somewhat more limited sense: Since we have so much wealth, what should we do with it? To what ends should our wealth be used? Thus far it is not unfair to say that the imperatives of our civilization have been to build roads no matter where they take us, and weapons no matter what values they attack or defend. If you want to know why that happens, at least one question might be the one introduced by Cicero more than two thousand years ago, *Cui bono?* Who gains by the arrangements of society? who profits, and who does not profit?

Figures prove anything. But there are no figures that can prove that in this country concentration of wealth and influence in the corporation is not enormous. General Motors, Standard Oil of

New Jersey, AT & T, Ford Motor, and Sears together in 1961 had assets of fifty-two billion dollars and sales of more than forty billion dollars. With the other forty-five companies on *Fortune*'s list of billion-dollar companies, their sales represent twenty-five percent of the Gross National Product. The five hundred leading industrials and the top fifty companies in transportation, utilities and merchandising account for no less than sixty-five percent of the GNP. In one year, New York had one-eighth the revenues of General Motors, General Motors had twenty percent of the revenues of the federal government. This kind of corporate power implies, first, a pretty free hand in the mere elements of production. Second, it means that the corporation irresponsibly—that is, in a formal sense irresponsibly—affects everybody's life because it decides the standard of consumption, the quality of goods, the drift of scientific research, the objects of production, the character of service, the schedule of obsolescence (that you have a car and that after three years it begins to break up has been planned). The opinions industries, what we now more euphemistically call the media, have also tended to obscure these realities of power, for the very simple reason that they are part of those realities of power. The press, the last vestige of family capitalism in America, is now becoming part and parcel of the vast corporate conglomerates. We have been told in recent years by Berle and others that corporations have developed a greater social conscience than in the past. However, to organize an economy for private profit—for which the economy is still organized and for which, I daresay, it will be organized for the next fifty or a hundred years—is not to organize it for public needs.

Third, corporate power's influence on legislation by Congress is, as even non-Americans know, enormous. There used to be a tendency to think of corporate development as a function of a Darwinian or Spencerian struggle for survival, and I suppose there is something to that, but the law has played a role. The Tenth Amendment to the Constitution reserved for the states and for the people any rights not taken by the federal government, and the

States began to give corporate charters, and those corporate charters, as influenced by the Fourteenth Amendment, were licenses pretty much to do what you will. There is in addition a whole fabric of law and administration which, despite a rhetoric of diffusion of wealth, has tended to maximize corporate concentrations: patents, import protection, immunities from antitrust prosecution, restriction of competition, direct subsidies, indirect subsidies, tax preferences, tax exemptions, stock-piling procedures, guaranteed profit and cost-plus procurement arrangements, research contracts, lax administration of monopoly legislation, and, of course, indulgence toward certain kinds of fraud. One of the guarantees that had been offered us was that there would exist in American society countervailing powers to that kind of corporate concentration.* I notice that the notion of countervailing powers has slowly disappeared, or at least receded, not least with my esteemed friend and colleague Galbraith himself. That may well be because we are less and less persuaded of important plural sources of power affecting the major decisions and non-decisions of American life. I hope that some of you will look at the pages on income distribution in my paper,† because they suggest how vast are the gaps, and how much larger they are becoming. Decentralization is now perhaps the most popular solution to the ills of society. But the decentralization of political powers, without touching the great concentrations of corporate and financial power, will leave America as close to being a *tabula rasa* for corporate and financial design as it was one hundred years ago. Given that context, and unless a new *esprit* develops among intellectuals, the universities are likely to be the mere handmaidens of the designs of the corporations.

BELL: Mr. Peretz has discovered something called economic power like a political virgin who has seen the primal scene for the

---

* See John Kenneth Galbraith's *American Capitalism* (Boston: Houghton Mifflin, 1952).

† See page 200.

first time and said, "My God, what's going on there?" The problems of America would be much easier, our sense of enemies much clearer, our targets more defined, if it were only a question of concentrated economic power and merchants of death who have sugar on their lips and have become proconsuls in foreign lands. Multiple revolutions are taking place in all countries, including this one, and it would be simpler were it only a matter of the old-fashioned notions of the *populus* versus economic power.

The first context for understanding change, as so often, is demographic. Since World War Two, sixty million people have been added to this country by the rising birth rate. In twenty years it has had to absorb as many as between 1789 and 1860. In addition, people have moved around so hugely that today seventy percent of the population lives in metropolitan areas. Many of the problems of the cities are due not only to hungry profit makers but to vast agglomerations of people, each one asking himself what he wants and, unfortunately, usually asking for automobiles, so that sheer numbers begin to overwhelm us. Then you have the migration of blacks from the South to the North, so that twenty to fifty percent of the central cities in St. Louis, Philadelphia, Chicago and even New York are Negro. This huge upheaval is an important factor to consider in trying to cope with this country's troubles.

The second context for understanding change is that this country has become in a curious way for the first time a national society. It's always been a nation, but for the first time the events in one area have an immediate impact on every other area. The third context is that this has become in some ways a communal society. Groups of individuals assert rights as groups, which goes against a large part of the history of this country, centered on individual rights. When people assert rights as groups this creates a series of specific social strains and adds to the danger of violence. I know I'm complicating the picture here. I'm doing it deliberately. We have to get away from the old simplicisms with which we have been bedeviled.

PERETZ: My discovery of economic power may be virginal, but

sometimes it is terribly important to emphasize the obvious when it is central. Some of you may remember about fifteen or twenty years ago when Mr. Bell's friends discovered sin. A senior colleague of mine at Harvard, Professor White, talked about that group of American intellectuals called "atheists for Niebuhr." After all, sin is a still more elemental issue and, frankly, lurks still, I suspect, in traditional analyses of what is possible in a democracy and in the distribution of economic power.

"Merchants of death" is a phrase I did not use, though I am glad Mr. Bell remembers his Marxist reading of the thirties so well. But is economic power really so irrelevant? I am struck that in all of the writings I have read on the Dominican Republic (and I must say we have all learned a great deal from Theodore Draper's writing on the subject), none of the writers, except for two left-wing kids stuck away in some university, has tried to find out the corporate and economic connections of the crucial decision-makers on the Dominican Republic. Is it not at least of marginal interest that Mr. Ellsworth Bunker had been chairman, president and long-time director of the National Sugar Refining Corporation, as well as a former owner of the Dominican Sugar Mill, or that his son is head of Holly Sugar and formerly the head of Great Western Sugar, or that Mr. Justice Fortas before he entered the court, but while he was Mr. Johnson's close adviser and we know just how close, had been for two decades director of Sucrest, or that Adolf A. Berle was chairman of the Sucrest board for almost eighteen years? That Roswell Gilpatrick, Deputy Secretary of Defense at the time, had been a director of the firm that was National Sugar's counsel, or that Joseph Farland, the State Department adviser on the Dominican Republic, is a director of South Puerto Rico Sugar Company? Are you really bored by the fact that Ambassador Harriman is a limited partner in the firm that is a large holder in National Sugar? Now, I am not saying that this explains why there was an American intervention in the Dominican Republic, but I am saying that unless we are trying to establish a new theory of human nature, those interests help to define ways in which American public officials see national interests. Horace Gray, who is a senior economist, rather a cranky old man, has talked about the power of the corporation as follows: "The new mercantilism today surpasses in scope, variety and ingenuity the achievements of the Tudor and Stuart kings of England or the autocracies of Europe in the sixteenth, seventeenth and early eighteenth centuries." There is developing in America a unification of economic with political power that is at least suggestive of the unification of economic and political power in the adversaries the United States has faced in the last four decades. I am not saying that it has come to that yet. I'm not saying that it will ever come to that. But it seems to me that for those of us who are concerned about the diffusion of power over the lives of men and women, this is an issue that should trouble us.

ALESSANDRO SILJ: I am disturbed by some aspects of the outburst of studies on the post-industrial society, the technetronic society, and so on. Three points worry me particularly. One is that the studies seem oddly irrelevant. If I were shipwrecked and trying to get to shore and somebody came to me and talked about all the future ships that would be built and their likely or unlikely colors or shapes, I couldn't care less, given the situation in which I found myself at the time.

The second disturbing thing is the fascination with the system as such, with technology as such, as if we were to do things only because they were technically feasible. We don't question whether it fits into some ethical or, for that matter, aesthetic framework for our future.

The third disturbing thing which I see in these studies is that the present order is taken for granted. It is as if it were solid enough, safe enough, acceptable enough to build on and extrapolate into the future. But what if this were not the case? We have been hearing people speak of the possibility of the system breaking down. What then? If in the next few years a black leader were to emerge with nationwide prestige and lead the black people to an open revolution, what kind of American society would we have then? What would be left of all the predictions about the so-called technetronic society in which we indulge today? I think there is a complete lack of human dimensions in all these projections.

There is a tendency among American intellectuals to pay too much attention to the year 2000 and too little to the many social problems of the industrial society in which we live. I'm not trying to say that we should give up the year-2000 studies, I am not suggesting Herman Kahn should be Nixon's Secretary for Urban Affairs. There is no shortage of talent. We can do both things. What I fear is that too great a shift of emphasis from present problems to the future may be psychologically dangerous. Futurism can become a synonym for escapism, a kind of moral alibi, because it's so much smarter to think about the year 2000 when the present is hard to take. We may well find that the post-industrial society will depend on what is young in the non-industrialized society.

DAVID MARQUAND: The debate between Peretz and Bell is fascinating to me as a member of the British Labour Party. I agree with a lot of what I thought Peretz was driving at. I agree with his distaste for the slightly castrated approach of the older generation, a sort of value-free social science. And yet it seems to me that he, and perhaps the whole of the American New Left, is busily digging himself into the same trap into which the British labor movement fell about thirty years ago, by concentrating too much on ownership, and has been unsuccessfully trying to escape ever since.

As I understand him, Mr. Peretz was saying, "You shouldn't bother with all this highfalutin crystal gazing. You should ask normative questions about society now." But the experience of our own Labour Party has shown that if you don't seriously try to predict future trends in society, you ask the wrong normative questions. The experience, if I may say so, of the British Labour Government has shown what happens if you don't have at the back of your mind a view of how society is going to develop and of what sort of strategy you need to make sure that your values can be imposed on these developments.

Let me give you two examples. My constituency is a mining constituency. Sixty percent of the male labor force there is employed by the National Coal Board. At the moment, going on right now on my doorstep, is a terrible problem of how to cope with the running down of the coal industry, the need to redeploy men, give them alternative skills and so on. The National Coal Board, a publicly owned corporation, is at least as unresponsive, bureaucratic and difficult to control, has at least as little sense of participation by the work force, as any of the great privately owned corporations. It's not simply a question of ownership. We have got to work out a philosophy of dealing with both publicly owned and privately owned corporations.

The other example is this: there has developed a great and growing gap between a minority in British society which is becoming relatively poorer and a majority which is pretty comfortably off. My great problem as a politician is how to persuade the skilled, relatively well-paid workers in my constituency to sacrifice some of the advantages they would otherwise enjoy, for the sake of the unskilled, underpaid, underprivileged, really poor members of their own community. In the past, it was possible to appeal to the myth of proletarian solidarity, and in this way you could, to some extent, persuade the better paid, better-off workers that they had some moral obligation to look after the interests of the less fortunate. But proletarian ideology has become less and less meaningful to them. The measures of the Labour Government which are most unpopular with working-class people in England today are aimed at redistributing wealth towards the less well-off members of society. There's no doubt about this at all. I think any British politician would agree. The American New Left has got to face this. It's no good saying the problem of poverty exists, unless you can get the votes to go and solve it.

We have got to get away from the obsession that there is one solution to all the problems of society, which takes you to your social classless utopia in which everyone can fulfill himself. This is not a very new thought, but the experience of the British labor movement and other Western European socialist movements in the last few years brings it home more than ever. What we have to do is to try to identify what are the particular obstacles now and in the future towards the socialist values of classlessness and individual self-realization and equality and fraternity. We can only proceed on the basis of a very tough, hard, rigorous, analytical sort of social-science approach. The kind of paper and talk Daniel Bell has presented here are something that, in my country, is not done nearly enough. We have a lot of journalistic speculation and idle gossip, but we don't have this serious systematic rigorous searching out of what are the trends.

PERETZ: I find one thing Mr. Marquand has said frankly distressing. He talked about persuading the workers to sacrifice something for the very poor. In America too the War on Poverty and reform in the cities are efforts to improve the lot of the poor on the backs of middle- and lower-class people. I was struck that you said that the sacrifice in England, as in America, should come off the backs of those who really do not have very much, and that little which they have, they have insecurely, and are obviously not terribly satisfied with.

JOHN MADDOX: Both Mr. Peretz, and Mr. Kennan last night, seem to have been saying that technology has an unpleasant influence in society and increases the gaps between rich and poor. This seems paradoxical to me. Technology has in fact borne out the futuristic optimism of forty years ago much more than one could have had any reason to expect. It is really quite remarkable that people can move about with almost undreamt-of freedom, can call each other up with almost undreamt-of ease, can look forward to a supply of power at perhaps a tenth of the cost it would have been twenty years ago. This is the sort of thing that poor people notice much more than rich people. It's their children who used to die at birth, it's they who were prevented from moving about and telephoning each other. The much maligned television set has helped enormously to open the horizon and feed the imagination of people who previously would have been cut off from society. We should remember these things. I find it paradoxical that people like Mr. Peretz and Mr. Kennan should say, "Let us do something to control television advertising, pollution and so on. Let's bring in new regulations." This rush to illiberalities seems to me to consist of trying to say that because we fear Big Brother in the world, that we don't know tomorrow, let's have him right now in the world we do understand. This seems to me extremely mistaken.

By insisting on the horrors and disappointments of technology, politicians cut themselves off from their constituents. The people who enjoy television like it that way and would like more of it. By insisting such things are bad, politicians patronize less wealthy countries in much the same style as Marie Antoinette talking about cake.

However, it seems to me that what Mr. Kennan said last night about the need for paying attention to the machinery of government is very important. One of the first things we could do is make better use of the existing machinery. I don't see why the regulatory agencies in the United States are not more thoroughly used, for instance, to control television. This country should also find new means of raising money for good causes. Why not raise more money for the transportation system when the Apollo program has obtained the lion's share?

MARTIN MEYERSON: If we were to judge America through the gloom that has so often entered our discussions here, the rubric of the American century would be the shortest-lived of any social order. Instead, I think we should judge the outcomes of our actions in America. In judging these outcomes, which Mr. Peretz failed to do in his paper, I see a series of mass or popular satisfactions. Intellectuals may hold them in disdain, but these mass satisfactions are remarkably real. A nation which has provided an individual house for almost all people has satisfied a goal shared very widely round the world. The universally owned automobile has a similar appeal, as do the conditions of work in the United States. Popular American culture is widely sought not only in the West but in Asia and Africa and even the socialistic countries. It is

not sufficient to say, as some Marxists do, that social consciousness derives from social existence and therefore what exists is what
is desired.

The desires satisfied in the United States are widespread ones
and looked to with great respect throughout the world. True, they
have not been respected by intellectuals outside the United States,
who scorn the so-called Coca-Cola culture the U. S. has produced.
However, the very scorn becomes dimmer as American higher
culture also becomes dominant in the world. There isn't, for
instance, an architect in the world who does not turn to the U. S.
for his models. The same is true in the visual arts generally.
Crozier, Shils and I have just come from an international meeting
on universities, and, to our surprise, the American model was held
out as the model for the world. The intellectual elsewhere has
become more sympathetic to the arts and intellectual life in
America in general, including, incidentally, music and dance and
the performing arts.

The American intellectual has gone through a kind of counter-
metamorphosis. He who had been on the margin of life has
suddenly found himself in the board rooms of corporations con-
sulting with the wicked men Mr. Peretz talks about (sometimes
they are wicked and often they are not), in the center of governmental controversy and decisions, and in a role, through our
universities, of a scale and kind that would have been hard to
imagine at the end of the Second World War.

Now we have suddenly found that many of the young have
rejected both the outcomes of the mass society we have known and
their intellectual predecessors, and rejected them with tremendous
turmoil. I think it is unfair at the moment to ask of the young that
they outline the future, although it is rapidly coming to a point
where we all should ask that futures be outlined. The kind of
organizational distaste that the young have requires a clear examination of alternatives which we have not seen previously and
which we are not seeing at this meeting. T. S. Eliot had some
lovely lines that—

We cannot revive old factions
We cannot restore old policies
Or follow an antique drum.

That antique drum has sounded long enough. It is time we began seriously examining the alternatives that lie before America.

MINOO MASANI: I must assure Mr. Peretz that in my country [India] there's no advertising campaign to make people appreciate the virtues of scooters or washing machines or other gadgets. Even the villager, given half a chance, grabs these because there is a real craving for them. But even putting aside the standard of life, I would like to suggest that the United States does not lag in regard to social justice, compassion and other nonmaterial values. Many years ago, Morgan Phillips, the secretary of the British Labour Party, said he thought the United States was a better socialist society than Britain or Scandinavia, not to mention the Communist countries. The inequality between the most skilled and least skilled workers in factories is less in America than in my country or Western Europe or the Soviet Union.

EUGEN LOEBL: Ownership is only one aspect of society. We in Czechoslovakia laid very great stress on the form of ownership and changed it. The result is that we have had all the negative aspects of capitalism and very few of its [positive] qualities. We assumed that a takeover by the state of the means of production was in itself a socialist measure. We forgot that once the means of production were concentrated in the hands of the state, or, rather, of the twenty members of the Presidium of the party, and they owned everything and had all the political power, the state ceased to be an organ of the people. It became the employer of the whole nation, and citizens had no rights. The question is not ownership but the system as a whole. We should see things in proportion. The freedom to discuss—it is a pleasure to discuss things—hasn't been generally accepted here as a problem. If I may speak on behalf of our laboratory experience in Czechoslovakia, the problem of our century is man himself. We can solve economic problems, we will

142

be able to solve social ones, we are not able to solve the problems of man. These are growing with the growing world. We should reformulate our old questions to ask what a society would look like in which man has the optimum space for self-realization. All other criteria should fall into place around this central value.

PERETZ: I did not say I was in favor of public ownership. I said that the concentration of ownership in our society leads to the irresponsible exercise of power by private institutions. I too am troubled by the irresponsible exercise of power in public institutions. I think we have to work out some form of democratic control of both public and private institutions.

JEAN-JACQUES SERVAN-SCHREIBER: Mr. Loebl, if, as I believe, you remain a convinced Communist, would you rather live in Soviet Russia or in the United States to achieve the human values to which you have devoted your life?

LOEBL: I would prefer to live in the country nearer the ideals of socialism, and that, permit me to say, is the United States. The first criterion by which to judge a society from the economic point of view is the level of science on which the economy is based. An economy based on private ownership at a high scientific level gives more social benefits than an economy based on a low level of science. If you have a water mill which is socially owned and a power station which is privately owned, the social benefit of the power station is far greater than that of the water mill. In socialist countries, because science and intellect have been discriminated against, our workers earn far less than the workers in, say, Austria, our neighbor. I feel that now that the Russians have decided to rely only on power, the United States, if they make full use of their opportunities, could take over the lead and show new perspectives to human society.

ANDREAS PAPANDREOU: I have the highest respect for Mr. Loebl—for what you have been through, sir, and for your courage —I countersign all he says; there is no disagreement in substance. But, Monsieur Servan-Schreiber, I object strongly to the question you put to Mr. Loebl and to the fact that you asked for a confession before this group. Where one wants to live and for what reason are not topics for which we have been called here. It is a highly improper question and a highly improper procedure.

SERVAN-SCHREIBER: There are no improper questions, since Mr. Loebl can always refuse to answer, and I knew beforehand that he would in fact answer.

LOEBL: I am very grateful to Monsieur Servan-Schreiber for giving me an opportunity to say, in my purely personal capacity, what the government and all my friends and comrades in Czechoslovakia are not able to say.

SERVAN-SCHREIBER: Does that satisfy Mr. Papandreou?

PAPANDREOU: No, sir, because the question was not addressed to Mr. Loebl, but to you.

AURELIO PECCEI: As a manager, I would like to criticize the method by which you Americans, and we Europeans, consider the post-industrial society. We choose the easy way out by examining the problems of this and other societies piecemeal, each one separately from the other, out of context. The problems of American society at this juncture are deeply embedded in the problems of the world. They belong to the general problems of humanity. You cannot isolate them as you do. We always consider what we may call the input of technology, of ways and habits and know-how and values pouring out from America into the other societies, and fail to see the elements conditioning American society, the input which is coming continuously and increasingly from other systems into American society. We generally fail to understand that all these systems are increasingly interacting upon one another. In the monetary field, the dollar is no longer in a unique position as the reserve currency of the world. The new international monetary system will condition the monetary, fiscal and financial policy of this country. We speak of trade as a world proposition. This means that purely internal, generally protectionist views we may have in any country cannot operate unfettered. The international company will mean more and more U. S. companies spreading all over the world, combining factors of production irrespective of national boundaries, and this will mean a redeployment, a relocation of industry from this country to other countries. Labor will follow suit; we are already talking about worldwide contracts and bargaining. Everything which happens in the world—today the Middle East, Vietnam, tomorrow perhaps Albania or Berlin or the oceans—has an input into this country. Instantaneous communications go across frontiers. The transnational is gaining over the national, especially in things psychological, in things that have to do with the future and therefore are of interest to the younger generation. The problems of this country cannot be taken in isolation, whether one is dealing with the individual versus the organization, or education versus confrontation, or employment and leisure, or the very important problems of planning. All these should be considered first in a general context, with European and other friends throughout the world, to find the best ways of dealing with them.

BELL: I don't think it's true that intellectuals, or even this organization, or its predecessor organization ten years ago, said that things were perfect in this country. I think something else was being said—that we don't know how to do things. We do have a rough notion of the goals we want, a more livable environment, better homes and schools and such. We don't know how to do it. We still don't know how to do it. Part of the crisis of liberalism is precisely the fact that we haven't realized the complexity of society and we don't know how to cut into it. We don't know, in a sense, what is a better school. We don't know really what is a better environment and how to plan it. Answers aren't always very easy. We want to clean up the physical environment. We want to have pure air and clean water. Well, it turns out when you begin to probe into the problem that if you want clean air you have to have more dirty water. When you take the effluents out of the air, you can send them into space, which is very expensive, or dig a hole in the ground, or dispose of them in water. It is too easy to say, "Let us do it." If that was at issue, humanity would have been satisfied a long time ago. Part of the problem is to realize these points of complexity. When you want to do one thing, you run into difficulties at the other end of the scale. These are the kinds of problems one runs into in this form of social engineering and social analysis.

I think, too, it's part of the way in which you understand the complications of society. We haven't been witnessing so much unification of economic and social power in the last twenty years. What we've been witnessing is the expansion of the political arena, a multiplication of claimants. You now have a scientific constituency, the poor, the blacks, farmers, laborers, business, all of them making claims on society. And to some extent the paradox is that the powerlessness of the people arises from more participation, not less. There are many more organizations today in American life, in the ghettos, in the communities, in the cities, thousands of them. Each begins to check the other out. As a politician, how do you begin to adjudicate among them? The odd thing is that we are in the middle of a revolution of participation, and that very fact makes it more difficult to decide not only where to go but how to do it. It doesn't do to sidestep that kind of problem by some kind of rhetorical sweep.

SABURO OKITA: What will be the major interest of the individual when you have a higher-income society and shorter working hours? Will his main concern be his place of work? Or the community where he is living? Or in cultural or sporting groups?

There is a growing gap between people active in society and average people. Elites in society are getting busier and busier running about all over the world. Average people are just contemplating what to do about the coming weekend. The type of society Mr. Bell describes may be very stimulating for small groups endowed with ability, but may become a very dull, unhappy society for average people.

BELL: After the events at Columbia, I turned to my colleagues and said at one point, "I finally realize the answer to the problem that has been plaguing Marxists for a hundred and fifty years. Marx said in *The German Ideology*, 'What will the workers do with their leisure time under socialism?' And the answer is very clear:

You serve on committees. Day and night, you serve on committees."
That is one of the things workers will do with their leisure time
under socialism, Mr. Okita. Another, of course, is what my [Co-
lumbia] colleague Steven Marcus calls "pornotopia," the utopia of
pornography which is part of the hedonism of the culture. This is
one of the dangers, if you will, of post-industrial society.

Then, with the multiplication of participation, there will be
more community conflict. When people are claimants in a society,
they will not take things passively. They will act. Part of the problem of the future society is how to stop this multiple conflict from
becoming polarized. Conflict could even polarize all society instead
of remaining divided in multiple conflicts which can be laid out
each in a particular way.

Finally, the question raised by Mr. Silj about the future. I don't
believe the future is a far-flung point out in time. Our present
problems in the cities come from the fact that we live in nineteenth-
century cities, we're constrained by the way the streets were laid
out in the past. This affects the way in which we can plan the
future. We have to begin now.

SERVAN-SCHREIBER: The problem of the human goals of the
industrial societies do not seem to Europeans always to be taken
seriously enough in this country. I was struck this morning by a
sentence of Mr. Bell's, when he said that the problems of goals in
the industrial society are not so difficult or important as the problems of means. This shocked me, and I would like him to explain
what he meant.

BELL: If one looks at the fundamental tendencies of industrial
society for a hundred and fifty years, there have been contradictory
thrusts. One has been towards bureaucracy as a means of organizing industry. The other has been political, towards equality.
Today, in the United States, the demands of the blacks are for
equality, and that continues one thrust. The reaction of the students against bureaucratization continues the other. That's why
they don't always converge. It is too easy to say simply that we are
against bureaucratization and for equality. For example, the arbi-

147

trary power of an official is curbed through bureaucratized rules. In the same way, trade unions introduced bureaucracy to establish rights inside the plant against arbitrary bosses. So while we are against overbureaucratization, those who understandably want equality neglect the fact that there is sometimes a tension between equality and liberty. Equality has a leveling effect, and liberty in the sense that you want to be alone means sometimes precisely that you don't want to be constantly forced into a leveling process. We run the risk today of setting up new shibboleths called "decentralization" and "participation," and assuming that by simply embracing them we are going to settle these questions.

When I say the goals aren't so difficult, I mean that they are not mysterious, we have always lived with them: We want community without conformity, privacy without isolation. But these aims diverge, and how one manages them in a complex society is the difficult thing. If you lived, for example, in an old rural atmosphere, you could take your garbage and simply throw it out of the window. You can't do that in an urban society. A man may say, "I want to participate in a democracy, I want to run my life the way I want," but should a man down South be able to say, "I don't want to have someone living next to me whom I don't like and therefore I'm going to exclude him"? You say, "No, you're a part of a moral community and can't practice discrimination." Or somebody may say, "I live near a certain road and I don't want another road to go by me," and you say, "But look, the community needs that kind of road, and you can't simply veto it." So we're left with the oldest of all questions of political theory, which is, What level of decision should be implemented by whom and in what way?

The question is one of means: How do you have effective social controls which best enhance individual rights? It's in that sense that I meant that the goals aren't difficult but the means are. One can't take entire blueprints and say, "This is the way the entire future is going to be," because you need a degree of humility to know that it is not going to work like that. One of the terrifying questions is how you avoid the bureaucratization of the basic intellectual work of the post-industrial society. We know in a sense what the bureaucratization of work on machines has done to many people. If the intellectual worker too becomes bureaucratized, it will be terrifying. An economist friend of mine, working on input-output tables, worked for five years on zinc and lead. How do you move such a man up from zinc and lead to platinum and diamonds and various other delights of the economic world? One has to begin to try to break up patterns of work. Many corporations are sensitive to this. It's much easier to work with a beard or at night for IBM than for General Motors, because they [IBM] need mathematicians more. You can work at your own pace a little more because what you do is in a sense respected. This is part of the problem of how to break up hierarchical, specialized detailed work and allow for different kinds of group and even individual formations. There is very little of that going on. The only realistic experiments took place in England, and those were the Glacier Metals studies done by W. J. Brown, the British-Labourite employer, with Elliot Jacques, who is now the president of, I think, Brunel University. They were never extended, oddly enough, by the British Labour Party, although it talks about humanization of work.

STANLEY HOFFMANN:* Mr. Bell has said that the society of the future, like those of the past, will be determined by the answer to the question not "Who rules?" but "How is it ruled?" He answers this by saying it will be ruled in terms of skills. Now, this is to me precisely the central mistake of the technocratic orientation so largely represented here. A society is defined by something else as well, by its culture, its political institutions, its leaders, and this is where choice comes in. The struggle for power is still with us. And here there are three kinds of questions we have somehow lost sight of. One is the social question of injustice and inequality: the vision of affluence, even in Western societies, has no relation to reality. Then there is the orientation of the political elite. How broad will the meritocratic principle be? Should one apply government by

* A comment later in the conference.

skills even in areas where it is very dubious what skills mean? Will the scientific intellectual elite be dispersed or concentrated? How will it be accountable? Third, there is the question of the individual. Society is more and more going to be managed by large organizations, hierarchies of unequal structures like the bureaucracy, the universities, the corporations. Nobody has really found an answer to the question of how these institutions will be made responsive or responsible. The old solution, which was to rely on one's central representatives, no longer works, even though many of the problems of society can be solved only at the center. The new myth, developed by the New Left, of community control is no answer, either, because of the various conflicts among communities, because some problems cannot be solved at the local level and because of racial tension. The seriousness of the problem of the blacks in America is that they are waging three battles at the same time: the old battle for equality of opportunity, the new battle for participation in the control of inequal organizations, and, finally, the battle for identity and dignity which may lead them towards separatism.

In this society of the future, what will be the role of the intellectuals? Will they be just the managers, the gatekeepers, the keepers of the status quo? Or will they continue to perform the critical function by standing outside and judging? This is a central problem in the crisis of the universities. What is indispensable for the intellectuals, whether they are close to power or not, is to play the normative function. I hope we would not lose sight of this even if we think the future is already determined.

ROY INNIS

THE DEBATE

The three-day seminar that is the basis of this book was held at Whig Hall on the campus of Princeton University under the auspices of the International Association for Cultural Freedom. The pictures of the participants on these pages were taken by Michael D. Sullivan.

SHEPARD STONE, JOHN J. MCCLOY and ROBERT J. LIFTON

ANDREAS
PAPANDREOU

JOHN KENNETH GALBRAITH

GEORGE F. KENNAN

NORMAN PODHORETZ,
SAM BROWN and
LILLIAN HELLMAN

JEAN-JACQUES
SERVAN-SCHREIBER
and CARL KAYSEN

ARTHUR M. SCHLESINGER, JR.

STANLEY HOFFMANN

DANIEL BELL

MARTIN PERETZ

6

THE NEW LEFT:

FEAR OF FREEDOM

AMBASSADOR SOEDJATMOKO: I speak out of a deep sense of frustration. I think this whole conference is in danger of missing its purpose. We came here because we all recognize that there is a crisis in America and that the way it will be met can affect the world. Now, we have discussed at length the Negro problem. But there is more to the American crisis than that. What of the New Left? How and why is the confidence of the American liberal faltering? What are the underground churches here? What is the nature of the discontent not only among militant protesters but in suburbia? What is going on subterraneously in the minds of the people who are part of the establishment? There is a deep malaise going through this country, and my superficial observations in the brief period I have lived here bring me to conclude that something very important is happening and that we have lulled ourselves at this conference by allowing ourselves to discuss deep motivations in familiar ways with familiar social-science jargon. I think we are overlooking the agony which exists in this country.

ROBERT LIFTON: I'm not going to *answer* Mr. Soedjatmoko, because I agree with him. I will only raise issues that seem to me implied by his question. I think the New Left and young intellectuals are trying to express dissatisfaction with what they consider the quality of life in America. This is a terribly hard subject to talk about, because most of our social science and psychological systems exclude it. What concerns me most about some of Dan Bell's projections about post-industrial society is that though he is aware of the risks, the psychological dimension may be excluded by his very model. That means we must change our systems of thought, not the problem which remains. An acquaintance of mine recently carried out a very imaginative study into the contents of the attaché cases of about thirty young executives. It's part of their uniform in America, like the briefcase but more elegant. He found expected things: some did have official papers in there, others had apples and pears, a few had pornographic books; all those things were quite expected. But some had ballet tights and other totally unexpected objects. This set me thinking in a new way about the degree to which one's job in a technological or industrial setup speaks to some larger sense of the rhythm of life. In traditional, pre-modern society, people lived with a shared cosmology, a set of symbols organized around family life, religion and various social forms. These have begun to break down in the West since the eighteenth century at the latest. They still exist, but in halfway and ambivalent forms. In America, the first post-modern society, technology has stepped into the gap and organized life in many ways around itself. But what if it fails to replace the symbolic content that exists in traditional society for the individual? What if, while providing goods, it leaves people with a sense of emptiness, of a counterfeit quality to existence? I think it is from some such sense of the need for a new search that much of the feeling behind the New Left begins.

Take an aspect of experience really typical of our world today; that is that everything and nothing is possible, that one can, in a sense, be anyone and no one. Dan Bell wrote in his paper that there will be three psychological types in the society which he described as post-industrial—the motor, the rational and the sensory. This reminds me of the way in which traditional societies used to segregate their women. There were housewives and mothers in the nurseries in the first place; seductresses and prostitutes who entertained men in the second place; and a small group of novelists and artists, the knowers, in the third. That worked fairly well then. But now all the mothers can watch television and know what it's like to be seductresses. They want to be mother, seductress and knower all in one. All are present in each mind. This is what I call the Protean style. Proteus was a sea god who could change his shape from man to fire to flood to beast and back to man again. The one thing he had great difficulty in doing, and never would do unless he were chained, was to carry out his own authentic function, that of prophecy. Well, Proteus, I think, is with us now. The Protean men of the contemporary world can shift from idea to idea, from experience to experience, and immerse themselves in a set of convictions or commitments, and then leave them, with relatively diminished psychological cost.

This engenders the whole train of experimentation characteristic of the young. The experimentation can be formal, through the arts and sciences; sensual and sexual; or ideational. It can and should be all of these, but in all the experimentation there is a great stress on the experience as such. Here's something Mr. Cruse was suggesting in terms of the influence of black culture on the American avant-garde: experientalism in music, in feeling, in dance, in ideas. In the process, there are several breakdowns, very disturbing to us, in the traditional separations between art and reality, between fiction and life and between theater and history. They produce, I think, the characteristic contemporary admixture of experientialism and radical politics which is really something new on such a large scale. They also lead to an enormous sense of absurdity and quality of mockery. Absurdity is not new (we've had a great literary tradition of it, particularly in French), but there's something new in the dimension of absurdity in recent experience. It can be seen in the graffiti of the student movement in France and in the slogans of the Columbia students and others in America, and it doesn't seem that we have yet grasped what they mean in cultural terms. The style of mockery is for the young at times the only authentic way of expressing the disturbance they feel and the relationship between self and world, and indeed between life and death. It may be that in the Protean style there are different relationships to those perceived in the old notion of ideas, relationships perceived not as wholes but in brief images and fragments. A gifted American writer once said, "Fragments are the only form I trust." There's something in the cultural style with us now that makes only fragments trustworthy. That doesn't do as a lasting solution to anything. But one has to recognize its importance especially to young people guarding themselves against the violation of the psychological realm that results from efforts to blueprint all society in a permanent form.

The style of mockery is, of course, often upsetting to the older generation. If I may say so, I think we saw last night, on the part of Mr. Kennan, a pattern all too frequent in America, and I'm sure elsewhere too—rage of the old against the young. This rage has to do with a sense of the world that one has known crumbling and with it one's own personal world. That doesn't do. Nor does embracing the young and putting more Protean style into the Protean. The third position, the more ambiguous one, is to be receptive to the Protean style, because it is essentially a desire to remain open to the enormous new possibilities now presenting themselves, and at the same time to bring to it what we have learned, our own history. Here universities become enormously important. They are not to be torn down, I agree. But they are a logical battlefield for ideas and for positions and commitments, and I don't think those of us in them should forget it.

WILLIAM GORDON BOWEN: There is one characteristic of the university scene in this country which troubles me: the tone of anti-intellectualism which colors university life these days. I would note first of all an increasing tendency for editors of student papers to print ringing editorials before they've even read reports dealing with the questions at issue. This tendency to state a position—indeed, to argue for it vigorously—before even having heard various sides can, I think, be observed among administrators, faculty members and trustees as well as students. I must say that trustees are learning faster than the others that this can be a dangerous procedure.

There's also an impatience with "respectable" subject matter,

ranging from classical archaeology to English literature to theoretical physics to much of modern political science, when it does
not seem to solve immediate problems or advance one's own
psychic development. It's the relevance, and that's the word, of
broad areas of intellectual inquiry which is at issue here. One of
the happy by-products of a recent trip of mine to another part of
this country was a catalog from one of the experimental colleges or
free universities now flourishing here. I mention only three of the
course titles. One was "Death to the Murderers of Che Guevara,"
which was scheduled to meet only once. The second was "Advanced Sensitivity Analysis," and the third was "Creative Chicken
Killing."

A much more serious manifestation is impatience with the use
of analysis in social and political problems. I can understand, even
sympathize with, the complaints of people who say we're trying to
apply sophisticated cost-benefit techniques to all problems except
the use of cost-benefit analysis itself. But I have a great deal of
difficulty with the argument that it is "obscene"—translated,
wrong—to try to sort out the consequences of a proposed course
of action and then decide, on balance, whether or not one ought to
do it, that instead of going through all this rigmarole one ought
simply to do what is obviously right. I have a strong feeling that
some of us in the universities now are practicing the same kind of
simplistic approach to complex problems for which we so roundly
criticize politicians such as Mr. Wallace.

I'm less inclined than some to put all the blame on Vietnam,
race and the cities. There are important contributing factors within
the universities themselves. There's the preoccupation, largely
forced on us by present circumstances, with financial and bud-
getary problems to the exclusion of educational questions. There's
the tendency for many faculty members, as well as administrators,
to work too hard and think too little. There's the extraordinary
conservatism of many academics towards proposals for educational change. Finally, there is a serious lack of really significant
intellectual progress in melding creative and humanistic and scien-

tific impulses in various fields of scholarship. I will not attempt to spell out the long-run consequences of this mood which I observe in many American universities. All that I will say is that I don't think all of them will be bad.

MICHEL CROZIER: I don't believe that the malaise foreigners like myself sense in this country,* and indeed in their own, can be sufficiently explained by the reasons usually given, such as fear of a growing oppression by an increasingly organized society. I come from a country, France, where we are burdened by organizations from the past which are much more oppressive than the American organizations of the present and even perhaps those of the future. Let's just recall what blue-collar workers had to endure in great American corporations thirty years ago and what they enjoy now. They have some power in the plant; they cannot be pushed around as they were. In France, government curbs businessmen much more than you do, and yet what happens? French blue-collar workers have much less power, much less opportunity than here to exercise their creative abilities. There is a lot of conformism in America, but there is more in France, at least in industrial enterprises. A few years ago, I spent a year in California and had some friends in the electronics industry. I was surprised to see people at one moment in one corporation and at the next in another, so I tried to find out what was happening. They told me that So-and-so had had a good idea but didn't see eye to eye with the people he was working with, and so had founded a new corporation. When I went home, I asked a friend what would happen in such a case in France. He answered that someone with an idea would have to sell it to the people he was working with. If he fell out with them, he could never get the credit from the banks to form his own corporation, because they would know from his employers that he was a bad risk; and he couldn't go to the government, because it was such a bureaucracy that the idea would get lost in the undergrowth. I don't want to emphasize these contrasts too much, because I know they are only one aspect of a complex problem. But I

* See M. Crozier's paper, pages 203–08.

do want to indicate that some kinds of individual freedom and power exist in the general framework of organization now and one can hope will do so in the future. This is not a lost cause.

I think the battle Galbraith and in another way Peretz are fighting against the corporation is the battle of 1948, Truman's battle. It was a good battle and it paid. But now it does not pay, because the corporations are responsible neither for Vietnam nor for the racial crisis. On the other hand, and here I come to my main point, there is a basic problem which can explain the malaise. During the past few years there has been a great development in America of a new kind of rationality of calculation, taking many forms, the most popular being perhaps cost-utility analysis. Those who are pushing to the fore and wielding increasing influence are mostly people who have a certain arrogance of rationality, who can calculate in such a way that everything is cut down to size. This is necessary because calculating one's operations more closely leads to new opportunities of progress and even certain kinds of freedom. But we have to understand that it creates a great psychological burden.

It's not that people are powerless or oppressed by conformism in the old sense, superiors telling them they have to do this or that and behave. As a Frenchman, I am struck by how much less conformism of that sort there is in America than there was before, by the much greater freedom of manner. But people are made utterly responsible for their own actions, they are forced to see the consequences of what they do and to live with those consequences. There are no scapegoats. This is much more difficult and produces a lot more tension than one thinks. I know there are many ways of escaping. Nevertheless, the pressures on the individual are very great. Human beings need protection against the consequences of their own actions. They don't want to be measured, they feel a great deal of antagonism towards a system which clearly weighs them by their acts. I think that, apart from the external accident of Vietnam, the current unrest is due to a backlash against the difficulties of meeting the new standards.

This is especially true of the students. As Daniel Bell has said, universities have become the basic unit in society where people are for the first time measuring up to their future, and this is very difficult for them. They do not have the protection of class and other barriers which helped them to hide from the pressures in the past. There isn't even the advantage intellectuals have in a less developed country of being few, and so able to play an aristocratic role. The more intellectuals you have in a country, the less each individual intellectual feels he has influence. It is natural to have a kind of backlash and symptoms like the retreat of the hippies and the explosions some students go in for. There is a lot of talk about the blue-collar, lower-middle-class backlash. I don't think one should make too much of this. One should pay equal attention to the intellectual backlash, which, in a certain way, you can find even in Ambassador Kennan's retreat to the Jeffersonian ideal of an unpolluted America. Many students are retreating into a dream of a community life because their real life is one of hard competition from which they cannot escape. I sympathize very much with their predicament, to some extent I even share it, but we have to find ways to build a society not based on retreat.

The problem as I see it, with perhaps some indulgence in the French taste for overgeneralization, is the breakdown of the liberal synthesis. The American liberals have begun to look complacent to foreigners and now also to American students and younger intellectuals because they have had too superficial a view of what it is to be rational. Too much stress was put on what could be counted and not enough on what required deeper analysis. All sorts of theories presented groups of people, even nations, as so many cells fitting into schemes where every variable could be set against every other variable. Foreigners, even ones who are not anti-American, could not help but feel American liberals were culture-blind and institution-blind, and saw all peoples as abstract pieces in the universalistic American dream, the great society of the free world. At home too, human beings were seen as abstract cells, deprived of their basic power drive and human warmth. This led to a lack of understanding of the kind of use people will make of their freedom. They will not always contribute to the universal harmony. People may even insist on doing wrong simply to show that they are free. It is too easy to talk about economic power and curbing corporations, like Professor Galbraith or Martin Peretz. Throughout the fabric of our society there are problems of power. If you curb it at one point it emerges at another. Everybody is going to fight for power in a certain way. The flaw in the liberal synthesis was that it assumed too easily that conflict and the basic difficulties of power could be resolved.

At the same time, there is the complementary problem of the capacity of society to face the difficulties of planning, analyzing and meeting the consequences of one's own calculations, and this is a problem of protection. The old privileges that provided protection must go, because many of them are sources of exploitation and very detrimental to human beings. But one cannot suppress everything at once, or there will be a backlash. Take the issue of school busing in New York. That was rational enough, but went too far because it endangered what many felt to be the protection of their families. We need to know more about social learning and how to build institutions which are responsive and open. We also have to work on values. I am not sure I agree with Daniel Bell about the importance of the theoretical creator. We are in urgent need of other kinds of creators, particularly in the field of implementation. The more we develop rationality, the more we have to deal with human problems, and in a much less categorical way than we are doing. We need to develop values of creativity not only in the theoretical but in the human sense. Here, I think, the values of spontaneity and creativity the student revolutionaries present may be a great help to a more rational society.

MARTIN PERETZ: I would like to take issue with Michel [Crozier] on what he has said about the rationality of our calculations. I think back on recent years of American history, and wonder about the rationality of our calculations. I remember a senior colleague of mine who explained to me how the strategists had rationally figured out how to pacify all the villages of South Vietnam when there were this many counterinsurgents and that many police experts distributed around. That doesn't ring true at all. Michel calls Vietnam an accident. What some of us have been saying is that Vietnam is not an accident but an organic outgrowth of ideological and structured elements of the American system. Of course, Vietnam policy is not a function of corporate decision-making. I would even say that, judging by the behaviour of Wall Street, the corporations would probably like the Vietnam adventure to come very quickly to a close. But the impact of corporate and military-industrial pressures on the political community has been such as to maximize the defense system and the capacity to engage in military activity. They have done this to such an extent that the easiest thing very often is to have an intervention. One of the impressions the confidence about tactical deployment made on me was that it supposed once you could move troops quickly round the world you didn't have to have diplomacy. Well, we should have the kind of defense system where it is more difficult to move troops and then maybe we'd even have some imagination in diplomacy.

STANLEY HOFFMANN: What we are in the midst of now, and probably for some time to come, is not a reaction against rationality, but a reaction against the limits of pseudo-rationality as in strategic decisions which have led us where we are. It is a revolt against the misapplication of rationality defined as the calculation of consequences in bureaucratic organizations, the misapplication of rationality to areas of life in which it has no business. What is missing is quite simply the good old question, "What for?"

EDWARD SHILS: Let me take my point of departure in the remarks of my friend Dr. Soedjatmoko. I myself live, as you may gather by looking at me, as a sort of rustic in a cave. I am not really a member of the underground or of an underground church, although I might look like a troglodyte. Years ago Miss Mary McCarthy said that modern literature was like a bordello with a glass ceiling, and I said that the difference between us was the company we kept. I don't go around much in these circles. Nonetheless, I wasn't born yesterday, and I'm not confined to a reformatory. I do get around a little bit. I don't quite see the anguish Dr. Soedjatmoko refers to. I am aware of these things, of course. They are more common, I daresay, than they were fifty years ago when I was a youth. At that time when it was thought that America was a happy country I used to go on Sunday afternoons and evenings around the mission houses of Philadelphia. This was a peaceful City of Brotherly Love. There were enough lunatics trying out new religions there to meet the requirements of the U. S. Census of Religious Bodies. If you think mankind is in a state of depression looking for a god because life has lost its meaning, read the history of American sects contained in the Census of Religious Bodies, an extraordinary collection of theology, fantastically irrational, mad, hopeless that they could ever hope to find God that way, still trying—and so many of them. It's an old thing. Human beings have had·a miserable time always. They're a bit more sensitive now. Here's where I come, I think, to some point of consensus with Dr. Soedjatmoko. Mankind has changed somewhat. There has been an increase in sensitivity, an increase in individuality—the very things which we think are ethically valuable. Of course, there are no answers. Individuality has to form itself. That is what we think is the justification for its existence. If it were to live up to received answers, it wouldn't be individuality but conformism. Man should find meaning in life for himself, not have a stereotyped meaning of life given to him. And that's what these poor devils (of the New Left) are doing. That is the fruit of the generosity, the productivity of the American economy, the tolerance of the American religious establishment, and a number of other things. It has led to a crisis of authority in the United States. What I'm struck by is the weakness of character of the American elite—extraordinary! Ruffians like President Johnson, rough, rude—using, I am told, rough language, very rough—and mean, and imperious and unsympathetic. This chap, who doesn't have much to do with the intellectual, comes from Texas; because a collection of young people in the West Side kibbutz, and a few of their offspring, are carrying on against him and abusing him, he suddenly gets his wind up. Now, what kind of WASP is that, may I ask? A WASP with the sting of a butterfly, and without its beautiful wings. The WASPS have often been derogated in this country. Now, I'm not one of them, but I was brought up to respect them, and I still would, if they would only live up to the standards which we expected of them. The WASPS have abdicated. What has taken their place? Ants! Fleas! You people may think this funny. I am dead serious about it. There is an abdication of authority in the United States, a weakness of character. The younger generation mention the failure of the liberal establishment—WASP, X, Y, Z and so on. Nobody mentions Mayor Daley—they're afraid of *him*. They don't know how the police used to behave in the United States. They've read books about labor problems; they've never seen the police in action against an incipient trade union in the United States. The United States is a jolly rough country, and I must say it is less rough now than it used to be, in spite of all these urchins on the streets enjoying themselves by intimidating cowardly middle-class people. The United States has always been a rough country, which is part of its exuberance, of its vitality, its energy and ambition. I was brought up in an age of squads for beating up criminal syndicalism. What was criminal syndicalism? Having a little meeting of a trade union or something. The police were extremely rough, and extremely mean-spirited. Whereas now what happens? Mayor Daley says, "Shoot to kill if you see a looter." Immediately, a terrific howl. Mayor Daley, who is not very nimble for a policeman, tries to get out of that statement. And nobody had been shot to kill! Most of the disturbances in the ghettos, as they are called now, with great respect to the Jews, have gone relatively unchecked. Of course people have been killed. But considering the disturbance of the Chicago race riots, let us say, of 1919, on which I am some sort of expert, it was all kid stuff, if I may say so. The police and the WASPS are very much less rough, much less repressive now, far more permissive. I don't know whether they've been corrupted by social psychology, or by sociology, or whether they're just strangled by the serpents of sociological terminology. But they can't move. Every time something goes wrong, they invoke a collection of sociologists. I'm one of the family. I know a lot about them. And what are they all preaching? The culture of permissiveness, the respect for the rights of the human being, and so on. A long secular trend in Western history is reaching its fullest expression in the United States now, of the desacralization of authority. Put that in your pipe and smoke it! That's a jolly important phrase.

WALDEMAR BESSON: Is there any specific quality of this application of authority in the United States different from the European situation, or is there a unique element in the American side?

SHILS: There are trends of desacralization characteristic of Western society as a whole. At the beginning of the century, Huizinga in the book called *In the Shadow of Tomorrow* wrote a section on puerilism—childishness, really. What he was referring to was the adoration of youth and boyishness in the style of life of adults. Youth has been made into a false god. Not that age deserves to be a god, either—I don't believe in earthly gods myself. Nonetheless, youth has been elevated in a further stage of the romantic movement into a principle of pleasure and the appreciation of spontaneity, hostility against tradition, against all that is received from outside the individual. That has a very positive aspect. It emancipates human beings from a large number of cruel, superstitious and bad things. But nonetheless it has its consequences in the dislegitimization of the authority of institutions, in the family, the state, the church and so on.

Further, in Europe, as in America, lost wars and unsuccessful economies dislegitimate authorities. You had revolutions in Russia, when the Tsarist regime failed in 1905 against the Japanese and against Germany in the 1914–18 war. Another in Germany, even Germany, after the failure in the First World War; in France, occupied, defeated, and that has left a very profound impact; in Great Britain, triumphant in war but shorn of its empire. Whereas one's chest swelled, one's stature rose, when one saw the large amount of pink on the map, now the pink space is a very small part of the map. That too is a diminution of the collective self, and therefore a diminution of the acceptance of those authorities who were responsible for the maintenance of the glory and dignity of the collective self. In this country, let's put it baldly, despite all its great economic triumphs there's been the failure of the war in Vietnam. It's not the immorality of the war in Vietnam, and I believe it is immoral in some respects, but the failure. You can get away with anything if you get away with it—that is, if you *do* it. Had Anthony Eden been able to carry off the Suez adventure, he would be one of the great men of British history, and Selwyn Lloyd with him, in spite of the iniquity of what they were trying to do there. But they didn't get away with it. And President Johnson and the rest of his associates have not been able to get away with the war in Vietnam. That is one of the reasons for the further dislegitimization of authority which is common to both the United States and Europe. But the United States is more progressive than Europe. Individuation has gone further. More of our youth are in universities. More of them are educated. Dr. Spock is an American product—I don't mean Dr. Spock as an antidraft man, but Dr. Spock as an attendant on infancy and childhood. Dr. Spock is carrying on the work of Ellen Key and all those other great reformers for emancipating children from the dominion of their parents, and permitting them to urinate and defecate as freely as they wish, and to eat when they want, and to develop their own rhythms—not the rhythms of society, but the rhythms which are natural to them.

This is compounded by another special American trait. We have a bad relationship in the United States between the intellectual and the civil order. We owe it to President Andrew Jackson that the educated classes of this country found the lower classes distasteful. We owe it to the Irish famine that the Irish, ignorant, vulgar, Roman Catholic, brawling, spawning, got control of urban politics in the United States and settled above all in New England, which was the seedbed from which American culture came. The reaction of the Boston Brahmins to the Irish untouchables has prevailed in American intellectual life for many years, and we are not finished with it yet. At the beginning of the 1930s Mr. Edmund Wilson, one of the greatest living American intellectuals, wrote a ridiculous article called "Let's Take Over Communism from the Communists." He said that "the lowest form of human existence since man emerged from the primordial slime is the American professional politicism." Just think of the attitude this bespeaks and what consequence it has for the intellectual's participation in the rough-and-tumble of politics. American intellectuals don't like that stuff. It still belongs in the lower classes. They may be as egalitarian as all get-out, but they still have an untouchable class in their society, namely the professional politician. America underwent what looked like an improvement first when President Wilson gave the intellectuals the feeling that the country had been restored to their possession and they could legitimately take a part in running it. Then came President Roosevelt, and he appeared to have brought about a great change because he brought so many intellectuals in under the name of the Brain Trust, but it is interesting to note how few of them entered politics; they entered public life under Roosevelt's coattails, as members of the executive, consultants, advisers, high civil servants. That gave the intellectuals greater intimacy with the processes of government. But it must be remembered that they had a lot to do with causing difficulties subsequently in the relationship between the executive and the legislative, because they taunted and irritated by their greater intelligence and cleverness all those roughhewn sons of the soil, the party members of the political machines who were sitting in the legislative bodies of the state and federal government. So that it wasn't a change in tradition, it was an adaptation of the tradition of anti-politics of the American intellectuals.

Things really have not changed very much. There have been brilliant exceptions, but one is very struck by the reluctance of the highly educated to associate themselves with politics except to be its critics. They think that they fulfill their obligation by being critics morally in a state of disjunction vis-à-vis the political order. What is lacking is the common ground of a language in which criticism can be made within the framework of a sense of common membership in society. That is singularly lacking in so many of our intellectuals, except those who are abused because they serve the public through the government. There is the establishment, and there is freedom. Freedom meaning negation. And in between there is nothing. There is no middle ground to stand on, there is no possibility for what could be called realistic and solidary criticism. I don't see a ready solution, and it is one of the things of which the world stands most in need. And now I think I must stop, as I am like Stalin, who could give a fourteen-hour report.

DAVID BLUMENTHAL: Professor Shils has talked of the failure of authority in the United States, and implied that the rebellion of American youth is a sort of fling of permissiveness. I would like to speak of the extraordinary authority with which President Johnson executed the Vietnam War. I would like to speak of the extraordinary authority with which Hubert Humphrey was nominated for the Presidency of the U. S., and also of the tremendous dedication and the tremendous involvement of the youth who worked in a tremendous mobilization for the nomination of Senator McCarthy. I would also like to talk of the moral outrage which anyone would feel watching an articulate black mother ask a school administrator in New York City why her child was not being educated.

I don't think American youth has been capricious or has not been suffering or has not been serious about its commitments. During March of 1968, I can remember the obsession with which large numbers of moderate—not New-Leftist, but moderate—students walked about campus questioning why we were still in Vietnam, why black students were not being educated, why President Johnson was still—though not for long, thanks to those youths—the prospective Presidential candidate. These problems are more basic than a crisis of authority. Professor Bell wrote recently about the crisis at Columbia. He noticed that a large number of the students who were occupying the buildings at Columbia were not SDS, but moderates who had been attracted by a sense of unease about American institutions. He also pointed out the failure of the intellectual community in Columbia to meet the arguments of these students and propose solutions. Youth is asking for solutions. The intellectuals of this country, youth included, must struggle to find them. I suggest that at a future conference we might concern ourselves, or the intellectual community in the U. S. might concern itself, with making concrete proposals. If solutions are not found, they will be solved anyway without the direction which the intellectual community might provide.

JOHN J. McCLOY: I rather hesitate to say that we in America are in agony. In the course of all this turmoil and ferment, a great deal of progress is being accomplished. This may not be a very significant factor, but when I first became chairman of one of the great banks in New York City, we employed, at that time, maybe a hundred Negroes. I checked up the other day and there were most encouraging reports of the way training and assimilation programs have advanced. We tend in this country to be inquiring, and then set about trying to attack the problem, and although it is a rather clumsy effort many times, and sometimes it may even take some pretty sordid aspects, there is a basic idealism in the country that has not been entirely fatuous. Some of our condemnations of suburbia are perhaps a little overdrawn. I have a place in Connecticut for weekends, and I am as impressed by the alertness of those communities to social problems as I am by the presence of drug addicts, the increase in crime and the confusion among youth. I don't mean to be a Pollyanna about it, but I am inclined to think there is a greater instinct for inquiry, for dissecting problems, here than in Europe. We are going through a terrible trauma, what with violence and the horrible record of our assassinations. It has brought about a self-questioning attitude and mood throughout all levels of society that will, I believe, be productive of a new form of morality that could even have an impact on the rest of the world.

PERETZ: I wonder, Mr. McCloy, what role you think racial

violence will play in the progress you see being made in race relations?

McCLOY: It has sharpened up our thinking. Whether progress would have occurred without this violence, whether the violence will create reactions that will be unfortunate, I don't know. There was a growing awareness even without the violence.

NORMAN PODHORETZ: Mr. Shils was lamenting the split between the intellectuals of this country and practical democratic politics. I think this is true. There are, roughly, two large groups in the United States which have not for about a century now felt that they belonged to the same society. One has been the party of opposition to the American way of life which has expressed itself through highbrow culture. This culture constituted itself originally around the 1870s during the rapid transformation of the United States into an industrial country. Huge numbers of immigrants were pouring in. All the usual dislocations of a great historical transformation were in evidence in the post–Civil War period. When we talk about America today, I think we talk about a country born at that time rather than in 1776. What some historians have called the American gospel of success—and the religious imagery is significant—was being widely preached in that era known as the Gilded Age. It is generally thought that the American dream of success was the achievement of a great fortune. This has never been the case except for extraordinarily ambitious individuals, of whom there are always fewer than is generally supposed. The dream of success was the achievement of middle-class comfort. The hero of a novel by Horatio Alger, who is the embodiment of this, is deemed a success when he gets to earn seven thousand five hundred to ten thousand dollars a year by today's standards. According to the gospel of success in the late nineteenth century the conditions already existed in America for the achievement of this dream. In the last hundred years the great struggle domestically has come from, crudely, the liberals, who insisted that barriers existed to real equality of opportunity and had to be removed by legislation if the dream was to be realized. This is the liberal–conservative struggle in American history. There was no disagreement that the objective was to achieve what in fact has already largely been achieved in this country, with exceptions we all know about: the spread of the middle-class style of life to as many people as possible. Now, the intellectuals, the artists, large and very important contingents within the universities, have for a hundred years been devoting themselves to saying that this way of life is corruptive, unworthy spiritually and aesthetically gross. It's almost impossible to think of an important American writer in the last hundred years who has not more or less associated himself with that view of middle-class American life. This opposition developed independently of socialist influences, and can be partly traced, as Ed Shils said, to a patrician disturbance at the introduction of barbarians into American life. For example, Henry James returned to America around 1905 and traveled around. He had been abroad for many years, and the book he published in 1906, *The American Scene,* describes a visit to the Jewish ghetto on the Lower East Side of Manhattan. James visited cafés where Yiddish was being spoken, and reflected that in fifty years these people and their children would come into possession of the English language, and he thought, "Whatever we shall know it for, we shall not know it for English." It has always struck me as amusing that the grandchildren of these people devoted themselves in large numbers to writing Ph.D. dissertations on Henry James. And he was quite right, a lot of these books are written in a language that one does not know for English. The fear of what would happen to the culture was very strong among people like James, Henry Adams, John C. Chapman—I could extend the list indefinitely. This opposition to a business civilization was very forceful and had extremely powerful adherents from the beginning. It had something like the force of a religion. With the infusion of socialist and Marxist ideas around the turn of the century, through the channel of H. G. Wells and Shaw rather than directly from Marxist sources, it was possible for the party of opposition to broaden its hostility toward what it then learned to call capitalism. It was also possible, as a result of the modernist revolution in the arts and literature, for it to deepen and universalize its extreme hatred of the bourgeoisie. This opposition, which was much more strongly cultural than political, was continually expressed and propagated in a despair over what America was becoming, the quality of life of the society. This helps to explain, I think, a curious phenomenon of domestic American politics, namely that it has been, with some exceptions, remarkably boring. It has taken on fire and excitement only when certain victimized groups have themselves taken the fight into their own hands, like the unions in the 1930s or the Negroes in the 1960s. For the rest of the time, a very important part of the American mind and the American imagination has felt that the struggle to extend equality of opportunity wasn't worth doing. What would you have when you had realized the dream, but the spread of what was already despised? There is a certain callousness in this attitude, a certain inhumane notion about what most people want and need, which one still finds today. In the 1930s this opposition expressed itself in terms of political radicalism. It did again to an extent in the 1960s. For the most part, however, it has expressed itself in one form or another of internal emigration to various bohemian communities and at times expatriation, to Paris largely.

This almost schizophrenic condition of the American soul has now reached the stage of confrontation politics. The party of opposition has finally found itself with enough divisions to mount an actual political challenge on the basis of its values, which is something it was previously unable to do. About ten years ago I wrote a piece very severely critical of the beat generation, and Allen Ginsberg, the poet, whom I knew in college, said to me, "We'll get you through your children." He was right, of course. We've only seen the beginning of a process in which the opposition culture, the adversary culture, whatever you wish to call it, is going to become much more powerful, both numerically and as a qualitative force inside the polity, with consequences which I believe it is impossible to predict. It has amused me to hear so many Europeans, Asians and Africans talk about the cultural dangers of Americanization. (I notice that there has been less talk of that at this conference than I am used to hearing.) Well, there has been scarcely less fear of Americanization in that sense among Americans for the past century, and the tide of anti-Americanism within America has now become as strong as it was in Britain in the early 1950s when I was a student there. I believe it will grow still stronger.

Now, when I say anti-Americanism, I mean America conceived as a bourgeois, middle-class, capitalist, nowadays imperialist culture, dominated in tone by Protestant repressiveness, gentility and prissiness. For the past century, this revolt has mostly manifested itself in culture. We are now beginning to feel it within the politics of the country. I think we shall be living with it for the next decade at least in a very immediate and urgent way.

LARS LANGSLET: We have heard during these days many American speakers, even Mr. Innis, call themselves pragmatists. I know this shouldn't be interpreted as a reference to pragmatism as a philosophy but rather to a pragmatic attitude, undogmatic in its openness to the variability of experience and always looking for practical solutions. But what I suggest is that these pragmatic attitudes, so characteristic of American culture, clearly reflect an ideology in the broad sense of the word. Essential to this ideology is the belief that conflicting interests can always be harmonized if the appropriate techniques are applied. Reality can and should be controlled and managed for practical ends. It is the ideology of social engineering and, if I may use a neo-Marxist catchword, of manipulation. The trouble is that this pragmatic ideology, however successful in situations of relative stability, seems unable to grasp the inner meaning of deeper conflicts where it is itself engaged as one of the poles of debate and is heavily criticized. If I may generalize in Hegelian terms, it is conscious but not self-conscious.

This somewhat shallow optimism and lack of deeper self-criticism has inspired much of the wariness and even antagonism towards American culture in the world. The spirit of practicability is too much oriented to purely external success. I have a feeling, confirmed by Mr. Podhoretz, that the spirit of pragmatism had driven the need for self-criticism into a kind of inner exile in art and literature where the American dream could be converted into an American tragedy. From that point of view, I must confess that this seminar has been a fascinating experience to Europeans like myself. It has been extremely frank and candid in its reflection of the profound self-criticism that is no longer a privilege of alienated artists, but a primary concern for the whole American intelligentsia, and even the American people at large. Self-confidence is giving way to self-consciousness. This may be experienced by some Americans as a sign of distress. I regard it as a sign of hope. I do not hope Americans will lose their sense of expediency and enter the wilderness of doctrinaire illusionism. But I do hope Americans will go on asking the fundamental, normative questions Mr. Peretz has called for, even if they affect the sacred ideological establishment of pragmatism. This process of questioning is extremely promising. It could create a mental coordination between the New World and the Old never experienced before, and dispose of much of the unease Europeans have traditionally felt toward American culture.

ANTHONY HARTLEY: There has certainly been an ideological impact on Europe of the American New Left which can claim precedence over other New Lefts in time, tactics and example. What strikes me chiefly about the American New Left is the extreme restriction of their ambition of reform. The less militant ones envisage a return to a kind of Brook Farm community separated from the rest of society. The more militant ones envisage the establishment of a kind of sanctuary from which political guerilla raids are carried out on the rest of society, with the aim not of governing it, but simply of annoying it, as far as I can see, and bearing witness. Probably this has to do with what Mr. Podhoretz has said of the attitudes of the American intellectual towards politics and with a conception of the state in the United States different from that held in Europe, but I feel some alarm when I see this infiltrating into movements of reform in Europe. In Europe we have a very respectable tradition of reform which has largely been one of state socialism. This has meant increasing the powers of the state, endeavoring by administration to redress social wrongs and to control the administration by democratic parliamentary government. This has not worked perfectly, but it seems to me a much more fruitful tradition than one which wishes to abolish state power. If you abolish state power, the result in a modern industrial society is that everything else is organized but that the state is not organized to cope with everything else. For this reason, I deplore the impact of back-to-Thoreau movements on European socialism, and do not wish to see the European left-wing movements becoming anarchist. I also deplore the retreat in ambition from a desire to rule society to a desire merely to annoy it.

GINO GIUGNI:* Both the movements which are so important in current politics, the black movement here and the students' movement everywhere, are dangerously exclusivist. When the socialist movement was born and the class struggle started, the main idea was that even though the workers had to form their own separate organizations, their message should be universal. That is why socialism has appealed to so many intellectuals and non-proletarians. But when the Black Power movement expresses itself in nationalistic terms, that may be fine for Negroes, but it disqualifies it as a liberating force for other people. Much the same goes for the students when they opt for a struggle between the generations. I don't want to generalize—I am talking only of the students I know personally as a professor. I sympathize when I think I see in them a will to put issues in universal terms. But when I observe some of the attitudes they take up, of power for power's sake or action for action's sake, I wonder if they fully realize who their philosophical ancestors are; and I am more than a little frightened. One was Georges Sorel, who was immediately reprinted in Italy by publishers who made good business out of student dissent. It was out

_____
* See also Signor Giugni's paper, pages 208–09.

...efusal of old values in the name of new values which ...wholly undefined that fascism was born.

...t the beginning of the century, many liberals in Europe wel-...omed the labor movement as a natural extension of the idea of liberty; but when they came to grips with it as a problem of power, they found themselves on the other side. I do not want to be on the other side. If I think a social movement is right, I want to be in a position to join it. But I fear that the present state of things does not make it possible to side with the students. At the same time, I dislike the position of many of us, of sympathy for social movements we do not propose to join. It is a rather paternalistic position, and in some cases conceals an ulterior motive—that is, to go along with these movements in order to achieve results which are alien to them.

PIERRE EMMANUEL: We have discussed the American image too much here in terms of power. We have too readily dismissed it in terms of psychology or the spirit—the soul, I would say. Among the participants, there are many professors, economists, sociologists, editors. There are very few novelists. There is one playwright, and, if I am not mistaken, one poet, myself. There is no painter, no architect, no film producer, no pure philosopher and no theologian. It shows some of the omissions of our meeting here. Between creative minds and academic ones there is a difference in the use of words. I have noticed here people who think fast and express themselves still faster than they think, and there are people who think slowly and express themselves slowly. This stands for a different approach to things altogether. These two aspects of language deal with very different levels of experience and even of reality. People who abstract and rationalize have a clear-cut view of solutions, at least theoretically. Those who cannot rationalize cannot do so because they feel that too many essential aspects of life are left aside by rationalization. I should have liked to hear some real voices of dissent here, people coming to tell us that they did not take absolutely for granted the future of the technetronic age. They might have agreed that it may be imposed upon them, but they would have shown also that they did not essentially believe in it. They would maybe have said that they did not even take for granted the idea of progress. It may be so, I may be attached to some aspects of it, I may even be prepared to defend it, but personally I do not fully believe in it. I would have liked someone to state that he did not take for granted the validity of the insights of science in the realm of thought. I respect scientific thought as a means of grasping some knowledge, not all, of the universe, but I do not want to be ruled by scientific thought, either the science of physicists or that of economists or sociologists, because I do not believe in such rule. The pretension of science, or, rather, of the techniques derived from science, to organize social life and even the psyche of the individual man seems to me to be grossly exaggerated and vague. I have the utmost dislike for such an idea. I will add something else. I am not entirely a man of good will, devoted to peace and to the creation of a stable order. I am that too, but equally I feel the tug of the restlessness, the chaos, the disruption, of life. I am not entirely against the disruptive forces that operate among us. That is why I would like to come back to this country and see tensions growing, flowering in forms that are sometimes absurd and shocking for the intellect. Here I see all the tensions of our developed world coming up to a point where they cannot be hidden any more. I may be wrong, but I think that law and order will be less and less able to cope with the repressed energies just beneath the surface of society and right here in the middle of each one of us. To me, America is prophetic of the tensions of the modern age.

I feel in my bones that it will have to suffer for this. The Americans will discover, or rediscover, and help the world rediscover, suffering as something which must have a meaning in the over-all process of change, and it is the task precisely of some who are not here, the American artists, to be those prophets and those dissenters. Not necessarily escapists. We all tend to escape. We build our universe on two levels, the worldly level and the personal one. I think that this division cannot go on forever. It increases the amount of suffering and the loss of belief. To push the situation to its limit, one could theoretically imagine a society where the pleasure principle would rule the individual self in its private and concealed life. The personality would be marginal to the social community. Drugs and pornography, for instance, would constitute, together with tranquilizers, the means to create a more or less isolated, egomaniac world. We would thus have two worlds instead of one: a world of power in the hands of a few and a world of pleasure for the many—pleasure being a means of control of the masses. I do not stand for such a partition, but the danger may exist. We tend to accept more and more the idea that man is not a person looking for his unity, his oneness, but is a succession or even a simultaneity of fragmentary perceptions in a fragmented surrounding. And at the same time we accept the idea of "scientific" control of this fragmented individual!

The fact is that men have ceased to learn how to dominate their own individual selves in the face of the ever-growing desires which assail them and drive them forward. Personally, in the world we live in, and particularly in this country, I feel pulled outside myself, uprooted, both by the growing pressure of the desires and needs of affluent society and by an abstract idea of man as a conqueror of the universe, before he has conquered himself and mastered the possibilities of this very earth. Going to the moon is one thing. Giving food to the poor is another. To create a better management of power is one thing. To tame the beast in man is another. The collectivity is one thing, a community is another. We now have the greatest collectivities that have ever existed, and we do not know any more what a real community is. I love this country, and I have been attached to it since my childhood. What I see here is a situation of anxiety, of frustration, but also a great urge to seek. I think that we will all have to go further in the direction of chaos. In that respect the twentieth century is not over and we must get used to a form of life with high concurrent contrasts between organization and disruption. It is not a very pleasant perspective. It is even a trying one. But without a series of traumatic experiences deeply felt by each one of us within our own society the deep forces of change which are among us and seeking expression will not be able to work their way out. To my mind, in this great continent the great ordeal of our times is being fought out, and my reaction to the chaotic aspects of American life is just as positive as to its superficial signs of success—probably more so.

BESSON: We have talked about the Negro and the New Left, but it is far more important to me that it is the far right that is apparently going to lead the country when this kind of crisis of authority of which Mr. Shils spoke appears. In all Western societies, we have a rising tide of authoritarianism. We can see it in Europe, we can see it here. The idea is spreading that the U. S. is in a stage of pre-fascist development, rooted not only in the racial issue but in the general crisis of authority. How will the abdication of authority affect the American political system and institutions? This kind of question is also part of the post-industrial society, and someone who has had experience of fascism must necessarily ask it.

7

EXTRACTS FROM CONFERENCE PAPERS

STRUCTURAL CHANGES IN THE UNITED STATES
by Daniel Bell*

These notes deal with social structure. This is not because I slight culture and values: on the contrary, I regard them not as reflective of a society but often as determining elements. Simply I have been working for the past several years in trying to identify persistent or long-run changes in the social structure. This does not include possible changes in values (e.g., the consequences of the growing hedonism in the society); nor account for new technologies and their consequences (e.g., the computer or biochemical engineering); and cannot assess the impact of crisis situations (e.g., the present entrapment in Vietnam) on the national will or the alienation of specific groups which such crises may engender. Thus, the flesh and blood of the future are omitted. If so, what remains? Perhaps the bare bones. But the skeleton holds up a system, and the virtue of structure—the nature of any set of institutions—is that it lives beyond the transient, changes quite slowly, and is more readily predictable.

I. The National Society

Most of our social problems have taken a new dimension in recent years because of the emergence of a national society. Only in the last thirty years have we seen problems generated in one

* See also Daniel Bell's "Notes on the Post-Industrial Society," in *The Public Interest,* Winter and Spring issues, 1967.

186

part of society (economic or social) have an immediate impact in every other and produce an almost immediate need to have recourse to a national, organized center. The national society can be looked at through the growth of four key elements:

A. A managed economy. Government fiscal policy and the budget set the environment of economic decisions and influence the rate and direction of growth.
B. A mobilized polity, turning in particular around (1) the military establishment commanding about half the federal budget (i.e., 10 percent of GNP) and (2) government support and potential command of society's scarce resource—scientific and engineering talent.
C. A welfare state.
D. A national popular culture, associated with television and the rise of national news weeklies.

Each of these four dimensions has many subsectors of its own, but for purposes of illustration we can say the following:

The main forces commanding the growth of this new national society have been, I think:

A. The demands of disadvantaged groups for a place in society— ethnic groups, labor, farmers, etc. (1930s).
B. The revolutions in communication and transport—jet airplanes, television, coast-to-coast telephone dialing, etc.
C. War and the demands of foreign policy, not least the revolutions in military technology.

Together these produce crucial structural consequences, the chief of which has been the expansion of the power of the Executive. Where power resides in a legislative or parliamentary chamber, the system is essentially *distributive* in which there is a balancing and deal process in the making of decisions: business, labor and farmers in the past have sought influence in the direct

187

electoral process. Where power shifts to the Executive, it necessarily becomes *aggregative* because the Executive becomes the mobilizing point of initiation of change: the new elite constituencies —science, universities, the military—work principally through the executive mechanisms for support.

The new changes—centralization, new command and control systems, future orientation through planning—all produce strains. The two chief ones, I believe, are:

A. The inadequacy of existing administrative relationships. The existing structure of fifty states with a patchwork set of boundaries clearly makes no sense. The 212 metropolitan areas of the country lack metropolitan governments to deal with the metropolitan problems that are being created.

B. The rise of plebiscitary politics to counter elite decision-making. The possibility of mobilizing tens and even hundreds of thousands of persons for direct pressure on the government in Washington and the possibilities of civil disorder which such mobilization tactics can provoke raise grave questions about the stability of the political system in the future.

We have seen over the past thirty years a significant *change of scale* in the institutions of government. The federal government is ill-equipped to handle, operationally, most of the new problems that arise in urbanization, the pollution of the environment, educational needs, medical needs and the like. Some new pattern needs to be developed which allows for local initiatives, adaptive responses by community groups and large-scale development. If the defense area can serve as some model (with due regard to the distortions in practice), it is that the function of government at the federal level is to serve as a *policy, standards* and *funding* agency, while *operations* and *adaptations* are decentralized. There is a crucial function of *evaluation*. I doubt that government can itself be the evaluating agency. Here one can conceive of a new function of *foundations*.

There is also the question of "participatory democracy." This provides a bridge to my next rubric, that of "the communal society." The concept of the "national society" focuses principally on structures. The idea of the "communal society" focuses on changes in values and functions.

II. The Communal Society
The two dimensions of the Communal Society are:

A. The growth of non-market public decision-making.
B. The definitions of social rights through group rather than individual mechanisms.

A number of crucial problems arise from the emergence of a communal society. On the theoretical side there is the problem, first posed by Kenneth Arrow in his *Social Choice and Individual Values,* that there is no "rational" way of combining discordant individual preferences into a combined social choice which represents an ordered scale that is democratic, transitive, etc. The consequences of this argument—in its own way a denial of the possibility of utopia—is that the political process cannot rely on "rationality" but on bargaining and trade-offs. Here we come to the nub of the problem. A market economy recording the divergent and discordant preferences of individuals through money bids disperses power and words on an impersonal mechanism. The political process, on the other hand, is open, visible and locatable. Hence the possibilities of direct conflict and confrontation are increased. A secondary consideration is that we do not have singular tests of efficiency or benefits in non-market decisions comparable to the economic tests of money purchases. For all these reasons, the rise of non-market public decision-making may be expected to increase the potentialities of community conflict in the next years. I regard this as a *central* problem.

Along with this comes the problem of defining *what is public* and *what is private*. The major private universities today are largely dependent on government funds for research. Public enterprises such as the Port of New York Authority operate little differently from private regulated utilities, etc. Increasingly as government finds it hard to handle operational problems, the lines between government and private areas are bound to blur.

The demand for group rights comes into conflict with older individualist principles. How do we reconcile them? For instance, as Nathan Glazer has put it so well, the Negroes have moved from a claim of *equality of opportunity* to *equality of result*. This results in demands for special quotas, preferential hiring, compensatory education at the expense of other persons whose claims are justified by having satisfied a merit principle. In the City College of New York, for example, there are about five percent Negro students, based on an entrance examination emphasizing intellectual competence. A demand is now made for a waiver of standards for Negroes in order to increase the number in college. Given the limitations of place, other students, normally qualified, would suffer. What is the distributive principle of justice? What do we do?

The broader question is one of participatory democracy, the theme that people ought to be in a position to affect the decisions which influence their lives. So far this has been raised only as a slogan by the New Left. In a striking way it parallels the older left slogan of "workers' control" in industry, or workers' self-management. In the industrial field some thinking has been done on the possible extensions and limits of workers' control (see the work of Hugh Clegg). But almost nothing has been done in the community field. This is a crucial problem. What sort of issues should be subject to local community decisions? The Bundy panel in New York proposes the break-up of the city school system into self-contained community districts. The teachers and professional groups claim this would disrupt civil service (an older reform against an arbitrary system!) and professional standards. If one were to follow the principle strictly, one might say that community groups would have the right to exclude Negroes, since by the community feeling this would disrupt the character of a neighborhood, and that community groups ought to have vetoes on road planning. In the broader theoretical and philosophical context, participatory democracy raises two kinds of questions:

1. What is the social unit for what kind of value decision? (E.g., clearly the national community must decide on a principle of Negro equality, not a local group.)
2. Where decisions have to be made in a broad *systems context* (e.g., roads, water, air—but schools?), what is the proper role and function of local community groups?

III. The Post-Industrial Society

There are three dimensions to the post-industrial society, of which the third is the most important:

A. A shift from goods to services.
B. The rise of a large-scale professional and technical class.
C. The centrality of theoretical knowledge as the source of innovation and policy analysis in society.

An entire range of questions is suggested by each of these changes.

The emergence of a service economy raises questions about the slowdown of productivity and the rate of economic growth, the change in the nature and character of the unit enterprise, a change in the nature of work.

The growth of a large professional-technical class—to about 14 million by 1980—raises questions about the relation of this class to others in society, and about the patterns of work in enterprises. The two major features, as I see it, are the emergence of a "bimodal" class system, in which education has served as the cut-off marker or as a gatekeeper, and the problems of bureaucratic structures in the organization of professional and technical work.

In a society increasingly organized around skill and education, a number of conflicts are bound to emerge.

A. A traditionalist-modernist split: the "small-town" moralizing mind, based on individualist and property values, versus the urban, educated, planning mind.
B. Conflicts between skill groups, traditionalist and modern—e.g., the military and the scientific communities.
C. The tensions between technocratic and political modes of decision-making.

Beyond all this are deeper changes in values which are in part responses to changes in social structure and, in greater measure, arise out of changes in consciousness about the world. In the first place is a hedonism made possible by, but not growing out of, economic affluence. The fundamental challenge here is to the delayed-gratification, personal-mastery character structures which a bourgeois, technological, achievement-oriented world emphasized in the eighteenth and nineteenth centuries. This becomes compounded by different kinds of challenges, such as the one to the "meritocracy" principle by the assertative need for group rights, and the acute generational differences which have developed in the last decade.

AMERICA IN THE TECHNETRONIC AGE:
NEW QUESTIONS OF OUR TIME
by Zbigniew Brzezinski

The world is on the eve of a transformation more dramatic in its historic and human consequences than that wrought by either the French or the Bolshevik Revolution. Shocking though it may sound to their acolytes, by the year 2000 it will be accepted that Robespierre and Lenin were mild reformers.

Men living in the developed world will undergo during the next decades a mutation potentially as basic as that experienced through the slow process of evolution from animal to human experience. However, the process will be telescoped in time, and the shock effect may be profound. Human conduct will become less spontaneous and more subject to deliberate "programming." Man will increasingly possess the capacity to determine the sex of his children, to affect through drugs the extent of their intelligence and to modify and control their personalities. The human brain will acquire expanded powers, with computers becoming as routine an extension of man's reasoning as automobiles have been of man's mobility. The human body will be improved and its durability extended: during the next century the average life span could reach approximately 120 years.

These developments will have major social impact. The prolongation of life will alter our values, our career patterns, and our social relationships. New forms of social control may be needed to limit the indiscriminate exercise by individuals of their new powers. The possibility of extensive chemical mind control, the danger of loss of individuality inherent in extensive transplantation, and the feasibility of manipulation of the genetic structure will call for a social definition of common criteria of restraint as well as of utilization. Scientists predict with some confidence that by the end of this century computers will reason as well as man and will be able to engage in "creative" thought; wedded to robots or to "laboratory beings," they could act like humans. The makings of a most complex—and perhaps bitter—philosophical and political dialogue about the nature of man are self-evident in these developments.

The transformation now taking place is already creating a technetronic society increasingly unlike its industrial predecessor.

1. In industrial society, the mode of production shifts from agriculture to industry, from muscle and animals to machines. In the technetronic society, industrial employment yields to services, with automation and cybernetics replacing individual operation of machines.

2. Problems of employment and unemployment dominate the relationships in the industrial society; assuring minimum welfare to the new industrial masses is a major concern. In the new society, skill-obsolescence, security, va-

cations, leisure, and profit sharing dominate the relationship; the psychic well-being of millions of relatively secure but potentially aimless blue-collar workers becomes a growing problem.

3. Breaking down traditional barriers to education, thus creating the basic point of departure for social advancement, is a major goal of reformers in the industrial society. In the technetronic society, education becomes universal and advanced training is available to almost all who have the talents. Quantity training is reinforced by quality selection for the most rational exploitation of social talent.

4. In industrial society, leadership shifts from the rural-aristocratic to an urban "plutocratic" elite. In technetronic society, leadership is permeated by individuals possessing special skills and intellectual talents. Knowledge becomes power.

5. The university in industrial society is an ivory tower. In technetronic society, it becomes an intensely involved think-tank, the source of sustained political planning and social innovation.

6. The turmoil of the shift from the rigidly traditional rural to urban existence engenders an inclination to seek total answers to social dilemmas, causing ideologies to thrive in industrial society. In technetronic society, increasing ability to reduce social conflicts to quantifiable dimensions reinforces the trend towards a more pragmatic approach to social issues.

7. The activization of hitherto passive masses makes for intense political conflict in industrial society. The issue of political participation is a crucial one. In the technetronic age, the question is one of ensuring real participation in decisions that seem too complex and too far removed from the ordinary citizen. Political alienation becomes a problem.

8. In industrial society, political attitudes are influenced by appeals to nationalist sentiments, communicated through the growth of newspapers, relying on native tongues. In technetronic society, the trend would seem to be towards the aggregation of the individual support of millions of uncoordinated citizens, easily within reach of magnetic personalities. Reliance on TV tends to replace language with

imagery unlimited by national confines and to create a more cosmopolitan, though impressionistic, involvement in global affairs.

9. Economic power in industrial society tends to be personalized in entrepreneurs like Henry Ford. Economic power is depersonalized in the next stage by a highly complex interdependence between government, scientific establishments and industrial organizations. Economic power becomes inseparably linked with political power, and more invisible, and the sense of individual futility increases.

10. Relaxation and escapism in industrial society, in its more intense forms, is a carryover from the rural drinking bout. Technetronic social life tends to be so atomized that group intimacy cannot be re-created through convivial group behavior. The new interest in drugs seeks to create intimacy through introspection, allegedly by expanding consciousness.

The American Transition

America today is ceasing to be an industrial society, and is becoming the first technetronic one. This is at least in part the cause of current tensions and violence.

The challenge in its essence involves the twin dangers of fragmentation and excessive control. Symptoms of alienation and depersonalization are already easy to find. Many Americans feel "less free"; this feeling seems to be connected with their loss of "purpose"; freedom implies choice of action, and action requires an awareness of goals. If the present transition of America to the technetronic age achieves no personally satisfying fruits, the next phase may be one of "inner emigration." Political alienation could increase the difficulty of absorbing rapid environmental changes, thereby prompting increasing psychic instability.

At the same time, the capacity to assert social and political control over the individual will vastly increase. With computers, it will soon be possible to assert almost continuous surveillance over every citizen.

The rapid pace of change will put a premium on anticipating events and planning for them. Our existing *post*-crisis management institutions will be increasingly supplanted by *pre*-crisis management institutions. This could encourage tendencies during the next decades towards technocratic dictatorship.

Yet it would be misleading to construct a new Orwellian piece of science fiction. New communications and computer techniques make possible both increased authority at lower levels and almost instant national coordination. It is likely that many functions currently the responsibility of the federal government will be assumed by state and local governments in the next ten years. The devolution of financial responsibility to lower echelons may encourage both the flow of better talent and greater local participation in more important local decision-making.

It is also hopeful that improved governmental performance and sensitivity to social needs is being stimulated by the growing involvement in national affairs of what Kenneth Boulding has called the Educational and Scientific Establishment (EASE). A community of organization-oriented, application-minded intellectuals, relating more effectively to the political system than their predecessors, serves to introduce into it concerns broader than those it might itself generate and more relevant than those articulated by outside critics.

The expansion of knowledge and the entry into sociopolitical life of the intellectual community have the further effect of making education an almost continuous process. In the new technetronic society, it will be necessary to require everyone at a sufficiently responsible post to take, say, two years of retraining every ten years.

Possibly, a society increasingly geared to learning will be able to absorb more resiliently the expected changes in social and individual life. Increasing GNP (which could reach $10,000 per capita per year), linked with educational advance, could prompt among those less involved in social management and scientific development a wave of interest in the cultural and humanistic aspects of life, in addition to purely hedonistic occupations.

Never truly an aristocratic state, the U. S. A. is becoming something which may be labeled the "meritocratic democracy." This combines continued respect for the popular will with an increasing role in the key decision-making institutions of individuals with special intellectual and scientific attainments.

The Trauma of Confrontation

The technetronic society could have the paradoxical effect of creating more distinct worlds on a planet that is continuously shrinking because of the communications revolution. Not only will the gap between the developed and the underdeveloped worlds probably become wider, but a *new* one may be developing *within* the industrialized and urban world.

Today America is *the* creative society; the others, consciously and unconsciously, are emulative. Approximately eighty percent of scientific and technical discoveries made during the last few decades originated in the United States. America has four times as many scientists and research workers as the countries of the European Economic Community, and three and a half times as many as the Soviet Union. The brain drain is almost entirely one way. Since scientific development is a dynamic process, the gap will probably widen.

American innovation is most strikingly seen in the manner in which the new meritocratic elite is taking over American life. Technetronics dominate American life, but so far nobody else's. This is bound to stimulate a psychocultural gap in the developed world.

At the same time, the backward regions of the world are becoming more rather than less poor in relation to the developed world. Their social elites tend to assimilate the life styles of the most advanced world, with which they are in close vicarious contact through television, etc. The international gap will thus have a domestic reflection, with the masses becoming more and more intensely aware of deprivation. With the widening gap dooming hopes of imitation, the likely development is rejection of the developed world. Racial hatred could provide the necessary emotional force. The writings of Frantz Fanon, violent and racist, are a good example. The result could be a modern version on a global scale of the old rural-urban dichotomy. To use a capsule formula: in the developed world, the nature of man, as man, is threatened; in the underdeveloped, society is. The interaction of the two could produce chaos.

It seems unlikely, given the rivalry between the two principal powers, that a foolproof system against international violence can be established. Some local nuclear wars between the weaker, nationalistically more aroused poorer nations may erupt before greater international control is imposed in the wake of the universal moral shock thereby generated.

The instantaneous electronic intermeshing of mankind will make for an intense confrontation, straining social and international peace. A three-way split into rural-backward, urban-industrial, and technetronic ways of life can only further divide man.

However, neither military power nor material wealth, both of which America possesses in abundance, can be used directly in responding to the onrushing division in man's thinking, norms, and character. Increasing attention will have to be given to improving the quality of life for man *as man*. The urgent need to do that may compel America to redefine its global posture. America is likely to become less concerned with "fighting Communism" or creating "a world safe for diversity" than with helping to develop a common response with the rest of mankind to the implications of a truly new era. Professional diplomacy will have to yield to intellectual leadership.

International cooperation will be necessary in almost every facet of life: to reform and develop more modern educational systems, to promote new sources of food supply, to accelerate economic development, to stimulate technological growth, to control climate, to disseminate new medical knowledge. However, the nation-state will remain for a long time the primary focus of loyalty. Regionalism will have to be promoted with due deference to the symbolic meaning of national sovereignty.

Even more important will be the stimulation, for the first time in history on a global scale, of the much needed dialogue on what it is about man's life that we wish to safeguard or promote. The search for new directions could be an appropriate subject for a world congress devoted to the technetronic and philosophical problems of the coming age.

Some Notes on the Present and Future of Power and Wealth in America
by Martin Peretz

This symposium has us concerned with post-industrial society, and I am not yet convinced, after more than a decade of the notion as virtually received orthodoxy, that we live in a post-capitalist society. If we ask who gains from American society, we are less struck by the divergences between the old and new orders than by the similarities. Not only does our system maximize the concentration of private economic wealth and power over public matters, it does so with much less risk and much greater official guarantee of profit than in any other era in modern economic history.

The top 500 industrial corporations in America control 70 percent of the production of the non-agricultural economy, which is approximately half of the manufacturing done in the world. One scholar, working from figures of the early fifties, reports that the 108 corporations with assets of $500 million or more had 49.2 percent of the assets of almost 3,000 public corporations. Moreover, out of these 3,000, the 163 corporations with assets of under $1 million controlled less than one tenth of one percent of the total assets of all 3,000. On concentration in banking, for which the facts as we know them are more startling still, even less data has been forthcoming; it is no small scandal and it is probably, as the Marxists used to say, not coincidental, that no foundation has sponsored major research in these areas.

Essentially, what this concentration entails is the establishment of formally and effectively irresponsible private government over public problems. The corporation's psychological test for employment, its country club, its "school tie," its psychoanalysts, its residential clusters, its chaplains, its implicit demand for conformisms of all sorts constitute impositions of power we would resist from government. Corporate concentration might be more tolerable in a democracy if one could argue that at least its profits were widely shared. "People's capitalism" was the quaint term used to express that hope. These very days' newspapers have been reporting the disinterest of brokerage houses in the small investor. And it takes only minimal common sense to realize that the ambitions of big money will always receive greater care and attention than that available for the more modest portfolio. To worry about the latter is, of course, still to care about only a minority of the population. But it is instructive to understand how even this relatively well-off fraction of the population is treated. I happen to watch the market with some care, and have observed with great interest the development of the new gargantuan conglomerates. To many, these forbiddingly call to mind the holding companies of an earlier expansive period in what is affectionately known as "the Street." "The main idea was to get so many layers of companies one on top of another that nobody could understand what was going on." Stocks were bought and sold "among the different layers, with some of the money falling off the table every time . . . The game was to carry off the waste-basket at the end of the day."

This is now being done to such an extent that for months the exchanges have had to cut their business week to four days so that they might catch up with their paper logjam. It is an inconvenience that the top one percent of wealth holders, who own 76 percent of the corporate stock, 77.5 percent of the corporate bonds and all of the tax-exempt securities, are willing to go along with. For while there has been a reduction in the inequality of income, there has been a parallel increase in the inequality of wealth. The one percent possesses upwards of 27 percent of the private sector. (This figure may be low because of the twilight zone of trusts, and the fact that increasingly wealth of the big rich is held abroad.) The top one half of one percent owns no less than 80 percent of that 27 percent share.

Now the question arises: Just how much wealth puts you in the top one percent of the population? According to Lampman's estimates a gross estate of $60,000 puts one into that category. This is crucial for the argument about the distinction between ownership and management, which had been apotheosized as the intracorporate protector of the public interest. The evidence of managerial independence from the largest shareholdings is far from conclusive. Moreover, the practice of offering large stock options to management is fast undermining such truth as the notion may have ever had. The same might be said of the growing stasis of mobility into high managerial ranks. In 1959, a *Fortune* study reported that the top executives of 834 corporations had median incomes of $73,584. That figure is considerably larger now. At that time, those with incomes over $50,000 held 35 percent of all stock and constituted but one tenth of one percent of the population. This is at least suggestive of how these managers become in effect "big rich," most especially when we realize that incomes in the $100,000 a year vicinity will probably be turned into wealth of at least $1 million. At these levels, it would be difficult to persuade that the interest of the manager is ultimately much different from that of ownership.

However natural the bonds between big ownership and big management become, the surest cement for them is likely to be their common relative position when measured against that of the remaining 95 percent and more of the American citizenry. In 1962, at an income of $18,000 one was in the top 5 percent and the average in that rank was $30,000. At the other end, the average income of the lowest quintile was $1,760 and that constituted but 4.6 percent of all family income in the country. The income of the second lowest 20 percent hovered in the vicinity of $3,900, and that of the third quintile at about $5,700. The average income of the fourth stood at $8,500. Eighty percent of the people fell below the income level of $10,400. (These statistics are before income tax, but the disposable income figures do not appreciably shift the curve.) Professors and other intellectuals who count themselves among the $20,000-a-year poor should be able to appreciate the dreary lives and anxieties of the overwhelming proportion of Americans who make do with roughly half that figure and much less. Viewed from the perspective of this scarcity among millions of Americans, Bell's version of the future and more especially Brzezinski's seem remote indeed.

The sense of crisis, however, is upon us, shared by everyone and most especially by the foundations. Decentralization is the rubric and lodestone under which most changes in the current winds fall. The schemes for decentralization are aimed at the diffusion of political power, not the diffusion of economic power. I am not hostile to some local diffusion of power, though I believe it to have some intrinsic limitations: the reactionary and the racist will also secure a firmer grasp on public decision-making. But the decentralization of politics which leaves corporate and other instances of private power untouched is a dreadful trick on those who yearn for some real control over the content of their lives.

Clearly the stranglehold of concentrated corporate wealth and power on the economy and its future direction must be eased. One way to reduce this would be to disallow as a business expense for purposes of taxation any and all costs of advertising and public relations. A corollary of this would be that no regulated industries or procurement suppliers could count such public relations as part of cost estimates. No public good is enhanced by these propagandistic activities: it is most clearly not a freely chosen enterprise, and it should not be paid for by the public. A government prepared to ensure this elimination of publicly subsidized waste would also be ready through its own policies in dealing directly with business to maximize corporate diversity and openness within the economy. One further step it might take is to prevent companies larger than some chosen formula from buying and subsuming other companies. Failing that, it might at least establish a deterrent tax on such undertakings, which if it did not deter would at least be a source of federal revenues. Beyond these, a government which makes these moves for deconcentration might exhume the old idea of an absolute limitation on income.

Any radical notion which strikes at the heart of corporate power will not easily gain currency, not for want of merit, but for want of exposure. Here monopolistic practices in the press and the fear of controversy on the air tend to narrow the limits of public discourse. The nervous will warn of the politics of impatience. The response might well be from Brecht:

> *Those who take the meat from the table*
> *Teach contentment.*
> *Those for whom the taxes are destined*
> *Demand sacrifice.*
> *Those who eat their fill speak to the hungry*
> *Of wonderful times to come.*
> *Those who lead the country into the abyss*
> *Call ruling too difficult*
> *For ordinary men.*

THE LONELY FRONTIER OF REASON*
by Michel Crozier

America has changed. One cannot otherwise explain the uneasiness that assails the returning visitor, and the new excitement that this time affects the spirit, the way life is lived.

One naturally thinks first of the political climate, of the moral fever agitating youth and troubling the nation over the war in Vietnam, and one is struck by its familiar European character. A French visitor in particular who has lived through the Algerian War is impressed by the extraordinary parallels. But if one dirty war resembles another, and if the interplay of politics and morality

* This paper was published in *The Nation,* May 27, 1968.

is so similar in America and in France, those who speak of the radicalization or the Europeanization of the United States tend to forget how effectively and speedily a country can wipe out all trace of the conflicts that have torn it apart.

Of course, the Negro revolt is a permanent phenomenon. The movement grows and its momentum increases; an unprecedented violence erupts, and the international brotherhood of the victims of American power is tied in with it.

All this is true, but one must not draw hasty inferences: America has never experienced a successful revolution, but it has always been a nation characterized by crisis and violence. Its many wars aside, riots of the unemployed, battles between strikers and police, witch hunts and anarchist attacks stand out in the history of a nation whose conformity has always remained on the surface.

The current explosions—a traditional form of protest—do not strike me as new in America; nor do the appearance of numerous militant groups, or the new romantic efforts to relate the class struggle (in the European sense) to the oppressed people of the Third World. Such efforts are made, in vain, whenever America suffers a crisis. What does strike me as new is the revolt of the individual against the system. This personal war, expressed through drugs, the repudiation of the American way of life and the embrace of psychedelia and the occult, attracts and fascinates the entire intellectual world.

Although we have in Europe numerous equivalents and imitations of this movement, it assumes in the United States a special character of contentiousness, of total challenge, unprecedented in brutality and radicalism. Every era has had its Bohemians, but compared to this new American Bohemianism, the surrealism of the prewar years and the Saint-Germain-des-Prés attitudes of the postwar years seem like mere gatherings of earnest young people looking for new ways to sow their wild oats.

I do not expect the students to undertake revolution, or even to threaten the established order. As I see it, their agitation does not even signify that the system is sick, but rather that it is in the process of profound change. What one can perceive behind a temporary crisis such as Vietnam, and a chronic crisis like that of the emancipation of the Negroes, is the reaction of the young to a mutation of society that affects them far more than it does their seniors, who are protected by their positions in the vast and relatively static economic and social system.

What most strikes the visitor is no longer the complacent and conservative prosperity of the United States, but its aggressive confidence in human reason and in the capacity of America to solve all problems by its use.

There has perhaps never before been such arrogant pride in the powers of reason. Never before has the world seen such an extraordinary capacity to mobilize resources and put them to work.

The practical successes of the science of decision-making are by now conclusively proven. Upon them rests the new surge of American confidence, which on the political level has completely upset the relations between the United States and the Communist world. The consequences are many; one is that the business world is in flux. Of course, the giants continue to grow; however, they no longer constitute the leading wing of economic thought. This role has been assumed by spectacularly effective new firms which directly or indirectly sell this decision-making capacity. Some specialize in the revamping of businesses that have lost their profit-making capacities. Others are pioneers in new relations of business with big science, with the government and with the universities, not only to earn their administrative fees but to exploit the advantages of the new kind of analysis in areas formerly unexplored. Government, education and health, areas hitherto paralyzed by bureaucratic inefficiency, will become more and more the preferred grounds of this new revolution.

This wave of rational decision-making which linked the actions of intellectuals to those of administrators, all in step and proclaiming the same faith (sometimes aggressively, but usually modestly), this belief in the omnipotence of reason, is in sharp contrast to the existential anguish of the young hippies and the Negro revolt. But the two movements are the opposite faces of America's transformation, of its passage, as it were, to a new form of society.

The real cost of rational progress is not at all alienation through bureaucratic regimentation, the loss of individuality. It would seem to me quite the contrary. The cost has to be sought in the growth of individuality itself, in the ever-increasing burden that comes from freedom of choice.

The cross carried by the American male of the *nouvelle vague* is not his submission to the large organizations (the latter having become increasingly flexible and tolerant); it is his submission to rationalism itself, the manipulation of himself by himself to which he finds himself condemned if he wants to succeed. Under the burning sun of a cost-utility system, there is no more excuse for failure; there is no longer a bureaucratic alibi, no protective niche, no privilege or handicap that is convincing either to those who benefit from the system or to those who suffer from it.

Naturally, the field of education is most profoundly affected, because the essential condition for survival in the new hyperrationalist world, in preparation for which training is indispensable, will depend more and more on a capacity for abstract reasoning, and to that the schools hold the key. Herein lies one of the aspects of the Negro problem which is least understood in Europe. The civil equality that permitted all the ethnic minorities to take their part in the game has proved to be of little value to the Negroes. The passport finally granted does not open the door, because it is no longer possible to make good through mere numbers, through the vote or through manual labor, but only through the ability to play the game of modern calculation. In that area the Negro is still fundamentally disadvantaged. His emancipation is of no use to him, because he is much less competitive in today's society than he was in the traditional industrial society. His relative situation tends to become worse; and for this to change, the Negro community would have to transform completely its mores and values. Only the extremist movements such as the Black Muslims have openly declared that goal, but the blind hostility of white society permits

Negroes to assert themselves in no way but through terrorism, and automatically abandons thousands of young Northern Negroes to the chaos of delinquency, drugs and political blackmail.

At this point the existential anguish of the students, though quite different, resembles the Negro revolt. Both include an element, metaphysical in nature, of pure revolt. More than others in American society, students are fascinated by the system through which they expect to benefit, and which provides their best weapon against their elders, still caught in a less rational past. At the same time it frightens them, for it already weighs heavily on them and they sense that they will pay dearly for the inheritance. It is they who must be the rational men in the demystified world of tomorrow. And this rationalism, which they absorb directly or indirectly in those intellectual hothouses that the great universities have become, offers them neither respite nor any secret corner, nor even the possibility of recrimination or contempt (as in France).

The extraordinary development of rational calculation appears irresistible, but it is limited by the tension it creates in the individual who feels himself incapable of directly coping with all the consequences of his own actions. Nowhere can this ambiguity be more clearly seen than in the extraordinary success of the books of Marshall McLuhan, who has become in the past two years an intellectual hero of the modern age. Prophet of the electronic universe, of television and of the happening, McLuhan announces the development of a new, synthetic tribal culture, to which we have access through the mass media and modern science. At the same time he signals the doom of analytical man, that limited product of the printed word and the linear and sequential reasoning it imposes. McLuhan almost puts science itself on the side of the hippies. But although the young American may dream with McLuhan of synthetic global communication, of short circuits which would permit him to escape the rational process, it is still a fact that he has never before read so many books or applied himself so thoroughly to the analytical disciplines. Through the study of systems, to be sure, he discovers further interlocking complexities, but he does not lose in them the identity that weighs him down. McLuhan's intuitions, if they prevail, will probably turn out to be new tools for integrating the logic of the new media into an all-powerful rationalism.

And yet the conflict remains, and will remain, between the rational and the spontaneous, the community and the individual, the desire for freedom and the fear of responsibility. There are no solutions to these dilemmas. An individual can join a marginal group, but there is no such thing as an artificial paradise where a society can take refuge. Perhaps, in order to carry the debate further, Americans will have to abandon this insoluble riddle and reexamine, through their institutions, the minimal degree of anarchy, confusion and inefficiency which must be tolerated if the participants are to withstand the rigors of the new rationality.

SOME REFLECTIONS ABOUT SOCIAL DISSENT IN POST-INDUSTRIAL SOCIETY
by Gino Giugni

Today's slogans like "participation" were conceived and became popular in the industrial shop. Do they have the same meaning in services, commerce, governmental offices, universities? Protest has shifted to social strata which do not even belong to the work force or, when they do, are strangers to the philosophies or to the experience of industrial conflict. Furthermore, while social dissent of the past, even in its most extremist expressions, was, after all, attached to sound rationalistic tenets, and was therefore typically Western, the new one, as it comes to existence mainly in the U. S., seems imbued with elements of irrationalism or even of mysticism.

The first possibility is that post-industrial society will push forward the process of integration into "one-dimensional culture," leaving room only to a mythical Great Refusal. This alienated society would be the theater of powerful social struggles, sectionalist in character. If we extrapolate some typical tendencies of militant white-collar or services unionism, we have already an anticipation of this. Short-sighted policies, factionalism, egotistic evaluation of group interests may be a serious challenge to society as a whole and, of course, to political institutions—even more than if these groups were committed to radical philosophies.

Another possibility is that present philosophies of social protest will maintain their grasp, going through a process of readaptation: it is the great hope of Western socialism and Communism; it was the hope of the Czechoslovak humanistic socialism.

Finally, new types of protest may come into being. We already have some anticipation of them. And there is a minor alternative: like industrial conflict, the new social protest may gradually set forth its rules, its adjusting machineries, its rites. On the other hand, it may act as a disruptive force, and perhaps cause a reaction, call a coercive order into existence.

Another challenge to "factory-oriented" philosophies looms at the horizon of social change. Leisure time will become larger and larger. This is a great hope, but also a great danger. Our ethics are based upon the assumption that work is the center of life. Our social doctrines draw their inferences from the image of man, whose values, feelings of solidarity, expectations, were shaped by work and the place of work. In spite of his alleged alienation, today's worker may develop high self-consciousness either of collective or of individual kinds, both drawn from his working experience and human relations on the job. How will he behave when the balance between free and working time will lean towards free time? What we may envisage for not too remote a future is the condition of man having lost his millenary link to society, namely work, and looking for a new one. The void, according to some gloomy forecasts, might be filled in by sophisticated techniques of manipulation.

III
GLOBAL POWER
OR

SELF-RESTRAINT

8

SELECTIVE DISENGAGEMENT

JEAN-JACQUES SERVAN-SCHREIBER: After the war in Vietnam is over, we shall certainly see a great debate here on how much and where America's forces should be present in the world. I suggest that the smallest possible presence will be the most reasonable.

Let us examine two different crises of recent years, Southeast Asia and the Middle East. In both cases, America felt it had to protect an ally threatened by external forces. In South Vietnam, America decided to go in physically, with its own men, and substitute its own determination and strength for the determination and strength of the South Vietnamese people. In Israel, America decided on a policy of indirect protection. The American government, at the request of the Israelis, is increasing the Israeli air force. But it did not physically substitute Americans for the Israeli army and people. These are, obviously, extreme situations; but the difference between them points the path to a more reasonable future. Your attitude might be to extend material help to any country that you consider, and that considers itself, your ally, but to accept that you cannot, and will not, take over its defense in its place.

This change of emphasis should be clearly made in Europe. Only if the Western European governments and peoples are certain that they cannot and must not count forever on the presence of American troops, and that they must progressively assume full responsibility for their own defense, will they act responsibly, and a partnership with you be possible. It is not rational that after last summer's crisis in Czechoslovakia, an American general in command of NATO should make a long and eloquent speech to beg the European nations to make greater efforts toward their own defense. That is a question for the Europeans themselves to solve. If the Europeans want to concentrate more resources on defense, if they wish to have more, or less, American assistance, whether by nuclear dissuasion or by the reinforcement of troops, let these be their decisions. If they debate whether or not they dislike Communism or are afraid of invasion or want to have, in time, nuclear weapons, let these be their conclusions. You should not attempt to solve the problems of Europe, but only be ready to respond to Europe's requests, so that a more responsible Europe should decide what its policies shall be. In the course of the next decade, Europe, as a great industrial power, should be able to dispense altogether with the permanent presence of American troops, since that presence is already more a symbol of alliance than a real factor of defense. I do not suggest that American troops should leave Europe now. But it is not in your interests, and not in ours, that you should continue to dictate the defense of Europe and decide its policies.

The great changes in military techniques of the last ten years allow you to abandon military bases on other continents without really reducing your capacity for military reaction. Why should you have to wait for crises in Spain or in Okinawa to decide that your bases are not needed there any more? They have been useless already for some time. The political and moral benefits that America would reap from exploiting these new possibilities of military technology might be enormous. They could become a major peace-making factor. A great deal of the disease now sickening the relationship between your own country and others in the world might be cured.

In a world dominated by nuclear weapons, the hopeful course is the "new politics" of nuclear peace. Once you start in this direction, the main confrontations will be in the application of the "new politics" in economics, industry and science. These will be far more complex, more delicate and even more important. There again, for a global power like yours, the problem will be to decide between direct and indirect presence, between control and partnership. If the United States becomes more and more the direct master of crucial industrial fields in foreign countries, this will lead to more and more irresponsibility and revolt. The lesson for great powers of the last century, such as England and France, has been that any system of direct command and management leads to all kinds of crises and is, in the final analysis, the most inefficient.

The modern answer on economic competition is far less simple than on military problems, since we all agree that the freest possible movement of men, goods, capital, industry and science is essential to development. We would by no means consider it reasonable or healthy to keep American industrial firms away from our countries. But we should jointly formulate the ways and means by which American industry can participate as much as possible in the development of all our countries without taking over or assuming control. American industry should always aim, if at all possible, not at majority control of foreign industries, but at a position of minority partnership. Self-restraint seems essential if your great economic power is to expand without fomenting political reactions and revolts. You should be careful not to create American "industrial bases" on foreign soil just when you are discovering you should maintain the fewest possible military bases abroad.

Far from urging American withdrawal from world responsibilities, I am suggesting that your country consider how it can make its most effective contribution to world development and peace. There are two possible orientations for American expansion. One is "on the surface," like your present physical deployment, military and economic, in the world. This diverts your energies and resources, creates tensions, and handicaps you in your efforts to build a humane post-industrial society. A new orientation would be "in depth." This would concentrate efforts on the formulation and construction of an ambitious civilization on this continent which would become more and more influential in the human adventure, for the benefit of us all. If you choose the former, you will simply follow our examples as colonial powers, with the same results in the end. If you choose the latter, you will help yourselves by investing in your own advanced society and cultural model, and others by a wiser authority and better leadership than you can ever attain by mere physical power.

ZBIGNIEW BRZEZINSKI: I presume the participants of this seminar have copies of my paper, and some of you have even read it. That paper is a distillation of articles I have written elsewhere, and I will now give a distillation of the distillation.

There are nine propositions. The first three pertain to the United States' internal situation as it affects American foreign policy. The first is that, in my view, the essence of the American crisis is not decay, but accelerated change, forcing America to confront fundamental issues facing humanity today. Can races coexist? Can man find dignity in the context of scientific society? This makes me on the whole optimistic about American society. Our discussions reveal more about the state of mind of the American liberal intellectual community than about American society as a whole.

The second proposition is that this evolution involves an emergence in America of a new kind of society, the parameters of which we still do not fully understand. Some of you yesterday talked about a society which you described as "technetronic," and I rather like that term. It catches the essence of the increasingly technological electronic processes which mold our behavior and make our society psychologically congested, interwoven and in constant change.

My third proposition is that because of all this change, America will continue to have an essential, illustrative impact upon the world. Concepts like imperialism do not capture this ambiguous, conflicting relationship with the world. It is, undeniably, in some respects exploitative. In others it is innovative, stimulating and positive.

My next batch of propositions pertains to external conditions in the world. The first is that the dynamic impact of American society on the world runs counter to the American policy preoccupation with international stability. There is a fundamental tension between our policy and our relationship to the world which is difficult to resolve. Eisenhower on the whole opted for order, Kennedy was searching for a formula to emphasize change. I doubt Mr. Nixon will find a creative fusion. Ambivalence will continue.

My second proposition here is that Third World chaos will probably intensify. I'm pessimistic there. Chaos and anarchy, mounting in the Third World, will probably cause a further gap—psychological, political, emotional—between America and the outlook of the Third World.

My third proposition concerns the Cold War. I believe it will fundamentally continue in the years to come. Third World instability will in itself revive it, but the basis for it is increasing ideological rigidity in the Soviet Union, which fears social evolution and has now become a conservative, in fact reactionary, political system. This is compounded by Western passivity. If the Soviet leaders can be said to fear internal change, Western leaders often fear external change. We have failed to take timely and appropriate initiatives in the last two years to redefine the East–West relationship. This too perpetuates the Cold War.

My last three propositions pertain to America's global role as I would like to see it. I see the task of the United States in the world as being basically that of ending the ideological civil war that has divided mankind in different ways since the French Revolution. This means persistent efforts to seek arrangements for such complex issues as arms control; a fundamental redefinition of our attitude toward China; and taking the lead in de-ideologizing international relations. I would like to draw your attention to the remarkable statement issued this summer by Academician Sakharov of the Soviet Union, who makes the same point with great eloquence and force; it could well have been the central paper at this conference. The ideological attitude toward international politics in the nuclear age is not only dangerous but fundamentally immoral. This is the lead that the United States ought to take. In many respects our society is suited for it, because by and large it has not been an ideologically motivated society.

My second proposition is that we have to search for the internationalization of foreign aid. We have to take it out of the realm of the Cold War and ideological conflict, and find a global basis for dealing with Third World problems.

The third proposition is that our ultimate objective in the forthcoming decade or so has to be the creation of a community of the developed nations. During the campaign, Vice-President Humphrey talked about an educational scientific common market as a task worthy of Atlantic initiatives. It's important to create a new sense of scientific, technological development in the advanced world. I do not mean Europe alone. I do not exclude eventually East Europe and the Soviet Union. But above all I mean Japan. Japan has to participate in the community of developed countries and not be left alone in Asia, hopefully assuming our burdens there, as so many Americans now speculate.

All of this means, cumulatively, a highly selective disengagement from different portions in the world, but not all-out disengagement. Some countries need disengagement today, but I also know many countries for which it would be highly unsettling. The worst thing that could happen to world stability would be general American disengagement. What is needed is redefined involvement in the problems of the seventies.

Many of you may shrug and say, "These are Brzezinski's private musings. Will the U. S. in fact do them?" I think we are going to move toward reconciliation on the East–West front. By and large the thrust of American public attitudes now is to think of the Soviet Union at most as an adversary but no longer as an enemy. The same is beginning to apply generally to Communism, though in a much more retarded fashion, and this may even include in the forthcoming years, if not months, China. I believe we're on the eve of a fundamental redefinition of our policy toward China. We will pursue arms-control measures, and I am fairly hopeful progress will be made. I also believe we shall move toward a community of the developed nations. There's a general recognition of our interdependence here, a willingness to search for new formulae, new institutional arrangements helping to end ideological civil war in the developed world and providing a basis, perhaps, for dealing with the problems of the Third World.

I am, however, profoundly pessimistic about the internationalization of foreign aid and continued American involvement in the Third World. I fear there is a growing feeling of detachment and lack of interest—impatience, disappointment, frustration and indifference. We now have an alibi, saying, "We cannot give foreign aid to the extent that we did, or even not at all, because we have pressing domestic problems." As a result, I fear, ambivalence will continue to characterize American foreign policy in the seventies and create difficulties of the kind with which we are already familiar.

MARION DOENHOFF: The peace is at present technically based on nuclear stalemate. We have to transform this technical security into a political one. So the West must go on trying a policy of détente. But the meaning of the occupation of Czechoslovakia seems to me to be that the Russians don't believe in contacts, only in the division of spheres of interest. What if they refuse to respond to efforts of cooperation? This underlines a certain contradiction between Mr. Brzezinski's Thesis Six, the perpetuation of Cold War, and his Thesis Nine, reconciliation of East and West. I would also like to ask what he means by a "community of developed countries." A community can be anything from the U. N., which is a bunch of nations, to the Common Market with all kinds of complicated laws and provisions.

BRZEZINSKI: I agree that the Soviets have opted for the maintenance of two cohesive blocs. They now have a concept of coexistence limited to bilateral reciprocally advantageous arrangements, particularly in arms control, and excluding ideological contacts. However, I do not see a contradiction between Theses

Six and Nine. Thesis Six describes the present situation. Thesis Nine is a normative one—that despite this the United States must promote reconciliation.

I don't believe that cooperative bipolarity is possible, nor that polycentrism is stable or desirable for either side. I think we're going to have a mix someday. Both sides will have to accept a loosening of their relationships with allies, a greater role for middle powers, particularly European ones, and greater multilateral institutional involvement over the long haul. The West must think creatively of the kind of economic, social-security and political-institutional arrangements that ought to be developed to span the abyss that divides the blocs. This is going to be slow, but it's the only solution. Attempts to impose American hegemony on Western Europe, or Soviet hegemony on Eastern Europe, however Machiavellian, will not work in the long run.

As for a community of developed nations, I have no blueprint. The Common Market's experience shows that it's dangerous to create too much of a gap between blueprints and reality. It causes counterreactions. But the Japanese, the West Europeans and ourselves have certain similar problems and should respond to them together. It would be extremely helpful to Americans to have Japanese and Europeans study and involve themselves in our urban and racial problems, realize their complexity and contribute ideas. We could try to develop a common educational system for the developed countries, to reduce present-day disparities which paralyze meaningful interchange. Last but not least, I favor more systematic political consultation. Consultations between Americans, Japanese and Europeans ought to be conducted collectively and not bilaterally by Americans with Japanese and West Europeans in separation.

STANLEY HOFFMANN: I agree with much of the meat of what Professor Brzezinski says, although I do not like the sauce. It is, however, the meat that matters.

American foreign policy in recent years has suffered from two flaws which could be summarized as "Nothing fails like success," in Raymond Aron's phrase, and "Nothing weighs like excess." Vietnam has been the payoff of both flaws. The United States has operated with a vision in black and white of the world which was accurate in 1948, gave a sense of mission to American foreign policy and led to great achievements, particularly in the Western alliance. But the very success of that policy of containment has altered relations between the United States and the Soviet Union, and within each of the camps, so it no longer serves. In Vietnam, its irrelevance to a situation of civil war has led to major troubles. The same irrelevance now exposes American policy to becoming more and more a defense of the status quo in areas like Latin America or Greece.

Then, nothing weighs like excess. The United States has developed a sense of world responsibility which was correct as a starting point. It is, or was, true that the United States was the only major non-Communist nation with sufficient power and sense of mission to man the front lines. However, the notion of being the unique power with world responsibility has often meant giving preference among allies to flatterers, sycophants and tyrants, when those who resisted American influence were more representative and progressive. It has also meant getting caught in a vicious circle of impotence of others and their dependence on us, and our conviction that they would always be incapable minors for whom we had to care. This has prepared the kind of fix in which we find ourselves now.

What way out can be found? There are two ways I would like to reject. The first one is the escapist way. There is today an interesting conjunction of the old isolationism of distrust of an ungrateful world and the new and generous idealism of contrition for what the United States has supposedly done to others. Both, I think, are examples of American moralism: "If only America removed itself from the world, evil would somehow disappear." This, I'm afraid, is incorrect. It may take two for an arms race, but it takes only one for an arms buildup and aggression. Also, all major powers in the past have had severe domestic problems. If a leading power had to wait until it solved all its domestic problems to wage foreign policy, we would have reached the nirvana of a world of isolationist powers which some of my colleagues dream about.

The other way out is the technocratic one. I would dismiss both Mr. Sakharov, whose views I respect because I respect the man, and Sakharov's echoes in Mr. Brzezinski. True, there are joint interests in technology and in decreasing the gap between rich and poor. But the scientific universalism Mr. Sakharov represents has always been negated by the fact that the state has nationalized science more than science has withered away the state. In a competitive situation, each power tries to manipulate the factors of interdependence for its own advantage and at the adversary's expense. The logic of diversity continues.

The problem is how to get to a situation in which the technological and scientific cooperation Mr. Brzezinski wants could even be considered. The basic question for the United States ought to be what kind of an international order we want, given what we have. The point of departure is a highly fragmented world. I do not believe that there is in the cards an American world empire—the world is not exactly ready for it. Nor do I believe we will get a return to the pure bipolarity of conflict or to a condominium of the superpowers—it's hard to see how it could be established or maintained. Our range of alternatives is narrower. Either the present international system will be perpetuated, in which case, unfortunately, since there is very little difference between partly impotent superpowers and largely impotent smaller states, we will have recurrent crises and overstraining of the superpowers, or there will be an attempt to establish a more structured international milieu with more middle powers, more hierarchies responding to different kinds of power—military, economic, technological, monetary— more regional decentralization, a world in which competition will continue, but within limits and restraints.

In this world, we must be careful about what the United States can and cannot do. It cannot act as though it could go home. It cannot act as a global power. Instead it must become more aware of its own important role in shaping the future, international order; it cannot help but have a shaping impact. We have not always been aware of this. I simply refer you to the extraordinary speech of Mr. McNamara in September 1967 where he showed how our miscalculations determined an arms race with the "mad momentum" he described. Precisely because explicit agreements between the superpowers remain difficult, our goal should be to affect others by our own behavior. Even if others want to isolate themselves, we should not contribute to it. We should make it clear that we are ready to talk when they are out of their present mood, even if there is no immediate response. It is very largely up to the United States, as a great power which has access to most of the states of mankind, to shape the environment. It is up to the United States to influence the moderation or brutality, intelligence or stupidity, even of the Soviet leaders. It is certainly up to the United States to instill in those parts of the world which are presently afraid of selective disengagement the sense of self-respect, of responsibility and of capacity to fill the shoes which the United States has been filling.

Now let me end with some specific imperatives, largely derived from our lessons in Vietnam. First of all, we have to accept domestic change elsewhere, even if American interests are the targets and if forces we do not like come to the fore. We cannot play the role of cosmic Metternichs. We must learn to distinguish between internal turbulence, which has to be tolerated because it's likely to continue, and the external outpourings of domestic turbulence, which are a legitimate concern for a great power. Here, indeed, there is a great deal to be said for greater emphasis on peace-keeping, regionalization and so on.

Second, we must critically reexamine the limits of American power: much of our military and economic power is not easily usable. We must also realize the limits imposed on our action by our style and our institutions. We have an overbearingly self-confident approach to complex problems, a tendency to reduce them to issues of management, and very often an underestimation of the way in which other people's history and customs condition their reaction to present issues.

Finally, we must understand that nations are more and more determined by their internal realities. Consequently, our social scientists should concentrate more on understanding foreign cultures and political systems and less on global visions. We have to learn to distinguish between kinds of interventions and understand that massive interventions in foreign societies are likely to be counterproductive.

The conclusion is the imperative of self-restraint, which is precisely what we can learn from past great powers. We can apply this to Vietnam and to East–West relations. There is a legitimate field of direct American–Soviet negotiations which is largely the arms race, in which convergent interests are developing. But when it comes to political settlement of the major underlying issues, the United States by itself cannot and should not do much. It should accept and recognize much more the need for diversity, the need for discriminating and the need for devolution of power to middle and potential middle states. This implies a reevaluation of the instruments of our foreign policy, a shift from unilateral to multilateral, from military to other forms of power—in other words, a reconsideration of everything that came to a head in what has been, to me at least, a culmination of some trends of American policy, the disaster in Vietnam.

ALASTAIR BUCHAN: Even if it were possible for the United States to impose a pattern of order on the world, this would require a degree of social sacrifice, in the sense of making the internal structure of the country like that of nineteenth-century Britain or France or contemporary Russia, which I, for one, do not believe Americans are prepared to contemplate. "Global influence," a "global impact," the United States has by reason of the dynamism of its society. "Global power" to affect permanently the pattern of international relations at a great distance from her shores, she does not have. She has neither the mandate nor the desire nor the ability. The United States really has very little alternative to building what Brzezinski called a community of the developed powers. If she can maintain a relatively stable and coherent power structure in the developed world, she will be doing very well.

Does America have the staying power for this? The reactions to Vietnam after only three years of relatively light casualties, though enormous financial cost, make one wonder, though I neither accepted the objectives nor admired the techniques of that operation. The American ally, who, if he is a West European, lives in a continent which if the Americans were not around would be Finlandized, permanently open to Soviet pressure, always has this nagging feeling that the United States might go home. Go home not in the sense of the old isolationism, but by concentrating on relations with the Soviet Union and later China, turning sour on the United Nations and NATO, and becoming increasingly unilateral and introspective.

It is here that the difficulty of defining American interests is relevant. If defined in ideological terms, they often turn out to be peripheral. Defined on any cold calculation of American well-being and safety, they may not be interests at all. The integrity of Europe is still regarded as a vital American interest, but nowadays both strategically and probably economically the United States could continue to maintain a balance with the Soviet Union even if the American–European relationship were hostile. The United States could maintain the security of North America, probably without any allies (except Canada). One of the arguments of twenty years ago was that even if she could, American society would wither away if isolated in a neutralist or unfriendly world. Is this still true?

Already, some redefinition of America's interests has taken place—for instance, the decision that every move in Africa does not affect her. As mass communications grow, there is going to be an increasingly cruel dilemma between our hearts and our heads on such things as conflict between Nigeria and Biafra, fury with the kind of brutality we see on television screens as against our cooler judgment not to get involved. What this demands is not a cynical policy towards the developing world but greater emphasis on multilateral aid and, above all, making the United Nations system, one of the most impractical in the world, work better. Few things have depressed me more in the last couple of years than the evidence of growing friction between the United States and the Secretariat of the United Nations.

Nevertheless, America's central problem will be to refine its conception of its interests with the developed powers. There is necessarily a dilemma in American policy between relations with Russia on the one hand and with the middle powers on the other. Let's face it, the Soviet Union is the only worthwhile interlocutor the United States has, the only country with whom it really has a special relationship. There is an important agenda for Soviet–American discussion, and it's growing: the stabilization of the arms race. There are areas where only the Soviet Union can help the United States redefine its interests: Vietnam and the Middle East. How in the circumstances can America maintain a confident dialogue with the middle powers, almost all of whom have potential conflicts of interest with the Soviet Union?

The sixty-four-dollar question is whether you can maintain stability in Soviet–American relations—the alternative being not necessarily war but superpower impotence—without articulating a spheres-of-influence policy. The problem is easier in Asia in the immediate future, because American and Soviet spheres of responsibility there are not necessarily contiguous. My own hunch is that the redefinition of American interests will draw it into closer relations with the countries of the Pacific, most of whom, including Australasia, are high-growth-rate countries, while the Soviet Union acquires an increasing sense of responsibility for the stability and security of the Indian subcontinent. (This doesn't necessarily mean that there aren't many other kinds of contacts between India, say, and the West.) The big problem seems to be the area in between, an area of a hundred ethnic minorities. Here the only concept that seems to me worthwhile is that of permeability: external powers should have cultural and political relations with this area without American or Chinese hegemony. It is a difficult concept to work and requires a dialogue with China as intimate as the Soviet–American dialogue must become. If you don't get that, if you get a very dynamic Japan and a level of distrust, or non-conversation, between China and the United States, then you'll have a reproduction, in a vast area and by vast powers, of the old European balance of power, with all its dangers.

In Europe, the dilemma between the superpower relationship and that of the allies is more difficult. Here, security relations are still dominant and the nature of the Soviet–American relationship inhibits real devolution of authority by either power. But I think most of us in Europe would agree there is little to be gained by opposing a Soviet–American dialogue—for instance, by heightening tension between them or opposing, say, the nondeployment of ballistic-missile defense. On the other hand, to accept it means, first, a continuing American leadership in the strategic field, for as far as the horizon takes us; and, second, explicit recognition that in certain kinds of crises the United States may have to give higher priority to its relationships with the Soviet Union than to those with its European allies. Continuing confidence between Western Europe and the United States lies in acknowledging this asymmetry, and in pursuing sensible functional forms of cooperation in Europe that diminish the power disparities where possible. There is a lot of sense in a technological and defense community that would not aspire at a separate strategic system from the United States, while recognizing that any concept of equal partnership (is Mr. Ball in the room?) is basically fraudulent and would be hotly opposed by the United States if it showed any signs of coming about. Much of modern American crisis management and control theory argues for the centralization of decision-making.

So, in the foreseeable future, America's central problem will be to preserve the strategic basis of political stability in the developed world, by building as much limitation as possible into what Marshall Shulman has called "her limited adversary relationship" with the Soviet Union, and perhaps with China too, without losing the confidence of the middle powers, of whose relationships with her Britain's is the easiest to maintain, France's the most difficult, and Japan's and Germany's the most complex. Towards these middle powers, the United States must make up its mind which it finds less intolerable: bearing an overwhelming share of the costs of running the non-Communist international system or sphere of responsibility, or seeing others take decisions which may affect the United States as well as themselves. This is a difficult set of requirements by any standards.

Because American–Japanese, American–European, American–Indian relationships are going to be under pressure of the super-power dialogue all the time, the nature of American society itself is very important. I doubt the United States can maintain them on its present amateur system of executive government. Over the last thirty years, I have had less and less admiration for it. It seems to me in the highest degree to divorce power from responsibility, to pursue dynamism at the expense of clarity, and to make it extremely difficult, particularly for a small country, to understand which of any one of half a dozen policies running in Washington at any time is likely to predominate. Brzezinski's sketch of government by professors seems to me a recipe for permanent divorce between aspirations and achievement. If war is too serious to be left to generals, foreign policy is too serious to be left to intellectuals. No one would argue for the mandarinate of Whitehall or the Quai d'Orsay. Professional public servants can give bad advice like amateurs, but they are less likely to be the victims of fashion, and they stay in office long enough to have to implement the consequences of their advice.

More broadly still, America's influence will depend on whether it can lick its problems and remain a free society. Many of us listened to George Kennan with great interest, but George's United States would lick its technological problems and lose its character as a free society. Many of the younger generation don't realize the extent to which American leadership during and after the war was a consequence of the immense admiration my generation of Europeans had for the New Deal. A great European intellectual, Isaiah Berlin, said about this, "It was really the first time a great modern democratic industrial society tried to reform itself in the direction supplied by what are ultimately abstract ideas in a not over-doctrinaire fashion, with due attention paid to the imperfections of the human beings who were being governed, or for whose benefit this was done, and, it seemed to me, with the most exceptional sensitiveness to the particular nature of the human beings, to the asymmetrical, to the irregularities, to the peculiarities, to the idiosyncrasies, to everything that could not be reproduced in a statistical form on the part of the people of the United States. As a combination of intellectual imagination, recognition of the value and importance of ideas, and natural humanity and empiricism of method, I don't think the period and the men concerned have ever been equaled." If the young generation of Americans who are here can do as well as that, they'll be doing damn well.

Louis Fischer: As a person who tries to write the history of diplomacy—especially Soviet diplomacy, and that involves the diplomacy of many other countries—I would like to add one new level to our discussion. This is that much of the history of the modern world is the record of the mistakes of governments in information or in evaluation. When one sees how many grave errors which result in world wars or minor wars have been committed, the question is what is the real function of an executive branch and whether there should not be some change in the whole manner of formulation of American foreign policy and the policies of other countries.

9

AMERICA'S EUROPE

WALDEMAR BESSON: I agree with the Brzezinski-Hoffmann desire that America should compromise between present overcommitment and the illusion of total disengagement. "Selective disengagement" is a happy phrase for this. But the problem of such a foreign policy is to get a political consensus behind it. That is not only an American problem. I would like to address myself mainly to our own neo-isolationists in Europe, who speak of independent European foreign policies. It's absolutely wrong to suppose that independent means of European defense can be found vis-à-vis the Soviet Union. The Soviet Union will never allow anything of this kind to appear on the scene. Remember the Soviet interference even in the MLF project.* I'm afraid that American troops in Europe are much more than a symbol, more so than ever since August 21st [the date of the Soviet occupation of Czechoslovakia]. It seems to me that we should not be so afraid of American hegemony in Europe. After all, if one gets protection, one has to pay something for it. We haven't fared badly with this kind of protection so far. We Germans must do our own share of promoting peaceful coexistence in Europe, by some sort of orderly coexistence between the two German states. But the precondition for this is the continued strong presence of the United States in Europe. I'm afraid I wouldn't exchange American leadership for a French one.

* MLF: The NATO nuclear multilateral force proposal put forward by the United States in 1963 and dropped, due to disagreements between the allies, late in 1964.

STANLEY HOFFMANN: I must say bluntly that I find Mr. Besson's position disastrous. It is precisely this kind of clinging to the United States which makes it more difficult for the United States to reshape its foreign policy in a more constructive way. It perpetuates the circle of dependency about which I was talking earlier. It confirms Americans in their conviction that only they can deal with European political problems. If I had to apportion blame for "Europe's identity crisis," it would be evenly divided between certain illusions of grandeur of Gaullist policy and the clinging to American leadership exhibited here. I wonder whether such a clinging does not make selective disengagement impossible. In my opinion, the only way to get selective disengagement will be for the United States to make it clear to those of its allies who could become responsible middle powers that they have to take a bigger part in settling their own affairs and that the United States is not prepared to play a nursing role forever.

BESSON: Mr. Hoffmann, I'm convinced the NATO structure will have to be changed, and that Europe is not the distraught province it was when NATO was formed. But in spite of all insistence on Western European regionalism, the balancing quality of the United States in Europe is necessary. It will not hamper American selective disengagement in Asia to turn back to a closer and better relationship with Western Europe. My main point is that West Germany can adjust to the territorial status quo which is necessary in Europe only if the United States is present there. I must tell my American friends that their neo-isolationism is not just a twist in American public opinion, but a deep crisis in the way America looks at the world, and might have dangerous consequences. The Germans are beginning to realize that they live in the center of Europe and that their future relations with the Soviet Union will have to be looked into. Selective disengagement including Europe might have disastrous effects on European morale.

CARL KAYSEN: You must distinguish, I think, you Europeans, as you have not, and as especially the officials and makers of public opinion and leaders of the [German] Federal Republic have not, between the following two questions. First, does the United States have a strong interest, which it perceives as its interest, in the stability of the present situation in Europe, and in particular in preventing the Soviet Union from using force or the threat of force to change that situation west of the dividing line? I think the answer is yes. We have that interest. It's *our* interest. If it's not our interest, no amount of cajoling, complaining, wheedling, whining, flattering, will make us perceive it. It *is* our interest. I think every American political leader of any substance, in opposition, in power, has asserted that interest. The second question is: What is the appropriate level of military deployment, organizational arrangement, command structure, this, that and the other technical detail to express this interest? If the discussion of the second question is used continually to reexamine the first question, the situation will become unmanageable. We have trembled so at every trembling response you have made to discussions of the second question, that we have encouraged you to believe that discussions of that question were discussions of our basic commitment. They're not. I would go further and say that it becomes more difficult for us to have rational discussions of the second question if you view it continuously as a questioning of the commitment.

ALASTAIR BUCHAN: I should like Carl Kaysen to substantiate his statement that the United States commitment to Europe can be taken for granted. American involvement in Western Europe arose out of the intensive process of thought in the forties when it was argued that Western Europe and an American role there were essential to the security of the United States itself, and, second, that with a sour relationship with Europe, or with a Western Europe in the Communist bloc, the United States itself would somehow diminish and wither spiritually. It's hard to maintain either of those arguments today, certainly not the strategic one. And since you yourself, Mr. Kaysen, have written so eloquently on the theme that the whole process of innovation and change arises out of a purely American process, our American colleagues owe us more substantial argumentation as to why the United States is going to remain committed in Western Europe, and why they regard it as a vital interest. Particularly in view of the fact that a Western Europe from which the United States disengaged herself is not likely to be a Communist one. It would simply be extremely vulnerable to Soviet pressure and diplomacy.

KAYSEN: The assertion was unsubstantiated, as Alastair Buchan has pointed out. Perhaps the first thing I should say is that this represents some judgment about what the political elites in the United States think. One reason is sentimental but has great political force. Most people in the United States feel a cultural kinship with Europe they do not feel with other parts of the world. If this were the only factor, one could argue whether it would be enough to provide the basis for the kind of political and military commitment we are talking about. But it is not the only factor. We are becoming economically more interconnected with Europe every day. If you compare the situation of the twenties (I won't talk about the disastrous situation of the thirties) with the current situation in terms of the volume and relative importance of international trade, of international capital movements, of joint enterprises, of traffic, of movement of people, of readership of other people's newspapers or whatever you like, there is a tremendous amount of interaction, and that is important. Now, at the politically operative level I would say that as long as the Soviet Union and Communism are perceived as hostile and only mildly dynamic, the sense that we should not allow this hostile system to expand at the expense of a group of states with whom we have such close ties will be extremely strong. This is partly a matter of military power—although, I think myself, less and less so—and partly a matter, if you like, of political and moral space in terms of our view of what the world ought to be like. I do think that the military component of this relation is of declining importance and that if we can't mutually recognize this and it becomes a matter of contention across the Atlantic, it would make for increasing strain and in the long run undermine the relationship.

JAN REIFENBERG: There is a fundamental danger here summed

up in the French proverb "Emotions are not a policy." We need the protection of the United States for the time being. But what is much more required these days is to get out of a pure security syndrome. If we go on like this, neither will there be some sort of United Europe nor will Germany contribute to reconciliation on earth. We should (a) look for ways to pursue détente and (b) understand once and for all that the United States does have a vital interest in Europe and will not relinquish it, no matter who sits in the White House. It is necessary to find ways to unite Europe in an intelligent way, so that Europe, even if she is only a middle power, can become the stabilizing factor between East and West. I do not necessarily espouse all General de Gaulle's theories of superintegrationists in Brussels, but something in between must be found. My country, which lies athwart the power blocs in Europe, has a very important mission to fulfill here, and it can best do it by practical steps, however tedious and slow. We shouldn't relinquish the effort because of events like Czechoslovakia, which are tragic, but part of the lesson of life.

SIMON NORA: I don't understand the role Mr. Reifenberg proposes for his country. Does he renounce reunification? I suppose not. If not, how does he propose to obtain this reunification?

BESSON: Mr. Chairman, I want to answer that question. Since 1945, we have all underestimated what Soviet power means in Europe. So long as the Soviet Union is a power equal to the United States there won't be a chance of eastward movement by West Germany—that is, reunification. The Soviet Union will not allow the other Germany to join the stronger, more prosperous, more dominant Western part. So, what can Germans contribute? The two parts of Germany might increase their contact if a kind of disengagement took place in the center of Europe. Quite possibly the Soviet Union doesn't want that either, because the continuation of the Cold War fits better into its scheme of things. But, in any case, there is no solution in the way we have been looking at the German problem for twenty years. So I agree with Mr. Reinfenberg, détente must continue. But how can we do this in the center of Europe unless the political and military stability of NATO is assured? You must understand, my position comes out of the experience of the last three years. We have felt in Europe that Vietnam has thinned America's presence in Europe, cut it down, and made it less reliable, and this has been a factor of unrest and instability.

ANDREAS PAPANDREOU: I take exception to the view that Mr. Besson's statement is a European statement. It is a statement of the view of West Germany, and more particularly of Mr. Besson.

The present arrangement in Europe means different things to different European nations. If West Germany is satisfied not to have a foreign policy, to live under an umbrella and look after its well-being, that is a legitimate choice, especially after its traumatic experiences in the past. The Germans have chosen, possibly correctly, that they cannot exercise leadership. That is a matter for them. But allow me to say that in Greece, which also belongs to NATO, the situation is very different. The arrangement of which we are eloquently speaking here involves in Greece today concentration camps to the tune of about ten thousand prisoners—not the figures reported to the press—and tortures that surpass those perpetrated in Dachau. This was documented in Strasbourg last week. The proceedings were *in camera,* but if you have friends in the Human Rights Commission of the Council of Europe, ask them what is going on in Greece. Is this an arrangement of which my German friend approves? Is it part of NATO's concept of order in Europe to turn Greece into a concentration camp and establish the first fascist beachhead in Europe since the last war? Those of us who have suffered under both fascisms may remind those who forget that, like cancer, it spreads. Without wishing to turn this into a discussion of the Greek case, I would like people to ask themselves, is this a contradiction in NATO and U. S. policy or not? What values are we really concerned with here? What is the meaning of the free world in its confrontation with Eastern totalitarianism?

Now a question, and not an academic one, to Mr. Hoffmann. Is it historically possible for a policy such as he suggests to be adopted in the United States? That takes us to another question: Who makes foreign policy in the United States? For me, this is fundamental. Policy requires a power propellent. Who are the people who make foreign policy in the United States? Is it the American citizenry? Congress? The President? I doubt it.

We should look carefully at the new alliance between the military, the intelligence services and the large economic interests, which is particularly evident in United States policy toward Latin America. It constitutes the social base of a new type of imperialism. Soviet bureaucratic socialism is not much different within its sphere of influence. The progressive forces released during the postwar period constitute a threat, real or imagined, to the interests of both superpowers, which have trampled upon them. A heightening of Cold War tensions tends to justify and encourage restrictive measures within both blocs, so that the process is mutually reinforcing and cumulative.

In 1947–48 the U. S. stepped into Britain's shoes in Greece by openly intervening there to "safeguard" Greek democracy, while the coalition regimes in Eastern Europe were converted into militant Communist regimes with close ties to Moscow. The emergence of the NATO Pact was countered by the emergence of the Warsaw Pact. In 1967, when Greece was on its way to becoming a democratic, progressive and sovereign country within NATO, the colonels associated with the CIA established a military dictatorship. A similar process of democratization and assertion of national sovereignty was under way in Czechoslovakia when the Warsaw Pact powers occupied the country. The Soviet military takeover provided the U. S. with a forceful argument for strengthening NATO. Neutralist tendencies on both sides of the Iron Curtain have given way to bloc-oriented behavior. While the actions in Greece and Czechoslovakia started out as interventions internal to each bloc, they may well end up by creating a new focal area of superpower confrontation in the Balkans.

There are differences, however, in two respects between U. S.

and Soviet supremacy. One is that the Soviet Union lacks the technoeconomic expansionism of the U. S. military-industrial complex—the complex dynamic which, while propelling the world to new technological frontiers, is creating a new managerial elite beyond the reach of traditional levers of political control exercised by the citizenry over the political authority and by the political authority over the bureaucracies. The other is that the Atlantic Alliance includes powerful advanced nations which are not dominated by the U. S. in the same sense as the Latin-American republics. The pattern here is one of rapidly growing economic domination hand in hand with political infiltration and control. This is the reason for the European concern over Greece. The U. S. employed methods there which so far it had not employed on the European Continent. Greece, since the military takeover, has become a U. S. satellite in the same sense that Bulgaria is a Russian satellite. A new and threatening pattern of United States supremacy in Europe is emerging.

While there is time, the democratic progressive forces on the European Continent should join hands to face the new gathering storm. They must work for a free, united and peaceful Europe in which each nation is respected as an equal partner and each citizen respected by the state as an inviolable individual. When a united Europe emerges and masters its technological, economic and political potential, it will be able to define its relationship with both the U. S. and the Soviet Union in a way which may well contribute to peace, progress and democracy in the world.

GEORGE BALL: I have to confess, I am getting a little tired of hearing the United States blamed for the problems of Greece. Some of the responsibility for the military coup must lie with the preceding government, its inability or unwillingness to face the hard problems which confronted Greece, including Cyprus, and discontent and strain within the country which made the coup at least possible. Some have inferred that because the United States was unhappy with the Greek regime, we had some responsibility for the coup. That is totally wrong and quite unacceptable. What is suggested is apparently that NATO should take some responsibility of a moral kind for the character of NATO members. This is a proposed interference in countries' internal affairs which requires some careful thought before we accept it at face value.

I don't think that my countrymen like the idea of playing a dominant role in Europe. The American ambition is to have a strong Europe which can look at the world with the same broad vision as the United States and take some interest in problems far afield. At present, the individual countries of Western Europe are very parochial. The degree of independence that Europe can or should assert depends on the willingness or ability of Europe to take the hard decisions to organize itself so that it has the command of resources, power and population to move toward greater independence. I don't see that occurring so long as the French government persists in its present policy with regard to British entry into, and commands such a dominating position over, the European Economic Community. Now the recent monetary crisis has tended to disclose what has been implicit for a long time, that French hegemony in Western Europe just isn't on. A bilateral Franco-German entente just isn't on, either, because there will inevitably be a more independent German policy as the new generation comes along, the commanding leader of France leaves the scene, and the French government is faced with problems of succession which are far from clear. What has always been just beneath the surface is going very much to emerge, and this is that West Germany does have the industrial capacity and manpower to play a leading role in Western Europe once it obtains the will to exercise it through a new generation without the inhibitions hampering the present, wartime one. Therefore it seems to me extremely important that Britain enter Europe and play an effective role as soon as possible. An edifice in Europe can be built on three pillars, not durably on two. With Britain playing an effective role, Western Europe can have a much higher degree of independence because it has the power, and the United States can modify its relations in a manner to give more self-respect to Europeans and so provide a more durable situation. Unless these arrangements can be made within the next two, three or five years, I see great difficulty. I see a growing reluctance by Germany to want Britain in Europe at a time when French objections begin to fade. Five years is an outer limit because if nationalism still appears to be the order of the day, the new generation of Germans will feel that nationalism, meaning the reconstruction of the prewar German state, is the wave of the future. A prewar German state is not something the West can secure to it. The logic of that could lead to some very great perplexities for all of us.

DAVID MARQUAND: It seems to me implicit in Mr. Ball's argument that Europe would develop, if Britain joined it, into a power which would make it more possible for the United States to withdraw. This too is a rather dangerous concept. Experience during the last few years has unfortunately shown that the impetus towards a really tight Europe unity has evaporated. I wish it hadn't. But we will be deceiving ourselves if we imagine that the mere fact of Britain's going into the Common Market will of itself revive the impetus towards European unity that existed in the middle fifties. I want to see Britain in the Common Market, but I feel it will be a very slow process before the Common Market develops into anything like a political unit making it possible for the United States to withdraw from Europe.

BALL: I wasn't suggesting the United States withdraw from Europe, nor limiting the length of time the process would take. All I meant was that if Britain does become a partner in the European Community, forces will be set in motion which over time will almost inevitably lead to a greater unity and make possible some revisions in the relationship between Europe and the United States.

KARL KAISER: I intended partially to criticize the remarks made by Jean-Jacques Servan-Schreiber. After this discussion I would like also to include my compatriot from Germany, Mr. Besson. Their two positions are reactions to each other. They represent two fundamental European positions. In Besson's I see the German fear that French policy may lead the United States to withdraw from Europe. In Servan-Schreiber's I see the French fear that German yearning for American presence in Europe may make it impossible for Europe to develop an identity of its own. I think these two positions are fears, and I don't think these two gentlemen meant them to be solutions. The crucial problem remains: what is America's interest in Europe? We have to get out of the syndrome of hysteric expressions of fear and declarations of love for Europe. I sympathize with Americans who are tired of this. Nevertheless, I would like to pick up Carl Kaysen's distinction between a fundamental reconsideration of the American commitment to Europe and the reconsideration of techniques. How are we going to know the difference? It is very difficult to interpret messages that come across the Atlantic. There is also a real difference in perspective. What to you is a technical question is very fundamental to us sometimes. Here is a dilemma, and we should face it. That leads to my main theme, the consequences of the changing power ratio in Europe. The recent crises in Europe have dramatically illuminated the rise of West Germany as the major economic power in Western Europe, and the relative decline of Britain and France.

I have strong attachments to both Britain and France. I am a product of their educational systems as well as of my own country's, and my concern goes beyond the usual *raison d'état* of European solidarity that we can expect of every responsible European. Britain's weakness concerns us all, because Britain's contribution is indispensable to a European state system that can accommodate a resurgent Germany. I do not share the feelings I often find, that Britain is finished. But, as a result of the French veto on her entry into the Common Market, Britain doesn't have a sense of purpose. It doesn't know where to go. If there were somewhere to go, Britain would be a very different country.

As for France, it seems to me that we are at the end of a period. The herculean effort of one man to lead the French nation to European hegemony has failed. In a way, it is touching, because it mobilized resources in the French we didn't expect. But it has overstrained French resources, mortgaged the social and economic stability of future French generations, and all but betrayed two generations of Europeans, those who died a meaningless death in the name of nationalism and those who have tried to build a community in Europe. I hope the *Götterdämmerung* which has begun to descend will not result in, first, colonels and, second, a destruction of the European state system. *Schadenfreude* about what happens in France is very shortsighted. Indeed, we have a very strong interest in helping even de Gaulle get out of the crisis—ultimately to help the next government avoid the colonels. But this must be done in a way to avoid the second danger, the destruction of the European state system. Above all, we must avoid the revival of bilateralism. If there is one blueprint for disaster in Europe, it is a positive American response to present French overtures for technical assistance in maintaining the French *force de frappe*.

This leads me to Germany. We Germans can no longer conceal from ourselves that we are now Europe's strongest power economically. We have recently heard voices from Germany, notably during the two monetary crises, which to many of us have not been very pleasant. We will hear more of them in the future, and some may have a Bavarian accent. We had better get used to them. Stability in Europe may be threatened not only by the mistakes of a resurgent Germany, but by those of the United States and of other European powers. The traps that existed in the interwar period are still present. I see two. The first is the refusal to satisfy legitimate national demands of a democratic Germany. This would encourage the nationalist forces which exist even in the democratic parties. We all know what happened to Weimar when the democratic powers refused to make concessions to democratic leaders, the concessions Hitler later extorted by force. Many of you have been annoyed by the recent refusal of Germany to revalue. The annoyance is understandable, but I have tried to think of what would have happened if the crisis had occurred two and a half years earlier with a weak Erhard government and, instead of

Schiller and Strauss, Schmücker and Dahlgrün as the German ne-
gotiators. I am sure the result would have led to a further revival
of right-wing extremism. In other words, we have to accept the
fact that the moment has come when German governments will
occasionally say no. German policy may be more independent in
the future. If the Oder-Neisse line is recognized, if the Berlin problem is solved, if Germany accepts the continued existence of two
German states, the Federal Republic will be freed from all the
chains that keep her a junior partner in the Western alliance. We
had better face this. But please do not see behind every German
cough a Hitlerian roar. A more nationally oriented Germany does
not mean an aggressive, expansive Germany. If we make that
mistake, we heavily mortgage the future. Every government says
no—the French, the American, we all do this when it comes to
legitimate national interests. Instead, we must avoid all the more
the second trap of the Weimar period, which is to leave the international framework too weak to accommodate Germany. The
tragedy of the interwar period was that France clung to the Ver-
sailles system, which was inadequate, and I am sorry to say that
de Gaulle's France is now trying to destroy the only possible
framework for Europe. The political, institutional, internationalist
and multilateral solution is the only constructive answer in Europe.

This leads me to my last point: the consequences of what I
regard as a new type of international politics. I call it transnational
politics. This consists of political processes where societal actors in
a relatively autonomous position move in an international environment where the governments are rather helpless because they
have sovereignty only over a fraction of the phenomenon. The
currency crisis is one example; investment is another; the multi-
national corporation; migration; tourism—all the things to which
Carl Kaysen referred when he spoke of the new rationale for an
American interest in Europe. Two reactions are possible to this
situation. A government can cut off the transactions, which is what
the French government is partially trying to do. This can be done
only at the cost of changing the system. If you push the present

Gaullist solution to the extreme, France has to become protectionist and give up hope of becoming a modern economic force. I don't
think this is acceptable to the French, or to the rest of us who also
have an important stake in a dynamic, prosperous France. The
other solution is some kind of regularization of these autonomous
transnational processes. It seems to me that three major monetary
crises in one year are an important warning. If we don't heed it, we
may head for disaster. The economists tell us that the crisis of
1929 is not going to repeat itself. I am less certain that our new
monetary techniques are so foolproof. I was very surprised that
when we discussed the problems of American society, almost
nobody mentioned to what extent this country is interlocked with
others and is losing its sovereign jurisdiction over societal processes. It would make a great deal of sense if the new Administration called a conference of the United States, the E.E.C., Japan
and Britain, to see how all our economic cooperation in the West,
including the monetary system, can be overhauled.

HOFFMANN: I always have the deepest respect for any European with a sense of tragedy, but I would say to Karl Kaiser that
his gloom may not be justified. There are absolutely no colonels on
the French scene, and the recent crisis is not such a disaster. What
it has shown is that even in the new world of transnational politics,
interstate politics go on. It is precisely the heart of what we have
been talking about that two kinds of politics are going on simultaneously—one the politics of interdependence which puts a safety
net under the antics of statesmen, and the other the old national
politics of each one trying to step on the other and trying not to be
stepped on. There is nothing particularly new about this. If Karl is
right and there is a revival of the national spirit in Germany, then
the kind of multilateral framework he advocates will, as Mr.
Marquand has suggested, not be very constraining or compelling.
But I do not find this particularly tragic, because I do not see the
German political scene quite as brutally as he does. The freedom
of movement of a slightly more national Germany in the present
Europe is, alas, or fortunately, depending on your viewpoint,

rather limited. A great deal depends on the United States. I see no future for the transnational world of Karl Kaiser if the United States fails to see that the purpose is to transform the traditional international struggle for power into something which resembles much more closely the struggles for power which obtain within domestic politics.

10

THE RAPE OF CZECHOSLOVAKIA

IVAN SVITAK: The Czechoslovak crisis is not the crisis of a
small country. It is the crisis of European and American values.
The important fact is not how fourteen million people will live—
they have spent years under the system of Novotny, and this one
will be analogous, or worse, or slightly better. The important point
is that twenty years after the war we must again ask, Is it possible
to defend the sovereignty of any small nation in Europe? An his-
torian or statesman must have the imagination of a Salvador Dali
to understand what has happened or may yet happen. In the International Year of Human Rights, the world has been forced to
swallow the most terrific violation of human rights. It has done so
passively on all sides. Biafra has caused more stir than Czechoslovakia. The Secretary General of the United Nations, who travels
all the time to trouble spots, did not even go to Prague. Bismarck
said, "He who controls Bohemia controls Europe." Perhaps that is
an exaggeration and the historical parallel is not reliable. I remember another parallel: Munich. Chamberlain thought he had
saved peace for a generation when he had put off war for one year.
Perhaps that too is exaggerated. But what we have experienced in
Czechoslovakia is a preventive war. We may be mild and call it by
other names and find excuses, but it was a preventive war and once
you start moving in that direction, where will you stop?

I say this because we must not underrate the consequences in
the Soviet Union itself. This is the victory of neo-Stalinism in the
Kremlin. I am afraid it is both a victory for imperialism—the

Soviet Union is now introducing a new form of colonialism in Europe—and a further stage in the transformation of the Soviet Union into a criminal state. For me the question is: Is it an international crime or a transformation of the Soviet state? In either case, it shows the crisis of Stalinist institutions. The Czech crisis is the future crisis of the Soviet Union. The Soviet authorities are afraid and when somebody is afraid, he is dangerous. The Soviet authorities are, I believe, more dangerous than ever before.

I've met many American students and intellectuals who are obsessed with the idea that they have to understand the motives of Russian behavior. Why? You have to understand the results. How can you understand absurdity? Albert Camus will tell you that you can't use rational arguments for explaining irrational outbursts. You are obsessed with projecting your ideas, your ideals, into the Kremlin. It doesn't work. I am sorry to quote those bad boys, students from Prague in August '68, but they will tell you, "Brezhnev is Hitler." Maybe they are wrong. Let us hope they are wrong. This is relevant to bridgebuilding, which was a good policy. Now you have to ask where you are building bridges. You can build a bridge over a river or narrows. You cannot build a bridge over the sea. The American intellectual cannot build bridges to the Kremlin. He can only build them to intellectuals elsewhere, East and West. He should help to build bridges to the Eastern intellectuals. Truth is the only revolutionary force in the cosmos.

EUGEN LOEBL: In the light of the discussions here, I think Czechoslovakia has had very great advantages. Our economy, our whole social life, were based on a theory which has proved totally wrong and an establishment which didn't work at all. So we have had to question all our assumptions and focus on essentials. Although we had discussed the shortcomings of our system for years, when Novotny fell we still had no exact plans for how to work out what we called "socialism with a human face." During the eight months to August we changed many views, and if we had had longer I am sure we would have changed many more. I don't think that I can offer any models. Nevertheless, Czechoslovakia has been a kind of laboratory experience for many problems. It is important not to see only a Czechoslovak or Czechoslovak–Soviet problem in the recent crisis.

In Czechoslovakia, the government had an absolute monopoly of economic and political power. The form of ownership was partly responsible for this. Being the one owner, the government ran the whole economy and couldn't do it otherwise than by directing enterprises to planned targets. So we found what central directive planning really means. We found that when all activities are concentrated in one planning body it is impossible to make use of the intellectual potential of the country, and the economy operates very ineffectively. Worse, we found that such a system forbids creative thinking at lower levels and so creates an antihumanistic society. From these experiences we discovered that the effectiveness of a modern economy and society depends on the intellectual level on which it is run.

Our revolution was in fact a synthesis of two revolutions. One was socialistic in the sense that it expropriated the expropriators, in this case the party leadership. The other was a social revolution produced as a by-product of the application of science. Our social revolution was that a new social stratum, the intelligentsia, took over the leadership of the country, while the old social stratum, the proletariat, regressed. We had to recognize that the proletariat, the manual workers, tend to diminish as the national wealth grows. I wouldn't like to be put in the position of being an opponent of the working class, especially as I am a Communist, but to glorify manual work and the proletariat is in this context to glorify backwardness. To accept this was a revolution in itself. It meant accepting that the intelligentsia, the mental workers, have become the center of society. It is not a question of their subjective qualities, but of their social role. It did not matter to the economy two hundred years ago whether schools were open or shut or intellectuals existed or not. Now the economy is based on intellectual work, and the intelligentsia is responsible not only for culture but also for material wealth. If we tried today to envisage the economy without intellectual workers, we would condemn the majority of the population to starve and the rest to live under the conditions of two or three hundred years ago. Research institutions, banks, means of transportation, schools, all are necessary today to produce the simplest commodity like a shoe. So the intelligentsia is steadily growing. The proletariat were a political power because, working in factories in large agglomerations, they could be organized. We must now expect the intelligentsia, already growing in the great agglomerations, to shoulder responsibilities the proletariat once had. So we came in Czechoslovakia to the conclusion that we must recognize the intelligentsia as the ruling stratum, which connects the citizen's interest with that of the whole nation. All the other social strata of the nation are a reservoir for it and it would have new qualities, leading not by power but by influence.

We paid a high price for not recognizing this in time, and another high price once we had recognized it, because we have now been occupied by those with political reasons for refusing to recognize it. In general, I think it is remarkable and sad that although the intelligentsia has created the cultural and material wealth of our times, they don't regard themselves as belonging to a social stratum. It is of the greatest importance that they should become conscious of their role. Here, in American universities, I am always told the intelligentsia can't be a leading force. Well, in Czechoslovakia it mobilized the nation, influenced the party apparatus and won over the majority of the Politburo. If the intelligentsia tries to solve the problems of humanism, then the whole nation will rally round it. After three months of occupation, you still see the strength of this unity. Just the other day I read of workers threatening to strike if anything happens to the newspapermen.

We also had to evaluate the problem of democracy. We learned, as Mr. Churchill said, that democracy is a very bad form of government but the best we have. But what democracy? We judged we could not rely on the mathematical form of democracy where a majority, the *vox populi* of the day, has the value of a decision of God. After all, in Germany the great majority joined Hitler in killing off democracy. Times have changed since the old days when the minority oppressed the majority and the majority wanted a quantitative democracy. We have heard from Mr. Marquand, the British M. P., that poor workers are a minority. Here in America the black people are a minority. A majority mechanism cannot decide what should happen to the Negroes. So there must be certain principles, a Magna Carta of human rights and socialism, which no majority can endanger. This duty gives government rights without which it cannot protect men. We have to define spheres where quantitative democracy can, and cannot, be applied.

Finally, freedom: We felt in Czechoslovakia that we must create a climate of freedom giving thinking people a wide space in which to act and react. We have, for instance, freedom of the press such as has never existed in any other country. In countries where there is legal security of the press, there are owners of the press who can restrict or prescribe what journalists do. In our country the owners, the trade unions, the rightist organization, the government, didn't dare interfere. The climate was also such that no journalist would have dared to abuse his freedom by writing on topics which may be popular but are not wise, like pornography. We learned that in a developed society people will act rationally if you give them freedom. To preserve this, one should not make an absolute, precise model in which everyone has to be happy, but build on a social stratum which, out of its own sense of responsibility to the nation, creates a favorable climate.

Yesterday, I heard Mr. Kennan put a very pessimistic view. I think we should be optimistic to see everything criticized here to the point where, if one didn't know the rest of the world, one would think this country is the worst of the lot. It is good to have such criticism. The intelligentsia has made this country the leading country in the world. The greatest weapon of this great nation is neither the atom bomb nor its dollars, but the intellect, and that is a tremendous weapon. A small country like Czechoslovakia, on the initiative of a few thousand intellectuals, has shaken a great power like Russia. At a meeting of party secretaries in Russia, the district secretaries asked the party leadership to do something about Czechoslovakia because of the danger of infection. In Russia forty percent of the intelligentsia is under thirty-five years of age, and we have a tremendous channel of communication, not by propaganda but in a genuinely democratic way. Here I see the greatest chance of the United States. I believe in the strength of the intellect and that sooner or later the American intelligentsia will realize that they can't be indifferent to what their intellect has created and must serve nothing but the truth and act regardless.

BRIAN WALDEN: The sympathy for Czechoslovakia in my country, Britain, is enormous. The personal sympathy that I and others feel for someone who has spent eleven years in prison for his beliefs is also enormous. But on your own confession you were, and are, a Communist. You didn't come from a backward fascist state. You came from the state of Thomas Masaryk and Beneš. But you chose to be a Communist. When the Communists took over in '48, rough things were done, as you know, to Social Democrats who wouldn't go along. Why did you ever get these ideas in the first place—some of which I detect you haven't wholly lost, when you talk about how the state should have rights over and above rights that citizens give it? Where did you go wrong? Or did you go wrong? Have I misstated the problem?

LOEBL: No, you have not misstated the problem, with one exception. I did not say that the state has special rights; on the contrary, I said it has no rights as such, only ones derived from its duty to protect the freedom of the citizen.

Now, as to why I joined the party and accepted the events of 1948. When I joined the party, we thought of fascism as a stage of capitalism. We thought that since capitalism was connected with fascism and all the persecution and misery typical especially of European capitalism in the late twenties and early thirties, the basic problem was to liquidate capitalism. It was an obvious form of logic, but things are not so simple. Even here, today, we have heard great emphasis laid on ownership. A related error is that we thought wealth grew by the exploitation of man, not scientifically through the exploitation of nature. The third mistake was to think that if the state takes over all means of production this in itself is a socialist measure.

We wanted to create a new society, but we made a lot of mistakes. As early as 1949 there was a group which tried to go what we called a specifically Czech way, meaning by that not a Soviet way. Only four months after the events of February 1948 (some call it a *putsch,* some a revolution), I was negotiating in the United States to obtain credits to compensate owners of factories we had nationalized. We were supposed to continue in November, but by that time I had been imprisoned and shortly after so were a lot of friends who had worked with me. Russians interrogated us and decided who should be imprisoned or not; they spoke quite openly about it. By then, Czechoslovakia was no longer an independent country. We had just one year of independence, from '48 to '49. After that anyone showing signs of independence was sentenced or executed, so that everyone should know that the slightest deviation from Russian ways would be punished by death or a life sentence. And, to be honest, even in prison it took me a long time (luckily, I had five years' solitary confinement, so I could think the problems over) to change my mind and clarify what had gone wrong.

MARTIN PERETZ: Mr. Loebl has all too willingly answered two outrageous questions today. I want, as an American, to say that I think it unseemly, and impolite, for an Englishman, who is therefore an accomplice to a wretched war against Biafra, in a room full of Americans, who are official and unofficial accomplices to the atomic bomb, to McCarthyism, and to Vietnam, to sit here and listen and judge.

QUESTION: Are the reforms in Czechoslovakia different from the ones in Yugoslavia?

LOEBL: Our reforms were influenced by the Yugoslavs, but in a more highly developed country we had other economic problems and put more emphasis on intellectual work and less on workers' ownership of enterprises.

QUESTION: Had the Soviet Union not intervened, what would you have regarded as the anticipated superiorities of the social system of Czechoslovakia as against, let's say, Britain under the Labour Party, or the United States?

LOEBL: I'll tell you where I think we would have felt better: in the formulation of our aims. We tried to construct a society giving a broader space for man to act. But we also needed a better managerial market system. So despite the fact that we would have tried to have a more modern theoretical conception, it would have taken us a generation at least to achieve the level of management in your country. As for democracy, we could have had a better constitution or laws, but, from my experience of living some years in Britain, it would have taken us many years to have as democratic an outlook as the British people. Democracy is in each man, and if we do not have enough democratically motivated people, then the best constitution will not create democracy.

QUESTION: You rejected majority rule and spoke of deducing the power of the state from moral and ethical principles. Who formulates these moral and ethical principles? The intelligentsia?

LOEBL: The United Nations has done remarkable work in this field. Naturally, in each country a number of experts would be entrusted to elaborate them. But what the United Nations has accepted would be acceptable, I think, for most nations and certainly for Czechoslovakia.

QUESTION: I was struck in Czechoslovakia by an apparent contradiction. The Czechoslovak Communists have been one of the most ignoble Communist parties, killing each other with great glee compared, for instance, to the Poles, who, under strong Russian pressure, did not kill each other. And yet Czechoslovakia had such a general resurgence of the ideals of freedom, decency and democracy among young and older leading Communists whose spirit and morale had not been broken by this long ten-year epoch. Did this resurgence come because of an ideal in Communism itself or because the Masaryk tradition of liberal democracy was so profound?

LOEBL: That's a difficult question to answer. A great deal depends on the relationship of the individual Communist parties to Stalin. The Czechoslovak government had accepted the Marshall Plan. Then Stalin rang up. He said, "I'm against that." And Gottwald, the Prime Minister of the government which had accepted the Marshall Plan, immediately said, "Naturally, we won't do that." And somehow the non-Communist ministers accepted it and it was a decision of the government. Once members of a government obey somebody other than the constitution or interests of their country, then they cannot stop sliding down the slippery slope. They have committed not only a political blunder but a real crime. The government, and especially Gottwald, knew the accusations against Slansky and his colleagues were false. He nevertheless approved the imprisonment of eleven Communists who were old friends of his. The reaction now has been a consequence of this. People have seen where abandoning the ethics of democracy can lead. If you had read what publicists wrote at that time! We must do anything to avoid a repetition of the fifties.

I want to prove to you that Gottwald knew exactly what was going on. Slansky was still secretary general of the party when the Russians told me to confess my criminal activities with him. I had never had anything to do with Slansky, only with Gottwald. A prisoner is a clever man, so I thought up what I thought was a very ingenious way out. I quoted all the conversations I had had with Gottwald as if I had had them with Slansky. Gottwald got my confession and knew that Slansky was innocent because he, Gottwald, had given the orders to me, and that I was innocent because I had acted according to his, Gottwald's, orders. One day the Russians told me that Gottwald had accepted my confession, which had helped the party very much, and they wouldn't forget it. I got only a life sentence.

QUESTION: Many enemies of socialist theory maintain that

socialism ignores human nature. How do you view this from your experience in Czechoslovakia? This is relevant to our situation in America because of the exaggerated value we place on individualism. For instance, most of the black militants in this country have not challenged the American value system in economics. They're asking basically for a piece of the corporate pie. Yet we look upon them as militants and revolutionaries.

LOEBL: Let me give you an example. We forced the peasants to go into collective farms and imprisoned many. That did not work at all and proved that human beings want and need freedom. So we gave the peasants freedom to leave the collectives, each would have got his share, and not a single one has left. This means that with care we could have achieved collective farms without force. It is possible to create a socialist economy by conserving human rights. The system we had, and Russia still has, and which I'm afraid we will have again, has nothing to do with socialism.

11

LATIN AMERICA IN THE SHADOW

ORLANDO ALBORNOZ: I will be brief. First, Latin America doesn't exist. I become a Latin American when I step down at Kennedy Airport; otherwise I am Venezuelan, and different from a Brazilian or a Chilean. To neglect the national identities and nationalism of Latin America (as the U. S. has neglected them) is to misunderstand its historical development. Second, there is the economic investment of the United States in Latin America. We all know Latin-American countries produce only one product, like oil in Venezuela or copper in Chile. However, there is a new type of development, which is investment in other areas of the economy. Rockefeller, for instance, is not only interested in oil in Venezuela; he produces all the eggs and chickens we eat in Venezuela, which makes my day very unpleasant every morning. Third, there is the United States paranoia about Communism in Latin America and the presence everywhere of the monster of the CIA, which takes many forms, from embassy officers to university professors. The United States is seen in Latin America as the imperialistic power. There are many European interests in Latin America. The British, for instance, may be decadent, but whatever is left of them is very much alive in Venezuela and other Latin-American countries. However, we see the United States as *the* imperialistic power in Latin America. Fourth, the foreign policy of the United States towards Latin America has been contradictory, and many people here know that. But between stability and change, the United States has always opted for stability, which means support for the upper class and oppression of the lower and middle classes in Latin America. It also means support for the army. Treaties with the Latin-American armies make them, or part of them, ready, with the U. S., to stop any nationalist movement. The Dominican Republic is a case in point.

The United States is creating in Latin America a number of tensions that might create a continental revolution and real chaos there. Many Americans ask me why there is so much anti-Americanism in Latin America. This is a very difficult thing to explain, but a large part is due, psychologically, to the way Americans behave in Latin America. Arrogant, full of power and money, always in the best hotels, they enjoy what the people cannot enjoy. We do appreciate the help of the naïve young kids of the Peace Corps, but they are a drop in the ocean.

ALEJANDRO MAGNET: The maintenance of the status quo has for too many years been the only policy of the United States in Latin America. From its inception the present inter-American system was related to the Cold War. The Rio Treaty, which provided for mutual assistance between Latin America and the United States, was practically a rehearsal for the NATO Treaty, which came two years later. The problem is that while other systems like NATO have evolved, the inter-American system has not. The many beautiful declarations about human rights, democracy and so on in the treaty have been for many years and in many places mere scraps of paper. When Mr. Papandreou spoke about Greece, I had to smile rather bitterly, because those things which shock people in NATO now have been common for us in Latin America for years. That's mainly because the inter-American system was above all a system of military security against Communism. We were rather too close to the United States and far away from the Soviet Union, and we were taken for granted. The United States was not aware of some basic facts about Latin America, such as the demographic explosion, the most dramatic in the whole world, the very rapid rise of expectations in a society which is basically Western combined with the rapid deterioration of economic circumstances. American policy was always behind the times, and reacted only to brutal facts. The first was the trip by Vice-President Nixon to Latin America in 1958. Mr. Nixon was hit in Lima and stoned in Caracas, yet he went on this trip because he was assured—this is in the records of the Committee on Foreign Relations of the Senate of the United States—that the political situation in Latin America was sure enough to permit him to make a quiet trip. That is proof that the United States government was simply not aware of things as they were in our countries. The other brutal fact was the rise of Castro in Cuba. After the Nixon trip the inter-American system, meeting in Bogotá, established for the first time, many years after the Marshall Plan, a beginning of inter-American help. After Fidel Castro, the Alliance for Progress was launched. I'm afraid that there is a direct relation between these events. The Alliance for Progress, which in the beginning correctly assumed that to promote economic progress in Latin America it was absolutely necessary to promote social change and a democratic revolution in Latin America, had a basic flaw. It was a system of cooperation between governments, and the American government continued to be obsessed by anti-Communism. Revolutions cannot be made by established governments. This kind of Maoism has too few disciples. We know now what has happened. And then one must take account of the enormous imbalance of power between the U. S. and the other members. The United States are condemned to intervene. They intervene if they act, and they intervene if they do not act. This point was brought out by an article in *The New York Times* when the United States recognized the regime in Venezuela about twenty years ago. It said: "If we recognize the Venezuela government, we back with all our power and moral authority a dictator. But if we don't recognize it, we intervene anyway, because we deny our recognition to a government that exists in a country." The problem, then, is how to organize the intervention of the United States: to maintain the status quo or to promote the revolution so badly needed in Latin America? The intervention in the Dominican Republic was an enormous setback because it returned to the old policy of simple anti-Communism and awakened a profound and ancient suspicion in Latin America against American intervention. Someone has said that the only way to avoid revolution is to make it first, and those who study Latin American circumstances are absolutely convinced that sooner or later there will be revolution in our countries. We do not want to have the United States disengage from Latin America. It would be unrealistic and would not help. What we do want is the United States to help make a democratic revolution in Latin America.

GINO GERMANI: I do not think the United States can disengage from Latin America. But I doubt very much whether their intervention can be in favor of a democratic revolution in the Latin countries. The social and political system in the United States is not likely to produce any coherent policy towards Latin America favorable to changes necessary to break the present stagnation and solve the tremendous and growing problems which now exist. The stagnation, which may be said to have begun in the last decade (after fifteen years of growth) in the major Latin-American countries, is quite similar to the stasis characterizing many European powers during the interwar period. The major Latin-American countries have reached a middle level of economic development similar to the level of those interwar European nations. The similarity, of course, is limited by many differences of economic, social and cultural structures. But what is analogous is the type of intra-elite conflicts, the crisis of the middle classes and the rapid mobilization and rise of the lower strata. In some European countries this configuration led to the pseudo-solution provided by fascism. It is not by chance that fascism was successful in three Latin countries—Italy, Spain and Portugal. The present danger in Latin America is not the rise of what we could call "classic fascism," a historical impossibility, but of a "functional substitute," mainly based on the military. The purpose, as in "classic fascism," is the forced demobilization of the lower classes. Now, the sectors of the Latin American elites which are ready for this kind of solution have their counterpart in powerful sectors of society in the United States, which are important in shaping the final decisions vis-à-vis Latin America.

True, the inconsistencies of United States policy affects even the various public agencies which intervene in foreign affairs, the State Department, the Defense Department, the CIA, et cetera, all of which may—not always—simultaneously pursue different goals. But, given the nature of the structural factors, the resulting orientation may well be to support the more reactionary sectors within Latin America. If this diagnosis is correct, the possibilities of peaceful social change are remote. The final outcome, perhaps after long delay and stagnation, will be catastrophic, not least for the United States.

I will add only one last point, a general one. The conflicting, contrasting attitudes towards United States intervention prevailing in the various nations of the planet can be explained on the basis of one single, simple law: The favor with which each nation regards American intervention is inversely proportional to the distance of the nation involved from the U.S.S.R. and directly proportional to its distance from the United States.

12

ASIA: DIALOGUE WITH CHINA

SABURO OKITA: Let me first give some figures of Japan's economic growth. In 1966 we had a Gross National Product (GNP) of 100 billion U. S. dollars. Last year, in 1967, our Gross National Product increased to 120 billion dollars.* This year, 1968, the estimate is that it will be 140 billion. My center, Japan Economic Research, produces eighteen-month forecasts every quarter, and according to our latest estimate the GNP will be 164 billion dollars in 1969. This is a rather fantastic expansion, and even if we assume a somewhat slower rate in the coming years, by around 1975 Japan's GNP will about equal that of the United Kingdom and France combined. I am not giving these figures to boast. We feel somewhat embarrassed with so much economic expansion. Recently, there has grown up a kind of GNP mentality gap among Japanese.

Ordinary people in Japan do not feel the rapid expansion in economic output. It somehow keeps on growing without them. Also, we do not know exactly how to use these enormous additional resources: sixty billion dollars, just for three years! There are three alternatives. The first is to improve our housing and urban conditions, which have been neglected for the sake of productive investment and export promotion. The second is to increase economic aid to developing countries, particularly in Asia. We spent some seven tenths of one percent of GNP last year for

* The GNP of Italy in 1967 was $67 billion, of France $109 billion, of the U. K. $108 billion, of West Germany $121 billion.

260

foreign aid, but this is still not sufficient, particularly when GNP is increasing so rapidly. The third is a military buildup, especially in face of possible disengagement by the U. S. from Asia and, as we see in the newspapers, of more emphasis on improving U.S.–European relations. This places Japan in a dilemma. Most people are not prepared for any kind of military responsibility. Partly because of our historical experience, partly because of our postwar education, most people are very much against military action of any kind. There may be some change in attitude, but, even in that case, I think this would be limited to some step-up in a purely defensive effort for Japan itself. The majority of Japanese will be very much against sending Japanese military force abroad. For the nuclear-weapon system, Japan will have to depend on the United States for many years to come, because we feel atomic weapons may bring danger rather than safety.

Given this background, it would be necessary for U. S. policy throughout Asia to have closer exchanges of views with Asian countries. Partial military disengagement, such as the evacuation from some bases, may be necessary for the sake of long-term considerations, but on intellectual and policy levels mutual understanding will be very much necessary. Any move by the United States to start a dialogue with mainland China will be a constructive measure which will make the Japanese position easier. What we do not like to see is the building up of too much military strength which may temporarily seem to strengthen security but in the long run may not be to the benefit of Japan, other Asian countries or the United States herself. In Asia we need more dialogue, and U. S. policy should encourage such a dialogue among Asian countries.

ABDUL GAFOOR NOORANI: It seems to me rather significant that while once upon a time there was an obsession in this country about America's image in the Third World, this has now ceased to matter. We have discussed America's relationship with her NATO allies and Soviet-bloc countries, but the relationships which she has forged with the countries of the Third World we have hardly discussed at all. In the Dulles era, there was an impatience with the Third World countries. Mr. Dulles had little use for them and branded nonalignment as something immoral. This was followed by the Kennedy Administration, which went to the other extremes of glorifying the attitudes and prejudices of the Third World countries and expecting far too much of them. In truth, the policy of these countries did not stem from ideological or moral considerations, and I say this very much as a person who comes from Nehru's India; they stemmed from self-interest, as anywhere else in the world. A stage has now been reached of subdued exasperation with the problems of these countries. However natural and even legitimate this may be, it would be a pity if it leads to a neglect of the problem altogether. To my mind, in the post-Vietnam phase, the Third World will assume not less but even more importance. The prospect of détente between America and China provides a challenge to America's foreign policy. The area in which American policy has been most subjected to criticism has been its policy towards China. It has been said, particularly by Asian countries, that America's failure to recognize Red China is at the root of Asian problems. Now that there is a prospect of America's opening up some kind of a dialogue with Communist China, it would be a pity if she were to embark on it alone. A test of her statesmanship would be to do so in concert with Asian countries and so make the challenge that is facing her their challenge as well.

MOCHTAR LUBIS: There has been a tendency in American foreign policy in Asia to support a long line of totalitarian corrupt governments just for the sake of containing Communism. This has done a great deal of harm. I speak with some anger of a small number of CIA agents who tried to influence the destiny of my people. America and Russia, by playing power politics, have kept the Middle East in turmoil for years. In Latin America the United States has supported Trujillo and very corrupt regimes in Nicaragua, Cuba, Venezuela. Things like that have struck us with horror and fear. What does the U.S. really want to achieve in the world? To me this is not clearly defined yet. Social fragmentation in the Third World I welcome, because this is a part of the process of nation building in our region of the world. Modern communications, modern industries, modern ideas frighten our traditional societies so that fragmentation is an essential part of building a new cohesive society. The danger is the continual intervention of outside powers. America, Soviet Russia and later Red China have all been guilty of this. As foreign policy is some kind of reflection of one's own domestic development, I am struck with dismay by what Mr. Roy Innis told us two days ago. It is tragic that a group of people in America, the most advanced country in our world technologically and culturally, should feel that they need to crawl back under the protection of the color of their skin, that only by doing that they feel they can live creatively and constructively. This will influence the attitudes of people in other parts of the world to the United States. How you solve this problem will have a great bearing on your relations with our countries.

On the other hand, I also think America has done a great deal in keeping a balance of sanity in our world. In Asia, for example, America despite all the negative examples I have mentioned has played a quite constructive role. Today my own country is experiencing continual subversive actions led by Red China and in some part also by Moscow, and we feel that the presence of America has greatly helped to allow us to stand on our democratic constitution and defend our own people. I wouldn't like to see America disengage herself from the Asian scene altogether. I would like to see her come to some arrangement with Red China and Russia so that big powers intervene less in the Third World. We need time to build viable democratic societies, and this is where I would suggest that American foreign policy be directed to less intervention and to more participation in building viable nations in the Third World.

SULAK SIVARAKSA: I agree that America should certainly have a selective-disengagement policy, there should be various power blocs, like a United Europe, Southeast Asia and so on, and a real dialogue must be established with Russia and China. I am quite convinced that this could be realized in the long run if America really wants to live in a more harmonious world with real understanding of other peoples' diversified histories. But will, and can, America do so? Unless America undergoes real self-criticism regarding values and man's part in the universe, she will go on, as now, policing the world, sometimes like a goodhearted uncle, sometimes like a wicked big brother, because she trusts none but herself. Unless America can get rid of her neurotic fear of Communism, which is not easy, the so-called "free world's" external policy will be dominated by fear, not by proper understanding. China and Russia too view the U.S. with fear and distrust, and they too have reason for their viewpoint. China used to admire America no less than we in Siam did when the U.S. was not a colonial power; American people, missionaries, philanthropic organizations did a great deal for China and Southeast Asia. China is in a vital revolutionary stage, perhaps more so than you, and its proletarian system makes it much worse. But I do not see why one must not take a reasonable view, try to understand China and develop the dialogue with her. If one has that in mind, one can plan the settlement in Vietnam much more effectively. In the initial stage, military and economic commitments to the region will have to be guaranteed by the U.S., so that the leaders of these countries feel secure. Economic aid must be given to develop the region as a strong unit equal to America in the long run. Australia and Japan must be persuaded to take more leading roles politically, economically and culturally, and, to some degree, militarily. Right now America is accused, with justification, of treating her Asian allies as junior partners. When you called a summit conference in Manila, the only summit power was the U.S. The rest went there under your leadership to join you in the Vietnam War. This humiliated the younger generation, as one can see clearly in countries with a free opinion. Where freedom is denied, many people join the underground movements and are accused of being Communist subversionists. Of course, there are Communist subversive elements—that is how Communism works. The early Christians did similar things. If the rulers are honest and capable, and listen to public opinion, I do not see how the Communists could take control of such countries. In the case of corrupt and inefficient leadership, the Communists have a good chance of gaining ground. Indonesia was a case in point. Siam could very well be the next. In short, the moral, economical and military commitment of the U.S. is needed in Southeast Asia, but the U.S. must also pursue a long-term policy of not letting us be dependent upon you and you alone.

MINOO MASANI: I would like to share a few thoughts about how the U. S. looks to us in Asia these days, first as a source of aid and economic assistance, and second as a guarantor of collective security.

As a voluntary contribution by the taxpayers of a great country for what may broadly be called purposes of altruism or intelligent long-term self-interest, the economic assistance given by the United States since the last world war, both in Europe and in Asia, is unparalleled in human history. But the fact is that much of this aid has been wasted. It is wasted when it is given unconditionally and diverted by governments to heavy engineering and high-cost showy projects of a gigantic nature while neglecting the fundamental needs of agriculture and the people. Therefore, I would urge not aid without strings, but aid with the right kind of strings. The German government has, in a declaration made by my friend Herr Walter Scheel when he was Minister of Economic Cooperation four or five years ago, shown the correct path. That is to restrict government-to-government aid and grants to infrastructure, and to ask that for everything else countries go to the money market and raise equity capital. Equity capital comes into our country at its own risk, while government loans come at our risk. However badly we use them, we have to pay capital and interest, with the result that today my country finds it difficult to repay loans and is really paying out more than it is able to get from now on.

Now, about collective security: we in Asia, as well as others in Europe, have been enchanted by the shield of the deterrent that the United States has been able to provide. It has even made it possible for us to indulge in the policy of carrying on dialogues with our neighbors of Communist China which resulted in 1962 in an invasion of our country. Under the stress of the popular upsurge that followed, our neutralist Prime Minister, Mr. Nehru, had to invite the powers of the West to give us military assistance, and we got instant response from the United States and Britain. The effectiveness of that became evident when the Chinese stopped their attack, and Mr. Khrushchev a few days later explained the Chinese cease-fire by the fact that, as he put it, the Anglo-American imperialist halter was on the point of being put round India's neck, to prevent which terrible event the Chinese desisted.

Professor Carl Kaysen has referred to the uselessness of military power. I wish it were so, but recent events do not seem to me to warrant such a conclusion. Did the victory of Israel in its defense or the brutal Soviet occupation of Czechoslovakia demonstrate the uselessness of military power? Even in the case of Vietnam, is it the failure of the military or the American public's lack of a will to win which is the real reason why this country has got sick and tired of that war?

There is a consensus, as you see, that all of us want the U. S. presence in our part of the world, as indeed everyone has agreed that the U. S. presence in Western Europe is also desired. What is lacking perhaps is United States maturity, will and conviction to use that military power. I notice that Mr. Buchan, in his paper, asks the question "Are the United States prepared to stand the strain of being the world's strongest power?" A little later he says, "The Russians seem to have staying power, still more the Chinese; have the Americans?" It is this element that seems to be lacking in making a security system credible in our eyes. To us in South and Southeast Asia, the defense of every country in our region is part of the defense of our own country. A concrete example exists with Indonesia today. If South Vietnam had not been defended all this time, Indonesia would have gone under. The Swatantra Party, to which I belong, has stood for the last seven or eight years for my country sending a detachment of troops, even as a token force, to Vietnam so that we could stand alongside your boys and the boys from Australia and Korea and other parts of the world who have been carrying on the fight for freedom. A vacuum has been caused in our part of the world by the British withdrawal. There is a need to fill it. Some of us are trying hard to bring about a system of regional security with India at one end, Japan in the Far East, and Australia and New Zealand down south. But this system of collective security will still need to be underwritten by the United States and the West. I think this is a necessary basis for building a future world order to which we can all belong.

OWEN HARRIES: I would like to say something about selective disengagement, as raised by Brzezinski. Most of the countries of Southeast Asia are by now reconciled, and I think "reconciled" is the word, to the fact that some degree of American disengagement is likely.

This poses a number of highly important and difficult questions. How selective will disengagement be? What principle or criterion of selection will be applied? On which side of the fence will a country fall in the process of making disengagement more or less selective? To say, like Kaysen, if I understood him, that the selection would be settled by United States national interests is to reformulate rather than to answer the question. I think if one examines the course of arguments that have gone on in the last two or three years over Vietnam, one can see that there are very considerable disagreements upon the sort of principles on which American commitment should be made. One line is that one should back only viable countries, stable countries, countries whose governments have popular support. That sounds fine. The trouble is that there aren't many such countries in the Third World, and they are the least vulnerable to the kind of attacks that one must expect against the countries in the Third World—indirect attack by subversion. In some way one should do almost the direct opposite and draw up criteria in terms of those areas where Communist expansion is most likely to take place. Not only are such commitments likely to be the most costly, the most numerous and, after Vietnam, I must say, the most unproductive, they are also likely to be morally unattractive in that the most vulnerable governments are often the least democratic.

Another important aspect people often point to is the nature of commitments. How deeply in the past has the United States gone in, how much did it influence the domestic situation and the regional situation? Certain parties and people and groups in such countries have gone out on a limb in support of United States policies. Disengagement reflects on the creditability of other commitments the United States might undertake.

I suppose the criterion most used by students of international relations is that of the promotion of the stability of the international system. What effect would the loss of one country have on the balance and stability of a particular region, and through that on the central balance? One finds the widest sort of disagreements between, say, what Mr. Kennan, Mr. Brzezinski, Mr. Buchan and Mr. Schlesinger have said about how important Southeast Asia is in terms of international politics. You get quite different answers. In short, if selective disengagement is going to happen, and it probably is going to happen, it is a process that is incredibly complicated and fraught with very great difficulties.

13

DILEMMAS OF DEVELOPMENT

LEO MATES: The short-term problems of Asia are connected with security, and it is understandable that this issue is in the forefront of our discussions. Nevertheless, security guaranteed from outside is in itself a form of permanent intervention. It may be understandable when there is a threat. But a stable situation calls for domestically or locally based security. Now, this brings in the long-term issue of the economic basis for development. It was impressive to listen to the incredibly fast development of an already highly developed country in Asia, Japan. But we haven't heard figures about the much less inspiring rates of development in other countries in Southeast Asia, and it is certain they would need that development much more. Now, this is where an outside presence is expected. Yet I believe that in the long term the ability of the great powers to promote accelerated development is greatly overrated. Mr. Brzezinski has said he is sad because the United States is not likely to internationalize foreign aid. I submit that even if foreign aid were stepped up and internationalized, this could not solve the problems of the Third World. We are deluding ourselves if we believe that this is the crux. The crux is the capacity for innovation inside these societies themselves. Of course, aid from the United States to Asian countries plays an important role. But innovations within their societies are the only base for any repetition of the Japanese miracle.

The truth is that not only is the economic gap widening but, more important still, so is the gap in the capacity of different

269

societies to innovate. If we arrange countries by levels of economic development, we see that we have more movement, innovation and modernization in the highly developed countries, and more rigidity and less ability and capability of introducing change in the less developed. I don't think this is simply a question of values, although these are important. Moral values and general views which have grown up in the more developed countries through history spread and become part of political life in societies where normally they would not have evolved. So development in recipient countries is a mixture. On the one hand you have a very low level of economic development and considerable rigidity in society; on the other, political forms spread from other societies as a result of the general tendency to share achievement and values irrespective of the applicability of one country's forms to another. The result is tension and change brought about violently and not by any kind of normal political evolution.

All this means that the interchange between highly developed societies and the rest of the world involves responsibilities which transcend material relations. I cannot say how highly developed societies can bring a sense of personal dignity and liberation and modern democratic attitudes into areas where they have either never developed or been lost in the past century. But I do realize that the problem exists and that, in the search for new approaches in industrial countries, values are created which will, whether one likes it or not, spread, and come into contact with realities in other areas different from the realities which engendered them, and that this creates a problem of communication. While the world is shrinking in terms of communications and transport, economically and socially it is becoming more and not less divided, in a kind of expanding universe of differences. And yet political forms and values tend to be shared and universal, at least as aspirations, because of communications. The result is great tensions within, and perhaps between, societies.

14

NOT BY COCA-COLA ALONE

ENRIQUE TIERNO GALVAN: America offers a unique example of the interaction of economic forces and political institutions. The basic model the United States has fostered has been the capitalist "enterprise." The consciousness of interests and the need to organize competition in accordance with these interests, as well as an overestimation of wealth as the mainspring of collective and individual action, have determined the formal structure of American politics. This is seen in lobbyism, in electoral campaigns and, above all, in the prestige that wealth carries in political institutions, and which is reflected in Supreme Court rulings. The intimate relation between politics and wealth has been the cohesive element in American society and the major force for social integration.

Something similar has happened in American foreign policy. The foreign projection of American power may be considered a direct result of private interests which are an integral part of the political apparatus. American imperialism does not correspond to traditional patterns of national imperialism based on an idealistic concept of the world. The Americans have never been fooled by what lay behind European imperialisms. They have been quite aware that foreign policy, trade and imperialism always coincided. They have been very naïve and frank about this link between politics and economics.

The consequence of the American conception of power as economic power has been to generate dislike among other nations.

271

For the Spaniard in the street, the United States is an exclusively quantitative economic complex. He does not see the moral conception behind its policies, for instance in Vietnam. Nor can he understand the strong links between the United States, a democracy, and the Spanish dictatorship, like many others in the world. The basic question is whether the ruling class and government of the United States have any conception of ends. Power is not a moral force. A global power without a global idea is not a global power. A ruling class unable to explain the future from a general conception is not a proper ruling class. Policies of compromise, of the interests of the moment, are not global policies. The revolution from policies to the mere exercise of power is an immoral revolution. The United States cannot offer the world "quality," only "quantity." The American model may be discarded as a model for future world organization.

However, things can change, are changing. Since World War Two, the "private enterprise" model has declined. The replacement of a free competitive market by monopolies and trusts as a result of the Cold War has changed the character of American society. The discontent among American intellectuals is also evidence of change. The decline of the "enterprise" model without a substitute being found has produced a sense of perplexity and distrust in regard to the patterns of behavior and political institutions that govern the country. European ideologies, traditionally idealistic and abstract, have invaded the United States. There is a very noticeable Europeanization of America, as can be seen in the progressive movement of students and intellectuals, as also in the totalitarian response on the right in the last Presidential campaign. On balance, America has been shifting towards the reactionary right. (By "reactionary" I do not mean conservative. A conservative thinks that progress may be destructive when it speeds up. A reactionary tries to build a barrier against progress, using the instruments of progress.) Most of the Western nations are going through a similar process, another sign that America is receiving its basic political stimuli from Europe.

In future, the United States can offer the world two different models or outlooks on life. One is to solve the internal problems now dogging the American people and provide a feasible model (positive or negative) for the West. These problems are (a) the intellectual rebellion, (b) racial disorder, (c) the latent generalized class struggle, and (d) how to harmonize U. S. foreign policy with the internal moral crisis. The other possible American example would be a change of foreign policy, based on a deeper understanding of and respect for other nations. This would mean drastic decolonization, economic and political.

In conclusion, there exists no strict American model, but an Atlantic model trying to reconcile material progress with man's moral and spiritual aspirations. In this model, the United States has something in common with Europe. It is not a traditional "nation," by which I mean a community held together by common beliefs that survive historical changes; it is a "people"—that is, a society which fuses a number of heterogeneous elements in the crucible of common interests. Europe too is becoming a "people" as the romantic nineteenth-century concept of "nation" begins to fade. In this sense, the United States might become the future "Atlantic model" and provide new answers to cultural challenges that are the common heritage of the old European nations.

EDWARD SHILS: America offers something more than quantity, as Professor Tierno Galvan believes. It has a strong cultural magnetism, which is a composite of two things. One is its association with material power in the world. The other is the exemplification of the ideal manifested in accomplishment.

The spirit is drawn by power, more than many would like to believe. Not just earthly power, but also transcendent power. That is what religion and science are about, the location of the final powers which govern our existence. Even intellectual and cultural activities not on that lofty level are concerned with power in the sense that they aspire to some ideal which doesn't exist in what already exists. Now, all of these things have a physical locus. In every society there is a capital the boys in the provinces yearn to reach, not just because the girls are easier to get or there are better jobs or restaurants stay open longer. There is a sort of golden life to be lived in the big city, the golden life in the culture. In the same way, some countries are metropolitan vis-à-vis other areas of the world, and that is the case with the United States today.

The United States does not simply impose its influence through institutions like the U. S. Information Service, which I think generally a discredit to American culture. It also offers a certain manifestation of the ideal. Naturally, no country could have a monopoly of creativity, though some societies do seem to me more stupid than others. Nevertheless, there is the extension outward of a powerful society with a powerful culture. It is in the nature of a strong culture to be expansive because other minds reach out for that which is thought to be richer, more life-giving, more connected with the center of vitality of the universe. And that's what we've seen developing in the United States. There has been a great growth of power and, partly but not entirely independent of it, growth of cultural creativity.

Before the Civil War, when Germany was beginning to establish modern science, the United States was nothing. There were a few amateurs, like Edison, but nothing very significant. The situation began to change, partly impelled by the feeling that if a country is powerful it must have cultural institutions corresponding to its grandeur. That didn't account for American literature, but the development of university culture, on which I want to concentrate, had a lot to do with power. American pilgrimages to Germany, which was the center of the academic cosmos at that time, ran on from the Civil War almost to 1914. By that time, new institutions adapted from Germany had become implanted in the United States and begun to generate a new type of intellectual culture. After the First World War this began to expand, and after the Second the American university became a model for the world. Our German friends have been witnesses to a titanic struggle to break what is now felt to be the bonds of those institutions which in their great days provided models for America. There is at least one reform proposed for each *Land* [German state] on the official side and one per professor or student on the unofficial side, all delivered in a great clamor, like contemporary music. But most call for the dissolution of the faculty system and the establishment of departments. Americans would regard departments as in the nature of things. Something as stupid and unimaginative as a department is thought by Europeans to be one of the secrets of American universities—and rightly so, I say it with all immodesty. By historical accident, not wisdom, the Americans hit on this thing. One could mention other reasons, such as giving representation in university government to the middle ranks, having more assistant professors and giving them proper academic tenure and status, and giving associate professors a vote in the department. Again, these things seem as self-evident as the Virgin Birth to a pious Christian in Italy in the nineteenth century. Yet that is what Europeans bring back from the Promised Land when they go home.

Or take a look at students. Indian students have been disrupting their more or less educational institutions for years. They had found all sorts of grounds for public disturbance—bus fares, cinema prices, insolence of porters, failure in examinations, difficulty in examination questions, all sorts of grounds. Indian universities may not lead the world in many subjects, but they certainly lead in student disorder. The Japanese are very good, too. But neither got any credit for it. Berkeley did. Then the Europeans took it on. The Indians were awfully good, skilled in all techniques of fighting, land fighting, water fighting, underwater fighting, everything. But the Americans, with one limited technique, the sit-in strike, because of its occurring in a powerful country, at a famous institution, inspired the ragamuffins everywhere, and now, as we know, there are established sitters-in as well as established anti–sitters-in.

The American standard, then, is *the* standard. If a country wants to make itself miserable it says, "We are only spending one tenth of one percent of our GNP for scientific research against the United States's three percent." The U. S. figure was arrived at entirely by accident and is probably not true anyway, but it is a kind of golden calf carried around in every capital where a chap with a test tube wants to have a bigger one. The same is true with the proportion of children in school. If the Americans do it, we ought to do it. If the Americans make a mistake, we ought to make it, too. Despite the animosity toward Coca-Cola culture, nobody questions such figures. They are standards by which a country measures its own movement into the center of vitality, into civilization.

There are plenty of unsatisfactory things in the United States my European friends aren't aware of. They don't see the enfeeblement of undergraduate education. They see the glories of research. They can't see the products of teaching. Who knows what the results of teaching are? Even more serious is the enfeeblement, if you can still speak of it as having any strength, of public elementary and secondary education in the States, and I'm not just speaking about Negroes, either. As everyone knows who has had experience in higher educational systems in Europe and America, American undergraduates come in knowing very little except by accident. Europeans see excellence in American postgraduate education and research. They don't see the extraordinary dilapidation down below. Nor do they see the most serious thing of all—the decay of the educated public; and in the presence of editors of highbrow magazines, I say that advisedly. Writers for independent periodicals now come almost exclusively from the universities. Public intellectual life in the United States, instead of being maintained by persons from a variety of professions—journalism, law, medicine, business, the government service, politics—is just another place where academics publish their reflections and research. This academicization is a very bad thing for the intellectual life of a society (quite apart from its ruinous effect on the language), and bad for the intellectuals themselves. It doesn't give them the connection with external reality they need.

Nevertheless, the world has benefited on the whole from America's intellectual ascent, because in many fields of science and scholarship American standards are extremely high. It has also gained to some extent in self-understanding. The merit of Americans is their outgoingness and curiosity about the world. American Sinological, Indological, Japanese, African and other studies since the war have greatly increased the amount of self-understanding. In India, for example, you have veritable hordes of Ph.D. locusts descending on the country. I don't think they do any harm, and in the end they do India good, though sometimes they injure sensibilities.

The severe problem of American ascendancy in science and scholarship is the brain drain. It isn't just the money, I want to emphasize that. It is the greater intellectual stimulation which scientists and academics have in the better American higher institutions. This permits them to realize their best qualities in the performance of something which is of universal value. Nonetheless, it is damaging. The recent receipt of the Nobel Prize by Professor Gabind Khorana, from the Punjab, who is professor at the University of Wisconsin, has generated pride in India that "one of our boys made it." But it also generates grief—"What is wrong with us that we can't keep such a man at home?" In their own countries, great scientists would generate the same enthusiasm— under greater obstacles, it is true—as among their pupils in Wisconsin or Imperial College, London. But as things are, they have British or American pupils, not Indian or Pakistani pupils. That is a major difference. The growth of intellectual institutions in underdeveloped countries is greatly hampered by the brain drain because awareness of being acknowledged by the world's intellectual community is a necessary condition for the development of one's own intellectual communities. When we speak about the autonomy of countries we do not mean just military or economic independence. Societies need to establish their own processes of creativity. These processes can't be ignited without having some of these genii who are being drawn into America or Britain. Then, of course, not all scientists or scholars are just scientists or scholars; they also work in industry and applied fields. These too are being drawn away. The National Health Service of Great Britain, one of the great humanitarian accomplishments of the postwar period, wouldn't be possible without Pakistani and Indian physicians. Nor would the American hospital system without the Latin Americans who come here and the Englishmen who can leave because Pakistanis and Indians man their hospitals. This is a very serious matter. In effect, the underdeveloped countries are paying a subsidy to advanced ones. This ought to be publicized much more. The advanced countries should take seriously some means of compensating the underdeveloped countries for this very great subsidy which they are receiving.

GEORGE F. KENNAN: I would like to put in a defensive word for U.S.I.S. and government efforts abroad. As ambassador in Yugoslavia, I was rather enthusiastic about what U.S.I.S. was doing there. The things it did were rather innocent. It operated three excellent libraries in three Yugoslav cities, superior both in selection and in quality to the libraries in any American city of equivalent size. They were enormously appreciated, the literary and reference sections were consulted by thousands of people. It also gave news broadcasts in the local language. These were listened to by an estimated audience of about one million and were better than any I have ever heard over the commercial media at home. They were not slanted, because our people were intelligent enough to know that a sophisticated public such as we find all through Eastern Europe wouldn't tolerate anything like that. They want facts, and this is what we were giving. We brought a variety of musical and theatrical functions, art exhibits, to Yugoslavia. I think we would all have been poorer without it.

The Yugoslavs were free to choose what they wanted out of this fare. This is true in the broader sense of the impact of the so-called American way of life. It is imposed on no one at all. All over the world, it flows from us outward because people abroad have a spongelike thirst for certain phenomena of our culture. If they feel anti-American, it is something in themselves that they are rebelling against. I remember Eric Erikson, when we crossed on a boat in

1933 from Europe and he was emigrating from Germany, saying the Nazi feared the Jew in himself. In nine cases out of ten where we find cultural anti-Americanism, it is because these people fear the American in themselves. What we throw up to the surface of our life and exhibit to other people is pretty ghastly, because most of it passes through a commercial filter which doesn't pollute it politically so much as give it a tinge of vulgar inanity. People who search in this country for other things can usually find them. Unfortunately there is nothing much we can do about this, short of tackling the domination of the whole process of mass communication by advertising interests. Even publishing companies are now falling like soldiers in the field before the efforts to buy them up of people like Time-Life and commercially supported magazines. This is where our problem lies.

LILLIAN HELLMAN: Like most people who deal in facts—facts, in my case, being imaginary characters in imaginary conversations—I dislike theories. But I am on my way to finding one that disturbs me: not one social scholar here, including Mr. Shils, in discussing our culture has made any mention of music, architecture, painting or movies. When Mr. Shils came to speak of literature only two people appeared in his talk: Edmund Wilson, and even there he chose one of the very few weak pieces Wilson ever wrote, and Lionel Abel. Nowhere at this conference was there a discussion of any art form. I'm sorry for that. But then I have long been puzzled by sociology, what it includes and excludes. Perhaps the difference lies in the gulf between education, as Mr. Shils describes it in American colleges, and true culture, which may not always have to do with formal education. In any case, I am uneasy that there are so few creative artists here. Saul Bellow was, indeed, invited, but we would have still been a very small number. This is all said too late to be a contribution. It is a complaint.

IV
POSTSCRIPT
INTELLECTUALS
AND POWER

15

LEFTS, NEW AND OLD

SAM BROWN: I spoke at the beginning of the conference with a certain sense of irony about being in such intimate relationship with the intellectual establishment. I come now with less sense of irony than of tragedy. To begin with, I am uncomfortable about the whole style of the conference, which says it's meeting to discuss serious problems for four hours a day and provides six hours a day to drink and eat. I'm intrigued by that schedule and the cocktail-party style it reflects. The question of style reflects a deeper problem. We come here with the conviction that rational and calm discussion must be pursued at all costs, when it seems to me today there is cause for passion reflected clearly among my contemporaries. Maybe it's because five thousand of them have been so passionate that they have been driven to leave this country because of the war in Vietnam. Maybe it's because another five thousand are either in jail or preparing to go to jail for terms of three to five years because of that war. It's very difficult for people facing questions about the rest of their lives, or the next five years of their lives, to remain calm and analytical.

One question about this conference was raised this morning by Mr. Emmanuel. The people here come with a degree of expertise, not because of their reputations for creativity. We discuss statistics and figures about where things seem to be going rather than where we might help to make them go. I'm intrigued that the people from the United States include Messrs. Ball, Bundy, Brzezinski and Schlesinger, all of whom were wrong on Vietnam from the beginning, and not Messrs. Morgenthau, Bowles, Lippman, Stone and others, who were right on Vietnam from the beginning. I find it symptomatic that people such as Norman Mailer, Mary McCarthy, Susan Sontag and I. F. Stone are not included. I'm intrigued that even a black militant showed up dressed and willing to talk calmly to whites in a fashion I find uncharacteristic of most black militants in this country. It would have been interesting to have had a man who has been very influential in the intellectual life of America in the last several years—Eldridge Cleaver. There are a lot of other people running around in fatigues and berets who might have given this conversation a different tone.

Then there are the people like myself who supposedly represent the New Left. I want to deny my role as any sort of representative Rennie Davis and others who have been influential in defining the of the New Left. I'm intrigued that Tom Hayden, Carl Oglesby, direction of the young left are not present. I find it symptomatic that when you look for youth, you look to the student establishment, the Columbia *Spectator,* the Harvard *Crimson* and the National Student Association, rather than to the more creative and more fundamentally critical trends in student politics.

When we look abroad, we don't find Juan Bosch or Michael Foot here; there are no Africans. We talked all day yesterday about United States foreign policy without any representation from the Middle East. I find that intriguing. CIA involvement in the history of the International Association for Cultural Freedom may have been another example of American overkill. It may have been unnecessary of the CIA to maintain a direction for a group which seems capable of maintaining itself, without the CIA, in a direction the agency would surely find agreeable.

Then, I have found the content of the discussion itself fascinating, especially in the Western European, NATO bias of the entire conversation. There seems to be fundamental commitment to NATO and mutual deterrence without any attempt to deal with the questions which are raised today about NATO kinds of alliance in the world.

A standard theme for discussion in the United States in young intellectual circles, the failure of welfare liberalism in the United States, was not discussed. Nor was leisure, and what's to be done about it; nor police—I'm intrigued that there are no police here, for *there*'s an intellectual undercurrent that will have more determining effects on American policy than all of us put together; education, and what you do at the primary and secondary level, has been raised in only the most superficial manner; as also the basic question whether liberal values inevitably lead to Vietnam. In short, we have not talked about the failure of the people in this room and others like them and how that reflects upon ourselves and upon society.

Another lack is the preoccupation with asking black people how to define black problems rather than asking ourselves how we can have some impact on white America's racism. That is related to a question which has been addressed several times here, but in the wrong way—the relationship of the intellectual to power. We talk about the failure of power to respond to our criticism, but we do not talk about how we should relate to power. Powerlessness is a false issue. Clearly the men in this room have in the past had power and influence. The question is how we find a way to define normatively what values we should employ in determining our relationship to power. I note that that's also a failure of most of my colleagues. The criticism that we attack society without being willing to run society is in some ways true. That reflects the failure on the part of all of us to deal with that demiurgic power within us all that can lead so easily to chaos. Because we don't know how to deal with power, we evade the question of how to deal with man, or because we don't know how to deal with man we evade the question of how to deal with power. Because of that failure, we are likely to be in for a period of chaos. In that chaos, the tragedy is that the people of America can't look to those of us gathered in Princeton this week and say, "Where is it we can go?"

ARTHUR M. SCHLESINGER, JR.: I've never been to a conference in my life which I considered a success. I think one measures a conference by what one learns from it oneself. On that ground I do not begrudge the days that I have spent here in Princeton.

One thing which has been of interest to me and other American participants is the extent to which the remarks made by our friends from other countries have confirmed an impression that there has been a subtle transformation of American power in the world. The instrumentalities through which America has sought to exert influence in the world in recent years—military power, economic power—have been played out in their current forms. The role in which America can hope to recover a measure of influence is going to lie in great part in the capacity with which we meet our problems at home. I was struck by the number of people who spoke of America as a kind of prophecy of the future, who felt that we are acting out on this stage the problems which industrial society in one form or another is going to meet. In any case, I think there is general response to Servan-Schreiber's suggestion of a contraction of the American physical military presence through the world, and of a reconsideration of the nature of our economic presence in other countries. I think one must express a feeling of understanding to those, some in Europe and more in Asia, who look with apprehension at the notion of a total American retreat from the world. This is certainly not the view of most Americans here; it is rather the sense that the American role is not, never in any rational sense was, the Messianic role described by President Johnson when he talked of the United States as "the principal protector of freedom through the world." It is rather a different relationship, dependent much more on political, cultural and intellectual influence than on physical power.

There's been a good deal of talk about the relationship of intellectuals to power, and so on. I rather regretted the implication in Sam Brown's remarks that passion exists on one side of the fence and rationality on the other, his evident disdain for what he contemptuously described as analytical discussion. I have never myself believed that passion and reason could be in any sense divorced. Passion to be effective must be controlled by reason, and reason to be effective must be animated by passion. This notion of a contempt for reason promises a defeat of every objective to which Sam Brown and his colleagues are professedly dedicated. If we are going to follow the exhortations of the young to convert intellectual subjects into subjects of emotion, if we are going to reject reason as the guide and the standard by which we attempt to meet problems, if we are going to make any kind of political discourse a competition in emotion, a competition in passion, a competition in hysteria, the one sure thing is that the winners will not be the New Left, will not be the students, will not be any of the minorities striving for a decent society. If the anti-reason thesis were to prevail, the winners in this would be the men on the right. If this is the politics to which we hope to reduce the United States, George Wallace is going to bring many more armed men into the arena than Tom Hayden.

I hold no brief for intellectuals. They are vulnerable, corruptible, easily deflected and unimportant as individuals. But I would say that ideas in the long run are the only thing which rule the world, and that for us to turn our backs on ideas and reasoned analysis as the means of tackling problems, and to assume that reasoned analysis is incompatible with concern, passion and commitment, would represent a betrayal in the long run benefiting only the most wicked and vicious forces we have.

There is no single role for the intellectual with regard to power. It's essential that some intellectuals participate in power and that some criticize. It's out of this balance and play of forces that power can be tempered. To take the view that intellectuals should have nothing to do with power is totally self-defeating. To take the view that they should all be accomplices of power is equally hopeless. What is required, not only among intellectuals as a group but, if their temperament enjoins this, within each intellectual, is the capacity to be both participant and commentator. The most defeating thing, and one which one discerns to an undue degree among American intellectuals, is the feeling of being rendered guilty by power. Power is one of the basic facts of the world. If people's reaction to power is one of guilt that such a phenomenon exists in the world, public affairs will be the worse for it. Particular exercises of power can well make anyone involved in them guilty, but the fact of power is a fact like every other fact. People who are rattled by power, discomposed by it, made guilty by its presence or its exercise, are not equipped to live in the public world. To feel guilty because power exists in the world is not just a handicap to public discussion, but a genuine *trahison des clercs*.

16

POLITICIANS AND MANDARINS

HENRY KISSINGER: I do not think that somebody in my position* should appear as a public advocate of a particular point of view or indeed should appear within the bureaucracy as an advocate of his own point of view. My primary responsibility, as I see it, is to make sure that every responsible point of view—and "responsible" is defined in a very generous manner—gets a fair hearing; to separate whatever recommendations I might make from the presentation of options that the President confronts. I want to say now that it is in providing this spectrum of considerations and to give a hearing to every point of view of significance that I would want the success of my efforts to be judged.

Policy-making in our society confronts the difficulty that revolutionary changes have to be encompassed and dealt with by an increasingly rigid administrative structure. Great, and increasing, energy has to be devoted to keeping the existing machine going, and in the nature of things there isn't enough time to inquire into the purpose of these activities. The temptation is great to define success by whether one fulfills certain programs, however accidentally these programs may have been arrived at. The question is whether it is possible in the modern bureaucratic state to develop a sense of long-range purpose and to inquire into the meaning of activity. This is one of the big challenges. The great danger of war seems to me not to lie in the deliberate actions of wicked man but

* Mr. Kissinger had just taken up his appointment as President Nixon's adviser for national-security affairs.

in the inability of harassed men to manage events that have run away with them.

The second and related problem seems to be how to deal with the element of conjecture in foreign policy, which I will define as follows: When the scope for action is greater, then the knowledge on which to base such action is at a minimum. When the knowledge is greatest, the scope for creative action has often disappeared. In 1936 it would have been physically possible when Germany reoccupied the Rhineland to stop Hitler. It would have been morally extremely difficult, because no one could know in 1936 whether Hitler was a misunderstood nationalist or bent on world domination. In 1941 it had become morally easy but physically very difficult. I am not saying that early action is always correct and that inaction is always incorrect. I am trying to say that whether one acts or doesn't act depends on some moral or philosophical judgment as well as on judgments of fact.

These are some of the concerns which have led me to accept the offer of the President-elect. He has insisted that he wanted to hear every point of view, that he wanted to make sure that the best talent in the country, whether or not it agreed with pronouncements he made in the past, would receive a hearing. I can tell you, speaking for myself as well as for the President-elect, that every effort will be made to give the best talent in the country an opportunity to present their views. Many of you have worked with me for many years and you know what I have stood for, and you know, I hope, that I will continue to stand for this no matter what my position is. I would hope that I can use this opportunity to tell you that the doors of my office are open to your ideas and to invite you to share them with me. I will try to enlist some of you from America as well as from abroad, but I also hope that you would volunteer your ideas, because after all it is not impossible that I will be caught up in the process that I have described and may not always get to make the requests.

BRIAN WALDEN: Just a few words about a topic that my colleague from the House of Commons, David Marquand, and I find we are discussing almost exclusively these days. I mean the mandarinism of the liberal intellectuals, the gap between the intelligentsia and the ordinary man, that growing army on the right to which Mr. Schlesinger has referred. I'm a politician, and have one advantage over most people here, only one: I do occasionally have to see ordinary people. Worse than that, I do have to try to persuade them not to be racists, not to listen to Mr. Enoch Powell, not to want to pull out of the world and give no assistance to underdeveloped countries, not to do the whole spectrum of things that you get from George Wallace and that we get from Mr. Powell. (Don't, by the way, write him down; he's a coming man, he's going to be very powerful.) I do have to do some of this. And I'm terribly worried. Not because I have an apocalyptic view of the world. I don't even think that America's problems are as bad as some people may have gathered from what has been said. Not because I have any illusions about the past. I know what the English working class was like. I was a member of it. I once lived in the very slums that I now represent. I know that life there was rugged and tough; there was drunkenness, there were a thousand and one problems. That's all got better. But I'll tell you what's got worse. That's the framework in which the ordinary man now thinks, which is rapidly ceasing, in my country at least, to have very much to do with liberalism or humane values at all. There are reasons for that in Britain. I don't know if any of you ever studied the history of English adult education. If you haven't, you should. Virtually every leading British trade-union leader was taught, when he was way down in the ranks, at an adult-education class. He was lectured on a disciplined weekly basis by a university professor. I'm bound to tell you that the movement that built all that now uses most of its resources putting on courses in flower arrangements for bored suburban women who don't have the nerve to commit adultery. The contact has gone. There is an increasing divergence between what intellectuals think about the world, even the framework in which they understand the problem, and what ordinary people are doing in all these regards. Amidst all the growing affluence, all the civilization that's growing up within family life and all the desirable changes, it represents nevertheless a complete collapse of the liberal values that underpin them. It's true in my country. Everybody still talks of Britain as if it were a great island of stability and sanity. Don't you believe it. Britain is cracking up in all of these respects. And we largely dug this pit for ourselves. Because we once used to have contact, and we've allowed it to rot and die, so that no intellectual is comprehensible any more, in my country, to an overwhelming majority of the people. I don't mean that they could pick up all the allusions, they never would have done that, but they did understand the framework of values. Now it's gone.

That's something every intellectual ought to think about. I'm struck very much in America, as in England, by the view that somehow this kind of thing is not the responsibility of the intelligentsia. It's some other guy's responsibility. Maybe the politician. Maybe if you can get a man with enough charisma, Teddy Kennedy, somebody like that, and he can get the votes that otherwise might have gone to Wallace, O.K., it can still be worked out at the government level. It never occurs to anyone that possibly too much is being asked of the liberal politicians; that there aren't enough to go round. Doesn't the liberal intellectual also have some responsibilities? Aren't there perhaps too many liberals waiting in Washington to structure the government once we get the right government in, and not enough out in Wyoming making sure we do get the white vote? Isn't it time that the liberal intelligentsia went out and made some liberals? I don't suggest the idea is just to go back and take some classes, that's much too simple (though perhaps it's not a bad idea: I put it forward as one tentative suggestion), but obviously we need something much better and wider than that. And, by God, we need it, and we need it quick.

MICHEL CROZIER: At times during this conference, I have felt we were almost about to issue a manifesto: "Intellectuals of the world, unite!" Intellectuals are a class, as some of our friends from Eastern Europe have indeed told us we are. And some of us seem to imagine that intellectuals are going to manage the affairs of mankind in the "technetronic" society. This kind of elite thinking is not only dangerous for the backlash it may produce; it kills off intellectual creativity itself. Abstract science and thinking are no doubt going to be more and more influential. But it does not follow that intellectuals should use their knowledge to rule the world. If they did, they would become less and less creative and meet the challenges neither of social change nor of innovation in their own fields.

Intellectuals are in a fix as a result of the breakdown of the liberal synthesis. The shallowness of the rationality which saw humanity as so many numbers in the calculus of happiness has been laid bare. The American liberal, with his ruined dream of the great society of the free world lying around him, is a kind of deserted man. He meets ingratitude all over the world, even at home. In the discussion over race, the emotional problem was the reverse of what I had expected: those who felt emotionally deprived were not the representatives of the black community, but the liberals. However, the opponents of the liberal synthesis also have a temptation, which in their case is the wholesale refusal of society. If we just say that modern societies are corrupt and nothing can be got out of them, our chances of building a better society will be very slim indeed. That too is excessively shallow and easy. Take the powerlessness of the individual. American organizations are in fact often more flexible and more open to innovation and to people who have a contribution to make than those of other countries. To reject all that leads to a leap into the unknown, an excess of confidence in one's own way of seeing things, a return to the very arrogance of rationality so often criticized in liberals. Intellectuals have to be more modest.

I may sound very pragmatic and narrow, but my own reaction is that we should be more careful and responsible in our use of intellectual methods. The liberal creed has fathered two general approaches, incrementalism and global policy planning. Incrementalism is liable to lead you down a blind alley: you add and add until piecemeal escalation lands you in Vietnam. As for the global view, its vice is often a purely superficial coherence. This is the

kind of thing which had led to the failures of the Eastern bureaucratic regimes which wanted to plan everything. Separately or
together, these approaches can neither meet today's challenge nor
sire the dreams of the year 2000. We need to use all our intellectual techniques not to set a goal—we have no right to define
solutions for people yet unborn—but to have a better view of our
own fragmented and interrelated world. The biggest lag is in our
thinking on how to manage change. We are very good at describing
systems, but not at understanding how to change them. We need to
look at institutions, cultures and all the different systems of which
people and groups are part, and at the processes for changing
them. The way to get at meaningful change is to focus on how
systems are regulated and where marginal action can mean a great
deal.

I would like, in general, to call for self-restraint, and to see
intellectual capacities concentrated on the key points where change
can be brought about. Internationally, I agree with Stanley Hoffmann that the United States should change its concept of global
power to one of global impact. It is a big animal and cannot
suppress itself. But it should not feel responsible for the whole
world. Instead, it needs to assume responsibility for its own acts
and realize their worldwide repercussions. In the same way, in this
or other countries, leaders and politicians should accept that they
are not responsible for the whole society, because they cannot
know and do everything. But they can know about their own behavior and the difference it makes. This requires confidence and
brings one to the problem of leadership. We haven't talked too
much about that, but it is one of the basic elements in human
innovation and cannot be lightly disposed of. Leadership, as I see
it, can be defined as the way to manage contradictions by going
beyond them and changing their context. In this situation intellectuals have a heavy responsibility; they are overburdened by it. But
if they recognize their limitations and get at the truth, even if it's
unpalatable, they may achieve something. This is the only way to
restore confidence.

INDEX

[Page numbers in italics denote photographs.]

297